PARTHENIA:

OR,

THE LAST DAYS OF PAGANISM.

BY

ELIZA BUCKMINSTER LEE,

AUTHOR OF "NAOMI," "LIFE OF JEAN PAUL," "LIVES OF THE BUCKMINSTERS," ETC., ETC.

BOSTON:
TICKNOR AND FIELDS.
M DCCC LVIII.

CAMBRIDGE:
ELECTROTYPED AND PRINTED BY METCALF AND COMPANY.

TO

THE REV. GEORGE E. ELLIS, D.D.,

THE FOLLOWING PAGES ARE INSCRIBED,

WITH EVERY SENTIMENT OF RESPECT AND GRATITUDE,

BY

THE AUTHOR.

PREFACE.

The period at which the events represented in the following pages occurred, or (as in one or more exceptions) are imagined to have occurred, was the middle of the fourth century; — the time when Paganism and Christianity were nearly balanced in their earthly forces; when a Christianized Paganism and a Paganized Christianity would naturally array themselves against each other. This was the time for a leading mind to appear as the vindicator or restorer of the old religion.

Julian, the person who enjoyed this unenviable distinction, received his early education under Christian influences. The causes of his subsequent opposition to Christianity may be easily found in the character of his cousin, the reigning Emperor,—who was a fanatical Christian, and also his deadliest enemy, — and in the influences afterwards affecting him. One of the tutors placed near him is said to have been a concealed Pagan; others were fanatical or hypocritical Christians, who exacted from the high-spirited and generous youth long midnight prayers and severe penances, rather than the genuine virtues of Christianity.

The movement which Julian represented is that which takes place when a powerful mind, but one of more warmth than penetration, observes in the present and the actual only its defects and shortcomings. The past in such a mind arrays itself in the attractive features of the departed, and the romantic enthusiast dreams only of resuscitating the past without its defects,—of bringing back the good only, divested of all its attending evils.

Paganism, as Julian wished it restored, was not the old religion of Greece and Rome. His ideal faith was natural religion as it was then understood, with a strong infusion of Platonism, softened by the tender precepts of Christianity which had clung to his memory from childhood, and arrayed in the gorgeous and attractive forms of the Grecian mythology.

It was scarcely necessary to depart at all from the truth of history in order to heighten the interest of this contest, when Christianity prevailed, and, in the words of tradition, "The Galilean conquered."

BROOKLINE, October 1, 1857.

CONTENTS.

CHAPTER I.

PAGE

CONSTANTIUS 1

CHAPTER II.

THE PRINCE 13

CHAPTER III.

THE MAGICIAN 19

CHAPTER IV.

THE VISION 29

CHAPTER V.

EUSEBIA 34

CHAPTER VI.

GREECE 49

CHAPTER VII.

ATHENS 59

CHAPTER VIII.

THE LECTURES 67

CHAPTER IX.

THE SYMPOSIUM 74

CHAPTER X.

THE ACROPOLIS 85

CHAPTER XI.

PARTHENIA 95

CHAPTER XII.

THE FRIENDS 115

CHAPTER XIII.

ADIEU TO ATHENS 129

CHAPTER XIV.

THE COURT OF CONSTANTIUS 140

CHAPTER XV.

HELENA 161

CHAPTER XVI.

THE BARBARIANS 168

CHAPTER XVII.

THE CHRISTIAN 177

CHAPTER XVIII.

LUTETIA, OR PARIS 192

CHAPTER XIX.

THE CONSPIRACY 199

CHAPTER XX.

ANTIOCH 214

CHAPTER XXI.

PHORION 223

CHAPTER XXII.

JULIAN AS EMPEROR 241

CHAPTER XXIII.

THE CHRISTIAN CHURCH 262

CHAPTER XXIV.

THE EMPEROR IN ANTIOCH 274

CHAPTER XXV.

JULIAN AND THE CHRISTIANS 287

CHAPTER XXVI.

DAPHNE 293

CHAPTER XXVII.

THE HOSPITAL FOR STRANGERS 314

CHAPTER XXVIII.

THE HERMITS 323

CHAPTER XXIX.

THE ANGER OF THE EMPEROR 332

CHAPTER XXX.

THEODORUS 341

CHAPTER XXXI.

THE SUBTERRANEAN TEMPLE 348

CHAPTER XXXII.

THE JEW 366

CHAPTER XXXIII.

THE CHRISTIANS 370

CHAPTER XXXIV.

JULIAN DEPARTS FOR PERSIA 379

CHAPTER XXXV.

"THE GALILEAN HAS CONQUERED" 399

CHAPTER XXXVI.

THE CONVENT 408

PARTHENIA.

CHAPTER I.

CONSTANTIUS.

THE Emperor Constantius reclined upon his couch in a lofty room of the palace of Milan. The imperial family, all except his cousins Gallus and Julian, under the pretence of avoiding civil war, and with the ready acquiescence of the Emperor, had been murdered. These murders were the fruit of different passions, combined with the policy of the despot, which taught him to seek repose in crime. But in preserving the two children, his cousins, Constantius listened to no pleadings of pity and to no whispers of conscience; he was sensible that the execution of the two orphans would have been esteemed by all mankind an act of the most deliberate cruelty. At the time of which we write, Gallus had been three years invested with the title of

Cæsar, but the writers most indulgent to his memory are obliged to confess that he was incapable of reigning, and he soon afforded the Emperor the fairest pretence for exacting the forfeit of his life.

In the deep embrasure of a window which commanded a wide prospect over the fertile plain surrounding Milan, and partially concealed by a crimson curtain, sat a woman of noble presence and proud, imperial beauty. A glance at her face showed that it was of the purest Greek type, and that the full and noble form possessed the grace which belongs to the highest birth.

The plain upon which she looked was not in the fourth century, as now, covered and glittering with towns and villages, but it was the most fertile country imaginable. Innumerable flocks, whose wool was of the finest quality, fed upon these plains, and the wine was so abundant that it was drunk like water.

Although the apartment was in some respects rude, being one in the temporary residence only of the court, the dress and appointments of Constantius showed the extreme of Oriental luxury. Formerly, the only distinction of the Emperor had been the purple robe, but now, since the introduction of Oriental splendor, jewels were appended to many parts of the dress. The under garment of the

Emperor, a late fashion, was of Alexandrian purple, of so dazzling a brilliancy, that it was said any other purple looked of an ash color by its side; and his slipper, which rested on a cushion embroidered in pearls, was incrusted with precious stones.

Constantius was silent, with moody and angry clouds overshadowing his brow. Occasionally he strode impatiently about the apartment, or nervously changed his posture on the couch; he was waiting, restless and gloomy, for some expected event. At last he started, as the usher hastily drew aside the curtain that covered the door, and announced that the Bishops of Milan and of Antioch craved permission to enter.

The Church had long since thrown off the simplicity of the Apostolic times. The Bishops had laid aside the staff and the scrip with which the Apostles travelled, and an ostentatious cortege brought them to the palace of the Emperor. Upon this occasion, their car was drawn by four Thessalian horses of spotless white. Their robes were gorgeous, and they were honored at the court of Constantius with more homage than the great officers of the Empire.

What officer of state would the Empress have received with such docile humility as she did these successors of the fishermen? As soon as they had paid their respects to the Emperor, she descended from her seat and stood humbly before them until a sign from Constantius required her to kneel for their blessing. The proud Eusebia knelt and bent her head, while the older of the two Bishops held his spread hands above her, calling her "blessed among women," "the mother of the Church," etc. Then he raised her from her knees, and, at a sign from the Emperor, she returned to her seat in the window. There, while apparently watching the crimson glow of the setting sun upon the snowy ridges of the Alps, her color changed with her varying emotions, now pale and now heightened by an angry flush as she listened silently to the whispers in the apartment, indicating that a subject of extreme interest for her or for her friends was under discussion by the Bishops.

Soon she caught the sound of a not distant trumpet, and the rapid click of the hoofs of approaching horses was heard. Preceded by guards, and borne by African slaves upon a gorgeous litter, Eusebius, the favorite eunuch, entered the court below. The Emperor's privacy was governed by this man, who received the infamous title of Prefect of the Bedchamber, and through his arts of flattery and intrigue, assisted by the fears, the indolence, and the vanity of Constantius, he ruled the court with almost absolute power. He alone had persuaded the Emperor to subscribe the condemnation of the elder of his cousins, the unfortunate Gallus, who, with his brother Julian, were, as we have said, all that remained of the house of Constantine.

Without waiting to be announced, and with haughty strides, as though entirely secure of the favor of the weak Emperor, the eunuch entered. He bent low to the Empress.

"What of the Cæsar ?" asked Constantius, impatiently.

"May all the enemies of Constantius lie as low as Gallus," he answered, as he made a significant gesture.

Constantius started from his couch and clapped his hands with violence ; the guards in the ante-room moved towards the tapestry. "For God's sake," cried the Empress, starting, and now for the first time speaking, "what would you do ?"

"In the first place, send an express, if possible to save my cousin, and next, order this man's head to the block."

The eunuch dropped upon one knee at the foot-stool of the Emperor, and the pallor of his countenance became, if possible, of a more deadly hue.

"Stay," cried the Empress, "are you in such haste to undo what you have so long desired to accomplish? Those whom you have feared as the sharers or disturbers of your government are now thrust from your path; no shadow —"

At this moment a messenger was announced, and pages entered bearing upon cushions the jewelled slippers and other ornaments of the Cæsar, Gallus.

"You have nothing more to fear, — Gallus is destroyed," continued the Empress, glancing at the empty slippers.

"*One* remains," said the Emperor, signing to the eunuch to rise, and dismissing with a nod the guards who had entered. "Ah! *one* remains, upon whom, if we believe report, have descended all the gifts of mind and person of the Claudian name. While *he* breathes in yonder fortress, the Empire is not safe."

"Julian! that poor-souled pedant," said the Empress. "Ah, Sire, give him his Homer and his beloved Greek poets, and you will have nothing to fear from him."

The eunuch turned his cold, sarcastic eye upon the Empress with an expression which made the blood rush over cheek and brow. She bent to conceal it upon the footstool of the Emperor. "Yes, Sire," she repeated, "the cool blood of Julian warms only to romantic dreams of Pan and his Fauns and Dryades."

"Cool-blooded, do you call the Prince ?" said the eunuch; "I have seen the proud young blood flush his cheek, and the fiery glance of his eye. I have much of import to reveal to you, Sire, from the report of those who observed Julian in Ionia —"

"Ah!" said the Empress, "spies and tale-bearers! how much more to be feared than poison or dagger!"

"The young dissembler is too cautious for outside and common reporters to fathom. He is yet zealous for the Church, but Maximus is his teacher," said the eunuch.

"Has he not been building the tombs of the martyrs?" asked Eusebia.

"Ah, yes, with one hand, and pulling down the cross with the other. He is no longer an obedient son of the Church —"

"That is, he no longer submits his conscience to the rule of those who curse him in this life, or in the future. He refuses to place his neck beneath the bare feet of the monks."

"By all the saints, as true as that sun will shine to-morrow," said Eusebius, "although, Sire, you have forbidden him to listen to the lectures of Libanius, he has put his soul into the hands of Maximus and the arch-sophists!"

"It is true," said the Emperor, "Julian would place Olympus above Calvary. If he should ever be Emperor, which the saints avert, he would bring back the old Gods, open the temples, renew the sacrifices —"

"Sire," said the Empress, "you mistake the character of Julian. The Prince is a night-dreamer, a star-gazer. Let him carry his owls to Athens; there in the midst of the schools and the philosophers, the wits and the necromancers, he will dream, and you will forget to fear him."

"I know the Prince," said Eusebius; "unstable as water, he shall not excel."

It was the purpose of the Empress to represent Julian to the Emperor as a dreamer and a poet, also as rather weak and uncertain in character, in order to disarm his suspicions, and induce him to spare the life of this, the last of his family. She had always been his firm friend. She was scarcely older than Julian, and certainly would have been captivated by the fascination of his character, had not destiny too early made her the wife of Constantius. Her penetration early discovered the real superiority of Julian's character to all the other descendants of Constantine. If she sometimes feared the bold, erratic fire of his genius, she saw beneath an ardor for truth, an enthusiasm of generosity, and a love of beauty, to which the quick sensibilities of her woman's heart responded.

The creatures of Constantius would have compassed the destruction of the Prince in order to remove the consequences of future anger at the death of all his family, should he at length succeed the Emperor. Eusebia's vigilance in protecting the young Julian had drawn upon herself cruel suspicions. In this corrupt court, her interest in him had been ascribed to motives degrading to the Empress; but the brave-hearted woman had never ceased her vigilance. She had always by secret message, under cover of sign or cipher, warned him of his enemies in time for the Prince to escape their snares.

Even at this moment, the countenance of the eunuch, although guarded as by a mask of clay, expressed suspicions dishonoring to the Empress. She was aware of the thoughts of his degraded soul, but she still interceded with the Emperor.

"In Athens," she continued, "Julian will be preserved from all ambitious thoughts. His beloved philosophy, his adored Homer, the arts, are all dearer to his visionary soul than all the toys of ambition."

"Ah! yes, send him to Athens, the forcing-house of Paganism, where we cannot enter a street, or turn a corner, without stumbling upon a naked God or a veiled Divinity," said the Emperor.

"Yes," said the eunuch, "in Athens, where the Gods outnumber the men! Ah! there this young heathen soul will expand and bear its accursed fruit."

Eusebia colored with indignation. Julian she knew had been a reader in the Church, and this direct charge of apostasy was to her as false as it was malicious. The Empress was silent, and the eunuch continued, in a tone of reproach, — "While the heathen temples remain open, and sacrifices are permitted, and the Prince has liberty to pass through all parts of the Empire, he not only gathers all the influences of Heathenism, but the prestige of his character draws after him all restless souls, and all who turn from the evening to the rising sun."

"Whither would you lead me?" asked the Emperor, turning pale, excited by the thought of having Julian within his power.

"Let him be *here!* Here he can be watched and guarded. His acts, his thoughts, cannot escape your knowledge."

"But how? every movement of the court would excite his vigilance."

"Send him under your own hand a guaranty of

safety, a guard of honor, — an escort to the court at Milan. Once here, under the surveillance of your trusted servants, it will be strange if we do not find the means to give the dreamer quiet dreams — "

The Emperor turned deadly pale! "Tempter," he hissed through his shut teeth, and the eunuch left the apartment.

"Liar! Poisoner! Assassin!" whispered the Empress, as she approached the Emperor, and knelt upon his footstool. She did not assume this place in an humble, but in a playful mood. "Sire, it is the very worst use you can make of the last of your family, the only one you could convert into a friend, to give him a prey to his slanderous enemies. Far better send after him the final mandate." She made a gesture sufficiently suggestive of her meaning.

"And can your transcendent wisdom suggest nothing better than the last sublime hint?"

"Sire! a thousand times better; send him to Athens. There, in the schools of philosophy, with his Plato and dreams of perfection, he will imagine himself the God-man that Plato has dreamed."

"It is too late for Roman women to imitate those barbarian Germans who dictate to their husbands, and assume the direction of affairs of state."

"Sire, I am only anxious for your own honor. Would you burden your conscience with the crime of your great ancestor?"

"The waters of the Jordan have washed away all the crimes of Constantine, and in future he will be hailed, 'the great, the good.'"

"Yet that golden statue bears witness to his eternal remorse,—'To my son, whom I unjustly condemned.' Sire, you have earned his fame, his renown; do not also earn his remorse, his unavailing repentance!"

At length Constantius yielded, and the Empress, before she left him, obtained a promise from him that he would send an order to Julian to visit the court, and a guard of honor to conduct him to Milan.

CHAPTER II.

THE PRINCE.

It was the purpose of the Empress, in order to save the life of Julian, to represent him to the Emperor as fickle, uncertain, a dreamer, an enthusiast for all that was unreal and imaginary, and as also deficient in practical talent. Perhaps in early youth he was so. She was not wholly ignorant of his secret disaffection towards the Christian faith. To this faith he had been rather devoted through baptism than truly instructed and educated in its precepts, while the Pagan poets and philosophers had been his daily food and delight.

"By his Christian instructors the young and ardent Julian was bound down to a course of the strictest observances; the midnight vigil, the fast, the long and weary prayer, and visits to the tombs of martyrs, rather than a wise and rational initiation in the genuine principles of the Gospel, or a familiarity with the originality, the beauty, and the depth of the Christian morals and Christian religion. For six years, he bitterly asserts, he was deprived of every kind of useful instruction." His Christianity was but the compulsory obedience of youth to the distasteful lessons of education enforced by the hateful authority of a tyrannical relative; thus taught and enforced, it was inseparably connected with the irksome and distasteful feelings of confinement and degradation.

His cruel enemy, the destroyer of his family, was a Christian, and this secretly excited his hatred, while the complete subjection in which he was held by the Church disgusted the mind of the young Prince, a mind eminently ambitious, and endued with the love of freedom. Julian, it is recorded, spent his days and nights in the study of the Pagan authors. His intense admiration for the great men of antiquity led him to wish their instructions might be true. Temptations, also, to forsake Christianity were everywhere around him. Idolatry was shaken, but not destroyed. The temples were closed, but not impaired. Sacrifices to the heathen Gods were forbidden, but the heathen games continued to be celebrated, and while they recalled the gorgeous festivals of poetry and music, perfumes and incense, processions of youths and virgins with scattered flowers and songs of triumph, they offered to the imagination and the senses the most attractive excitement.

Pagans shared with Christians some of the highest offices in the Empire. Although a very large number of educated persons had been drawn into the Christian Church, still, men of letters, poets, philosophers, sophists, teachers, held their faith in the Pagan superstitions, and taught them in the schools and academies where resorted the youth of the Empire. From his love of what they taught, Julian made these his companions and friends; and such was the fascination of the young Prince, that all whom he sought, he attracted irresistibly to himself.

Where now was the object of all this solicitude of the Empress and of Constantius, which we have mentioned in the last chapter? After the death of his brother Gallus, Julian had been allowed to inherit the fortune and the estate of their mother, and had also received permission to travel in certain parts of the Empire, it being tacitly understood that he should not present himself at the court. Attention was drawn towards him as the probable heir of Constantius, and this made him the centre of attraction to sycophants and flatterers; added to this, the singular traits of his character drew towards him all that was strange and eccentric, as well as much that was distinguished and intellectual.

Now that he was permitted to travel, he would appease that burning thirst he felt to penetrate the secrets of the future; he would explore the occult sciences; he would visit the magicians and philosophers; he would anticipate what of good or evil time had in store for him, and rifle from the hands of the future the destiny it concealed.

Edicius, the chief of the Platonists, dwelt at Pergamos. Julian, Prince of the Empire, determined to visit with a splendid retinue the venerable man, who, although bowed with years and infirmities, yet retained a healthy and vigorous mind. The Prince had caused his visit to be preceded by costly presents, hoping thus to propitiate the ancient Stoic; but his mortification was great, upon entering the vestibule of the house, to find them all returned.

"Amiable Prince," said the old man, "you know that my heart craves the happiness to serve you, but my body will not second its efforts. It is, as you see, an old edifice, ready to fall into ruins."

"I ask only words from your mouth to direct me where to find the truth."

"Noble Prince! you, a follower of the Nazarene,

a disciple of Matthew and of Paul, — do you come to Edicius for wisdom ?"

"I am tired of the long prayers, the fasts, and night-watches, to which I have been subjected. Look at me. Is this robust form, this blooming health, to be consumed in kneeling at altars and in repeating long prayers at midnight ?"

"But philosophy demands long night-watches, and the subjection of the flesh to the spiritual nature."

"I seek divine philosophy as a beneficent guide to the truth. Christianity has been to me only a scourge in the hands of tyrants and hypocrites."

There was so much of bitterness in Julian's invectives that the aged philosopher perceived that the enmity and persecution of the Emperor were driving Julian to excesses, which would perhaps end in rebellion.

"I cannot help you, said the old man; "I advise you to seek my true disciples, — you will find with them an inexhaustible source of light and wisdom."

"Ah," said Julian, "to whom shall I go ?"

"Procles has gone to Greece," said the sage. "Maximus is at Ephesus, — he will initiate you into those sacred mysteries which will make you blush to be anything but a noble man."

Julian bent and kissed the hem of the old man's garment.

"Maximus," he continued, "is one of my oldest and most skilful disciples, but he admits follies, and dark mysteries such as I can never adopt."

"Adieu," said Julian; "you have shown me the man whom I seek."

"But remember," said Edicius, impressively, "that the essential aim of all philosophy is to purify and enlighten the reason."

"Ah, yes," — and he hastily embraced and left the old man, who turned from the door, his long white hair streaming towards the Prince as though it would again recall him.

CHAPTER III.

THE MAGICIAN.

With all the impetuosity of a young man seeking an unknown but priceless good, Julian travelled to Ephesus. The luxurious gardens that surrounded the city imparted a new charm to the lovely climate of Ionia, and perhaps furnished an excuse for the effeminate character of its inhabitants. The robust nature of the Prince preserved him from yielding to the softening influences of climate, or to the indulgences of effeminate habits.

Although he was now travelling with a retinue becoming his princely rank, he knew that Maximus was not a man to be dazzled by external splendor; he therefore laid aside all indications of his station, and, clad in a simple Greek dress, on foot, and followed only by Mardonius, the slave who had been the favorite of his mother, and from his infancy his own attached attendant, he traversed the environs of Ephesus, and entered one of the gardens, in which a lowly building stood alone, detached from all others.

Small but luxuriant was the garden of the philosopher, the sophist, or rather the magician, whose long pursuit of the occult sciences and of divination, which, in this age, was relied on to reveal the secrets of the future, but tended to shroud the possessor in deeper mystery.

The heat of the noonday sun was excluded by overhanging luxuriant vines, among which was heard the sound of busy insects and innumerable birds, sometimes interrupted by the tinkling of fountains and the lapse of running streams so dispersed as to cool the heat of noon. It was late in the afternoon when Julian entered the garden; indeed, the lights and shadows were becoming mingled and indistinct through the softening shade of twilight, that seemed still to linger as though reluctant to veil so much beauty in the darker mantle of night. The falling dew had condensed the fragrant perfumes, scattered in the hot beams of the sun, and the flowers, their beauty thus veiled, still gave out tokens of their love.

Maximus dwelt in the humble edifice belonging to this garden. He was a man past seventy, although his robust frame seemed to bear well the weight of years. A venerable white beard reached to his girdle, and his eyes, of an indescribable color, in which youth and age seemed strangely blended, flashed from beneath the overhanging brow. These eyes were penetrating in their glance, and overpowering in their fixed expression, and his voice was capable of the most insinuating and varied melody, so that, when voice and eye united to captivate those who addressed him, none could resist the enchantment. These external advantages, together with the report of his researches into the hidden mysteries of science, caused him to be regarded by the Pagans as one inspired by the Gods, and by the Christians as one under the influence of the Prince of Evil.

Maximus had received secret information that the Prince, in this crisis of his life, would seek counsel from him. As he approached the old man, the contrast of his blooming youth, his fine, although not altogether symmetrical features, and his bright, penetrating eye, was felt by the philosopher, always accustomed to remark the peculiar personal advantages of different men. Julian also affected the Grecian costume, and, contrary to the Roman fashion, his yet scanty beard was cultivated with the utmost care.

Maximus rose from his seat, an unusual act of deference to the near relation of the Emperor, and displayed by rising the tunic, embroidered with exquisite workmanship, which he had assumed upon this occasion. Upon his breast a triangle was wrought in gold; beneath that a single eye, the pupil of which was formed of a priceless sapphire; the lashes of thin, dazzling rubies; over the upper lid, formed of small diamonds, was the single letter Beth. The outer garment consisted of a long purple cloak, and upon his feet were embroidered sandals, faded and worn. Divers crucibles and other appurtenances of his art lay upon a table, together with elixirs, salts, and perfumes, while instruments, and books half unrolled, were carelessly thrown about the apartment. Even the Lares and Penates were not omitted. Upon a low marble altar stood a small statue of Apollo of pure gold, whose radiated brow showed that it was intended as an emblem of the orb of day; by his side was a still smaller silver statue of the twin sister of Apollo, the Goddess Diana. Maximus was also a worshipper of nature as represented by the heathen Divinity Pan. In a small grotto-like recess stood an image of Pan, with the face and breast of a man. Upon his breast there shone a single radiant star; his robe was also sprinkled with stars, and he held in his hand a pipe of reeds.

Julian approached, and said in a voice rendered

tremulous by feeling: "Pardon, O Maximus! this intrusion. Thy great fame has reached me even in the place of banishment to which my august cousin has condemned me for so many years. I would not leave Ionia without communing with thy wisdom."

Maximus saw at once that Julian was in earnest, and he was instantly confirmed in the plan projected by Crysanthius and other philosophers to augment the Prince's delusions, and establish his faith in the heathen Deities.

"Welcome!" said the old magician; "this is an auspicious day that brings to my humble roof the heir of the empire of the world."

"Pardon," said Julian; "not so fast, venerable Maximus. I come as the humblest of pupils, to learn of thy wisdom. I come to be helped to decide the great questions now burdening my thoughts."

"That is? — These are?" said Maximus, affecting ignorance. "Ah! is it the question as old as the world, — What is truth?"

"No," said Julian, whose thoughts were always too rapid for his utterance. "Do not affect ignorance! I wish to make the inward revelation of the Divinity, which I feel in myself, universal; and to give new life to its expression in many beautiful forms. I would also revive its worship in the ancient Divinities."

"You believe *yourself* favored and protected by these Divinities?"

"Whether a favorite or not, I receive from them daily benefits. Apollo, in his living image, the sun, sends his rays to enlighten me. Diana's milder light cheers me at night —"

"But these blessings," said Maximus, "are common to all."

"Ah, yes! But Minerva, the virgin Goddess, is ever near me with her whispered counsels. Apollo, the glorious, inspires me with poetry and wisdom. Can I desert these beneficent beings to worship a mere man, a malefactor, crucified between thieves?"

"One truth must be granted," said Maximus, "wherever this new doctrine of the Galilean has been received, the condition of society is ameliorated, industry revives, quarrels cease, marriage is pure, the poor and the sick are sheltered. Even in this city of Ephesus the example of the Christians has checked the extremest of immoralities."

"The immortal Gods grant me but life and opportunity," said Julian with impetuosity, "and we will unite this order, this industry, this humane spirit, this purity of manners, which does not belong solely to those you call Christians, with the Grecian spirit of beauty, with the living Divinities which are everywhere around us."

"Your mind is then fixed? you are ready to avow your faith in the old Divinities?"

"No! most venerable Maximus. I demand from you a proof, a sign, a voice, — something from the celestial, or the infernal powers, which shall be irresistible —"

"Noble Prince, have you prepared yourself for this revelation from the invisible world by silence, fasting, and purification from all earthly dross?"

"I cannot avow that I have spent, as you demand of your disciples, twenty-five years in unbroken silence in the desert, abstaining from all food except that which Nature's bounty provides for the humblest of her pensioners. But for the twenty years of my life, the pure fountain gushing from the earth has been my sole beverage, and my food only bread and fruits."

"Prince! in what form shall I answer your demand?"

Julian mused a moment. "Let me behold my mother, and faith in your art will follow."

"Basilina? the beautiful wife of Julius Constantius?" said Maximus.

"Alas! she left me too early to imbue my young

soul with her own strong faith, or these doubts perhaps would never have tormented her son."

"She was a Christian?" asked Maximus.

"In that fearful tragedy, when all were slain but Gallus and myself, I was torn from my mother, and her death soon after effaced from my memory all but the deep impression of her beautiful features."

"Come what may," said Maximus, in a tremulous voice, "follow me."

He led the way to a very small apartment, which appeared dark and empty; but as Julian's eyes became accustomed to the obscurity, he saw, occupying one side of the room, a mirror of intensely polished steel. As Maximus kindled various colored lamps about the room, the splendor of this metallic mirror would have been intolerable, had there not been suspended between it and Julian divers veils of gossamer almost as transparent as woven air, or like the gossamer that trembles upon the grass in a dewy summer morning. Maximus made certain signs, and instantly, like meteors, streams of white light were reflected from the mirror, dazzling as the meridian sun. The light again faded to the softest moonbeams. Unseen by Julian, various drugs were thrown upon a small lighted altar, which instantly filled the room with thick fumes of vapor and smoke. As this opened in the centre, and Julian's attention was riveted upon the mirror, there was gradually recalled to him the interior of a Christian church. Kneeling upon the steps of the altar, where she had fled for refuge from assassins, was a young woman, pale and beautiful, with two children clinging to her. One, of about six years old, she held in her arms; the other, older, stood trembling at her side. An old man, apparently their sole guardian, stood over them; and in him Julian recognized Mardonius, the faithful slave, who had been given to his mother as her instructor, and to himself as a tutor and guardian, who had never left him, and was now watching over him in Ephesus.

Julian gazed with intense feeling; gradually the whole scene returned to his memory. It was the church to which his mother fled for refuge, when driven from her palace with Gallus and himself, her only children. The face of Basilina was turned from him, but Julian felt intuitively that it was the semblance of his mother. He became a child again, concealed his face in his robe, and wept.

When he looked up again, the room was dark, the whole vision had vanished.

"It is enough," he said to Maximus, who stood

at his side. "When will you condescend to give me other proofs of your science?"

The magician approached the clepsydra and seemed to count the hours. "To-night, at the hour of midnight, I will meet you in the cloisters of the Artemisium, or the great temple of Diana."

CHAPTER IV.

THE VISION.

At midnight the Prince did not fail to keep his appointment. Mardonius followed his footsteps, for he yet felt that Julian was his pupil, and that he must watch over him. The philosopher was waiting, and, with his finger on his lip to impose silence and awe, he desired him to follow him into the temple of the great Diana of the Ephesians. The magnificence of this temple exceeded many of the most gorgeous of the fanes of the ancient Deities. The statue of the Goddess was not that of the sister of Apollo, with bow and quiver, her robe gracefully girt around her, with the trusting hound reposing at her feet, surrounded by beautiful nymphs who have consecrated themselves to perpetual virginity. This famous "Diana of the Ephesians" would rather inspire disgust and fear. She resembled more an Egyptian mummy than the virgin sister of Apollo. Upon her head reposed the turreted crown of Cybele, surmounted by the lunar bow. Her breast was covered by the signs of the zodiac, surrounded by flowers and acorns. Between her outstretched arms were the odious fountains of many milky streams, and upon her robe, reaching to her feet, were images of all the tame beasts subjected to man's power; while birds and flowers filled every vacant space. It was for this idol of the Ephesians that Demetrius made those shrines of gold and silver, whose decrease at the preaching of Paul, three hundred years before, had so much alarmed her worshippers. Their number had indeed very much diminished, as Christianity gained proselytes, but yet her influence in Ephesus was great, and her priesthood corrupt, and, like Maximus, deceivers and deceived.

The old man desired Julian to choose a position which was rather obscure, in front of the image, and, selecting a censer from the hand of one of the priests, he seemed to inspect very closely the contents, and then, waving it before the Goddess, a smile immediately illumined her face. Julian, suspecting some deception, desired that the lamps of the temple should be lighted. Instantly, as though by magic, without human hands, every lamp was kindled, and the whole temple flooded with a blaze of light.

Julian, astonished and agitated, seized the hands of Maximus to assure himself that he was a man like himself.

"Pshaw!" said the magician, — "this is but a bagatelle, — here is nothing which ought to astonish you. It is only essential to keep your reason enlightened and then be convinced."

"This is all that I wish," said the Prince.

"Then follow me," said Maximus; and he led the way, descending innumerable steps beneath the temple into an obscure grotto, which was wholly prepared and furnished for magical purposes. These, however, were not seen by Julian, in the nearly total obscurity which prevailed. No word was spoken. The awe inspired by the indescribably palpable atmosphere, which seemed filled with invisible spirits, caused Julian to grasp the warm, beating pulse of Maximus. His own hand was icy cold, and he felt more than anything else the need of a human heart near his own.

Maximus cast upon the altar various kinds of incense, invoking the celestial and infernal Deities. Distant sounds like thunder, that gradually drew nearer, filled the grotto with flashes of light, which left the darkness more intense, till, in forms like fire, Julian saw pass before him the spectres of his ancestors, from Claudian, the founder of the family, to Julius Constantius, that gentle prince, his father, and, last of all, his murdered brother, Gallus. Julian, still a novice, was overpowered with terror, and, forgetting all but his Christian education, made continually the sign of the cross.

Immediately the spectres vanished. Maximus, afraid of losing his pupil, presented another and more entrancing image,—Constantius on his death-bed, and Julian clothed with the insignia of Emperor receiving the crown from the Roman Senate. Julian, overpowered with terror, sank trembling upon his knees, and repeated again and again the Christian sign. Again all vanished, and Julian stood alone with the magician.

"Acknowledge," said he, "the power of the cross. The spectres that you invoked in the name of your Gods fled before the mere sign of the Nazarene!"

"What!" said Maximus, observing that Julian trembled; "think you that the Immortals were afraid of your pitiful sign? No, my Prince, the Gods will have no commerce with a profane person, who trembles at the thought of that malefactor of Galilee!"

Maximus saw that his pupil was steeped in credulity, and he seized the occasion to place before him in pictured representations the glories of the restored heathen superstitions. He impressed and reiterated the idea that Julian himself was preordained by the Gods to rebuild their altars, restore their temples, purify their ceremonies, reunite the ancient Grecian beauty with the worship of nature, and symbolize again that worship in the beautiful forms of nymphs and dryads, and all the exquisite creations of genius.

Thus before he left Maximus he had mentally renounced his allegiance to Christianity. But for a time he must conceal the change. He was indeed a simple youth, without a shadow of influence. His next move might be to a prison provided for him by his cousin the Emperor. He knew that he had but one *friend*, and that one was the Empress. Humility was his safest guardian: he therefore shaved his beard, and assumed the simple dress of a Christian stoic.

CHAPTER V.

EUSEBIA.

JULIAN, on the point of renouncing Christianity, was apparently unconscious how much of it he retained in his transfigured Paganism, and how much his character had been moulded by it. He believed in a Supreme Divinity, in the divine origin and the eternal destiny of man; he wished to revive the old heathen religion by means of that internal revelation upon which the Platonists insisted, and to give new life to that from which the living spirit had fled. He possessed that philosophic tendency which strives to penetrate into the natural causes of things, and rebels against all unnecessary belief. To him the Supreme Creator was manifested in the various forms of nature, which were portioned out and ruled over by the heathen Divinities, and he was superstitiously credulous in his belief in their care and guardianship of himself. He imagined himself their favorite, and he held perpetual communion of love and worship with them.

This arose from the pride of his character; — he could not admit the idea of a divine nature in the humble form of a servant, with a crown of thorns. He had no ideal conception of true holiness, which manifests itself in humble love, in disinterested service, in hidden, unassuming goodness. With all his striving after an heroic virtue, he was unacquainted with his own heart; he was unconscious of his own imperfections, and he constantly allowed in himself a biting, sarcastic tone, the strongest weapon he was at this moment capable of wielding against Christianity.

Julian met Mardonius on the steps of the great temple. The latter was pale as death, and whispered in the ear of the Prince, that he had seen the captain of the secret police of the Emperor lurking about the temple.

"Have you seen the eunuch Eusebius?" asked Julian.

"God forbid! he is not with them, my Prince."

"I fear no other!" said Julian; and, fortified as he was by the predictions of Maximus, he determined to meet his enemies boldly.

"Concealment, flight, — anything is preferable to the tender mercies of Constantius," cried his anxious servant.

"Think you that Minerva will desert her worshipper? or that Apollo, who makes it light to me, will not make it dark round about my enemies?"

"I should place no confidence in God or Goddess; the Lord of Hosts will protect his own, if it be his will that you, my Prince, should not fall into the hands of your enemies."

Mardonius was no Christian, neither was he altogether a Heathen. His soul was imbued with Homer, and also with the study of the Jewish prophets and poets. He was himself a follower of Plato, and led what he called an "orphic life," and taught his pupil those abstemious and even ascetic habits which so offended the Antiochians.

It was too late for concealment or flight, as the guard, which the Emperor had ordered to conduct the Prince to Milan, were already in one of the avenues of the temple waiting for him. He was conducted secretly, but without violence, to Milan, where the Emperor and court were then established. The place appointed for his residence was a castle strongly fortified and guarded; and as he entered it, the fall of the drawbridge, the clash of the weapons, the measured tread of sentinels, told him but too plainly, as darkness settled down upon the castle, that he was a prisoner in the power of his deadly enemy. He had sufficient thought to conceal his grief for the murder of his brother, and prudence to repress every complaint; and thus, for a person impetuous and not usually master of his indignation, he proved that it was not in vain that he had learnt self-control or dissimulation in the school of Maximus.

Surrounded by spies and reporters of every word and every gesture to his deadly enemy, the eunuch, he longed for death or exile to the country of the barbarians.

The night had fallen, a night without moon or stars; Julian had lighted his lamp, and by its aid was examining the small apartment forming his prison. In a recess of the wall, lighted by a high window, he found cases containing some of his beloved authors. "Ah!" said he, "here is the providence of my noble friend, the Empress; no other would have thought of so precious a solace for my solitary hours." In comparison with books, man and woman also were worthless to Julian. He unrolled his favorites, and soon everything else was forgotten, till the watches of the night were nearly over.

At length he looked at the clepsydra; the midnight hour had passed, and, without the least desire for sleep, he drew aside the heavy curtain and looked into the darkness. No star was visible, and the only sounds were the measured steps of the sentinels, and the word as they passed each other, guarding the fortress of his prison.

At last he fancied he heard lighter footsteps and whispered words; he perceived also a peculiar perfume, which he remembered years ago, and was endeavoring to recollect under what circumstances, when, turning towards the door, a form enveloped in a robe of black stood before it.

"O blest Minerva!" he cried, "thou knewest that thy servant was without consolation, and hast sent this angel to assure and comfort me."

Eusebia — for it was the Empress — smiled at this mingling in thought of Christian angels with the Pagan Goddess of Wisdom, but a shade of sorrow passed across her noble brow.

"Ah!" she said, "the same faithlessness in woman's friendship and in God's protection!" — and she made the sign of the cross as she seated herself upon the couch and signed to Julian to sit near her.

"I should be ungrateful indeed, did I not believe in you, noble friend; this last proof of your regard takes from me all words to express my gratitude!" — and he stooped so low as to kiss the hem of the Empress's robe.

Julian, the lover of beauty in the abstract, was singularly insensible to the beauty of women. He had never been enthralled by the lovely maidens attending the Empress, and for Eusebia herself, to whom contemporary history assigns exquisite beauty and grace, as well as singular loveliness of character, he felt only reverence and gratitude. She was not spared by the licentious tongues of that age; selfish and unworthy motives were assigned to all her noble efforts to serve and save him.

"Slanderous and venomous tongues are even now busy; but who can warn and shield you, should I be silent?"

"Noble friend, tell me, what shall I do?"

"Prince, this last step you have so unwisely taken has made your position still more dangerous, — this resort to sorcerers and magicians —"

Julian turned pale. Was he, then, so closely watched? were secret spies all around him?

"Was there no assurance from Christian teachers, no miracle of Christian faith, to teach you to rely upon God's protection?"

"Ah, your Majesty! no miraculous cross has appeared moving before the unworthy descendant of our great ancestor, Constantine, to lead him on to conquest as well as crime."

"Julian, you are young; you do not understand

the terrible anarchy and the atrocious crimes of this age, and you do not see in the new faith the dawn of a new era, when a purer religion shall bring purer lives, and — "

"Pardon me, beloved Princess, if I am deaf and blind to that which is so clear to your vision. Did Constantine's new faith prevent the murder that destroyed the young life of Crispus, his own son?"

"Julian, that was a fearful crime, and fearfully was it repented! Constantine wept away his life, after being convinced of his son's innocence. Constantine committed sins; but compared with those Emperors who preceded him, his was a divine soul."

"The new religion," said Julian, with scorn,— "did it utter a whisper to stay the murder of all my family, or a word to prevent that last act which has left me alone in the world,— Gallus!" — and the Empress saw tears in the eyes of Julian.

"Those were cruel acts of state policy in those who think they must reign *alone*, or perish," continued Eusebia. "We must look to private life for reforms; the humble religion of Jesus begins there. All women should be Christians."

"Yes, your new faith is suited to women, and to men like women. Pardon me, Princess,— it is worthy of the abject, the cowardly. But are these the *humble* followers of the Nazarene, before whom your Majesty kneels to beg a blessing, and in whose presence the *Empress* dare not sit, till bidden by the successors of the fishermen? My blood boils with indignation."

"Ah! Prince, I obey the order of the Emperor! He would conciliate the Church. But all are not so—"

"Many of these fishers of men have caught in their nets only fine pearls, and have fished for diamonds rather than for lost souls. See your Paul of Antioch driving to the Basilica with his snow-white mules and golden harness. Even the jewels upon his sandals are worth a kingdom. The proud Bishop calls himself the disciple of him who trod barefoot the stony paths of Judæa. See him in the pulpit; the perfumed handkerchiefs of the women waving before him, and their white hands clapping his eloquence."

"Look rather, Julian, at the noble Bishop of Cæsarea. See his whole fortune given up to the poor, the aged, the orphan, the blind. Look at his houses for the sick, the destitute, the stranger! He calls to all the suffering to come to him. His houses for the destitute form a town of themselves."

"Yes, they form a town," said Julian, "and eat

up the country. Empress! the expenses of the Bishops, their carriages, horses, servants, food, as they travel at the public cost, from council to council, to reconcile quarrels, and to decide upon articles of faith in this new religion, which was not dreamed of four hundred years ago, threaten to destroy the Empire. This carpenter's son, who perished as a malefactor, will cost the Empire more than all the gorgeous worship of the true Gods. O that they would again take possession, and put down these idle, vain conceits!"

"Prince, have you forgotten that any institution, Divine or human, which would rouse and interest the multitude, must either surround itself with splendor, with gorgeous rites, sacrifices, incense, or must work moral miracles. The majority are incapable of appreciating the simplicity, the true moral sublimity, of him who, though equal with God, made himself the servant of all—"

"And could not protect himself or escape the death of a malefactor," interrupted Julian.

The Empress made the sign of the cross. "Are you, also, Prince, dazzled by success? Are you capable of appreciating only that which is made known by fame? Must the *aureola* rest upon a head that you may honor it? Do you forget your own Plato's definition of a divine man?"

"I remember Plato's definition of a perfect man,—'one who is the servant of all.' Noble Princess! the pride of your Bishops is not the only stumbling-block to my belief. The discussions of your Church appall me. Ah, you are more cruel to each other than the Heathen have been to you. Then your differences are upon subjects so open to ridicule, that they furnish comedies for the theatres of unbelievers."

The Empress would not enter upon the defence of the Church in this particular, with so keen a satirist as Julian. She was an Arian in faith, and abhorred persecution. They were both silent for some moments; at length Eusebia said, looking earnestly at the young Prince, "Julian, I have placed precious hopes upon you. Educated a Christian, but instructed in all the learning and philosophy of antiquity, I hoped that, like Paul, you would place yourself at the head of the new era and lead on that blessed period, promised to the Church and the nations."

Julian laughed that scornful laugh which so distorted his features that even his admirers found it hateful. "You forget, Princess, your Galilean said, 'I came not to bring peace, but a sword.' Certainly his words have been prophetic. Look at your so-called Church, rent into a hundred fragments.

See bishops and deacons grasping the portion of widows; virgin orphans sold to the highest bidder; Arians torturing Athanasians; Athanasians piercing the hearts of matrons and maidens; old men broken upon the wheel!"

The Empress would not answer, but went on. "How glorious would it be for a young Prince like yourself to check all these horrors; to be able to understand the signs of the times; to see that the old religion is utterly powerless to cure the horrible disorders and crimes of the age; that it is like a decayed and hollow tree, dead and rotten at the root, but here and there showing a tuft of beauty at the extremities of the branches, as you refresh it with costly wine, and heap treasures about the root: it cannot revive; it must fall and be thrown to the furnace. The new era has begun. O Julian! you must lead it on."

"Ah, that will I," said Julian, his eye flashing and his whole frame expanding, "but with the Olympian Jupiter as fellow-leader; with Apollo and his virgin sister, with the divine Pallas, the celestial Venus, the Loves, the Graces, not in company with the Galilean and his fishermen and magdalens. Yes, Empress! to bring back that age of heroism would reward the ambition of a God; — again to crown the temples with beauty, and to spread over the rough and stony paths of life the green and flowing veil of poetry;—to restore the time when in every form of nature we saw the impress of a God. Gentle beings, the friends of man, dwelt in every thicket. Juno reposed upon the fleecy clouds, and tender doves bore invisibly the car of Venus. Lovely naiads poured the rivers from their urns, or sprang from the silver foam of cascades. The brooks were swelled by the tears of Ceres, as she wept the loss of her beloved daughter. The virgin priestess knelt praying at the altar of the Graces, and made vows for others to all the holy Charities."

"Yes," said the Empress, "it is easy thus to represent the fair side of Heathenism; this worship, for I cannot call it a religion, is beautiful in subjects for art and for the poetry of Julian, but it is powerless and worse than powerless against the wickedness of the age."

"But the soul, the fire of genius! they are not in your Christian literature. Where is the immortal spirit which inspires the hymns of Pindar. Who has carved the dead stone into the godlike forms of Phidias?"

"Prince! you are a stranger to the inspired hymns of the Hebrew?"

Julian hurried on, as was his custom, without

listening to the Empress. "Dearer is every gift when we know that it comes from the bounty of a God. How lovely is the pearl-covered field beneath the bow of Iris; the glow of morning with Aurora's saffron-colored robe! How sweet is youth in the happy features of Ganymede and Hebe! how dear to lovers must be the form of Hymen, when he knits the bond of love's eternal union! Even life's tender thread is severed by the hand of the Parcæ, and the genius of death, as he extinguishes his torch, receives the last sigh with a kiss!" *

"Ah yes! but where in your Elysium is found the soul, so gently borne away. *There* only are your heroes and sages. There is no place there for the gentle and the humble, — the suffering souls. The mother will not find again her innocent child. No reward is promised there for heroic souls enslaved by the despots of earth. But in the Christian Heaven, all, the oppressed and the humble, the noble souls of whom the world was not worthy, shall be recognized beneath the white robes of martyrdom."

"By the Gods," cried Julian, "a reason for not desiring to go there! Ah no! beloved Empress! keep your Christian Heaven for priests and monks."

The Empress rose, and checked abruptly the sar-

* See Schiller's Ode.

casm she saw upon his lips. "I have not yet made known my errand, Prince," she said. "Constantius at length has consented to grant you leave to pursue your favorite studies in Greece, in your beloved Athens. He demands only, in return, that you avoid all political questions, and abstain from all expressions of opinion."

"Enough, enough, Empress! It is all I desire! Athens! my beloved Athens! the eye, the heart of the world! Eternal thanks, noble friend! It is to you alone I owe this boon. The immortal Gods reward you! But how soon am I permitted to depart?" The impetuosity of the Prince almost checked the current of his words as they rushed forth to express his gratitude.

The Empress smiled. "Are you so anxious to leave your friends, — so hastily, without a word of farewell?"

"Ah yes! beloved Empress! add one more favor. Obtain leave for me, that I may go unattended, — that I may journey as a humble individual, without these hated guards, without these disgraceful bonds!"

"For such a boon the Emperor demands of you eternal silence; that you abstain from all remark whatever upon his actions, past or present."

"Ah yes! I understand; oblivion of wrong, forgetfulness that in my veins alone flows the blood that should be beating in many murdered breasts."

"Julian!" cried the Empress, "you forget that spies are all around you; even at this midnight hour are listeners."

"Thanks, thanks, noble friend! but the ear is not curious at the door of the disgraced. One more question. Must I beg an audience of the Emperor? humble myself before his sycophants, his trembling slaves, the company of his pale monks? Must the proud Eusebius witness my humiliation?"

"I think the Emperor would avoid a meeting while the memory of Gallus is fresh. But look towards the east. Is not that the faint gleam of returning day?" said the Empress.

"Ah no! it is but the northern Aurora"; and as he saw the Empress turning the key of the heavy door, he cried, "Minerva, and all the immortal Gods, for ever bless you!"

"Rather the Almighty and his Son!" said Eusebia, as she made the sign of the cross, and looked back with a smile.

CHAPTER VI.

GREECE.

When Constantius restored to Julian the fortune of his mother, he permitted him also to retain in his service the slave, now the freed man, Mardonius, who had also been his tutor, and Oribasius, his faithful and long-attached friend, who united the offices of librarian and physician.

The Prince now stood, together with Mardonius, upon the deck of one of those deeply laden corn ships, which was returning from Egypt to Athens, with a cargo of wheat. They had embarked in a small vessel upon the river Padus or Po, and crossing, at its whole length, the Adriatic Sea, they went to one of the ports of Crete, where they met and embarked upon the larger vessel, it having stopped there on its way to Athens. They were now drawing to the close of their long and tedious voyage.

The calm, almost waveless Ægean permitted their heavy craft to make but slow progress. Julian, in his simple student's dress, remained unrecognized, as he stood conversing in a low voice with Mardonius, whose venerable appearance attracted far more attention than the Prince. The old man's high and wrinkled brow subdued the expression of deeply piercing Jewish eyes, while wisdom seemed lurking behind his beard and gray locks. His dress was simple and elegant, and in his hand he bore a small lyre. Among other accomplishments, he had taught Julian music, a science of which the Prince was always passionately fond.

"How poor would have been Constantius's gift to me of my mother's fortune, if he had not enhanced it by the gift of her friend!" said Julian, in a low voice.

"The fortune was yours by right, my Prince, and the friend was yours by the act and will of that friend himself," said the other.

"Ah! but the Emperor might have withheld from me, as from Gallus, that treasure more precious than all the others."

"Basilina —"

"Ah! tell me of my mother. I was too young to remember aught of her, except two large mild eyes always turned upon me."

"We differed only in this, — that she was a Christian, while I — I still wait for the coming of the Messiah! Her father was the first Roman Senator who publicly professed his faith in the new religion; induced to the act, I verily believe, by the loveliness of its fruits in his own daughters."

A dark cloud passed over the face of the Prince. He trembled as he asked, "And you were sought to instruct her in the language of the Jewish Scriptures?"

"No; her thirst for the poetry of the heroic ages was too ardent. Homer and the Greek poets were her daily food; but while she pursued these studies, she retained the heart of an angel and the language of a seraph."

"Ah, Mardonius! I sucked with my mother's milk my love of Homer and Sophocles."

"That was not all, my Prince. How often did noble words fall from her sweet lips! 'Inspire my son,' she said, 'with modesty and gentleness, with contempt for sensual and trifling pleasures. Let pure nobleness, truth, gentleness, be his virtues. Let him love a retired and studious life.'"

"Thanks, thanks, my mother!" cried Julian.

"But with your vivid imagination and ardent passions I was afraid, my Prince, of inspiring disgust rather than love," said Mardonius.

"That fear was vain; my passion is to learn. I do not readily forget what has once made an impression. I learnt to lisp the noble language of the poets from my mother's lips, and I long to make those poems my own. Homer, Pindar, Sophocles, are my masters. I love them as an ardent youth loves his mistress."

Mardonius smiled, and, from the instruction he continued to give him, one would have thought that Julian was still his pupil, had not the resolute and manly expression, and the dark eye which flashed with intensity from beneath the thick eyebrow, showed that the Prince could be, and that he *was*, the master spirit. They stood thus in the mild air of the summer night, till the first flush of the crimson dawn began to break over the Ægean.

It was reflected in the almost waveless mirror of the deep waters, and upon the projecting headlands of the islands, giving them the appearance of vast flashing gems, rising above the waters. A transparent curtain of vapor was just lifted as the morning breeze curled over the sea, disclosing the enchanting landscapes of the islands, while Hesperus, the morning star, large and calm, the single star in the sky, hung like a brilliant lamp over the whole magnificent scene.

As they approached Sunium, whose promontory was crowned with the white columns of the temple of Minerva, the vestibule as it were of the still more crowded temple of all the Gods, which would open upon him in Athens, Julian's cheek glowed, for these Gods would not be to him merely objects of taste and admiration, but of that secret faith which he in his soul avowed. He was silently contrasting the splendor and power of the classic mythology with the homely and despised symbols of the new faith, — the manger and the cross, and, between these, the humble life, the obscure and unrewarded labor, of him he called the "Galilean."

As the breeze freshened and filled their sails, and their ship neared the coast, Julian saw the central rock of the Acropolis, round which Athens is grouped, crowned with its immortal temples and the colossal statue of Pallas Athena. The form and color of this rock, surmounted by its marble temples beneath the transparent sky of Greece, were more grand, and of more entrancing beauty, than anything Julian had imagined. He began, by its silver light, to trace the winding course of the Ilissus, and to perceive upon the west of the city the olive groves of Plato's Academy. The mountain peaks of Hymettus were now touched with a rosy light, and at last the golden helmet and spear-top of the Goddess, as she stood upon the Acropolis, flashed back the beams of the risen sun. Julian stood entranced by so much beauty.

The sun was high when they entered the harbor of the Piræus, already crowded by vessels from every port, with ships of war and ships of burden, the latter heavy and bulky in order to carry great quantities of goods ; also, square-rigged vessels, loaded with wheat from Egypt. The little pleasure-boats of the Athenians were skimming from port to port, distinguished by their sails of brilliant dyes and rowers with gay liveries, the prows bearing some tutelary Deities of gold or silver, wreathed with garlands of natural flowers.

Julian landed at the port nearest the sepulchre of Themistocles, and, as he desired to preserve his incognito, he determined to walk, accompanied by Mardonius, the four or five miles that led from the Piræus to the gate of Athens. But, said he to Mardonius, "I cannot proceed till I have entered these temples of Zeus and Athena, and offered my homage to the glorious Divinities, more worthy of worship than anything the Piræus contains."

"More worthy than the Cnidian Venus?" asked his companion, "whose temple is close to the sea."

"Venus is no Divinity of mine, as you well know," said the Prince.

"The Venus to whose homage I would direct you is not the Goddess whose worship has been perverted into sensual delight, but she who is the ideal of moral beauty, veiled like pure love and adorned by all the graces," said Mardonius.

Along the walls of the Piræus were colonnades of marble, and also the tombs of the great men of Attica, their poets and tragedians. Julian, the enthusiast, could not pass the tomb of Menander, nor the empty sepulchre of Euripides, without repeating aloud the great thoughts and the inspired lines with which his memory was stored. But he soon found himself involved in the throng and pressure of the market-place, the great bazaar, where merchandise of every species, and every production of the known world, were collected.

Merchants from every climate here met travellers from every land Here were crowded taverns, inns, wine-shops, workshops sending forth a din of metal, and mechanics plying their craft in the open air. On one side were heaps of common pottery, and, not far from them, collections of vases of exquisite form, of varied and beautiful designs. Shops filled with costly stuffs, cloths of gold, and the Alexandrian purple, of such brilliancy that all other colors appeared faded by its side. Here were silks and spices from beyond the Euphrates, heavy cargoes of marble, innumerable objects of art of exquisite beauty, statues, sculptures, bassi rilievi, ready for packing in order to be sent from Athens, as was the custom in the fourth century, to every part of the known world.

Julian and his companion threaded their way through the crowded streets and no less crowded colonnades towards the Piræenian gate. The Prince was nervously anxious to attract no attention; but the quick-witted Athenians soon discovered that he was a stranger, and also inferred from his youth and the intellectual expression of his features that he was a Roman and a student. His cloak was often plucked from behind, which was the usual fashion of attracting attention, and cards of the various sophists and teachers of the schools of philosophy thrust into his hands.

They diverged to the right towards the Phalerian road, and Julian felt that he was indeed in Attica, the country of the Gods and of beauty, when he saw the Ilissus flowing pure and transparent in its rocky bed, bordered by low bushes of the agnus cactus, its snowy blossoms filling the air with fragrance. The grass was high and luxuriant, and, passing from the busy, noisy market, there was a quiet summer air brooding over the country, where lovely springs of water flowed, and the song of the cicada was heard.

Julian had now passed the gate and found himself in the labyrinth of temples, monuments, statues of dazzling marble, of ivory and gold, the representations of Gods and heroes. A colonnade of marble extended the whole way from the gate to the Cerameicus, where throngs of people walked sheltered from both sun and rain. Along the margin of this colonnade were small altars dedicated to various Divinities, with votive offerings, sometimes of great value; busts of great men, poets, philosophers; beautiful vases; stones exquisitely cut; and all adorned with the freshest flowers.

"What a refined and cultivated people must these Athenians be," said the Prince, "that such exquisite works of art can remain from year to year in the most crowded thoroughfare, where thousands pass every hour, and yet never incur the smallest injury."

"And thousands like yonder man," said Mardonius, pointing to one abject in appearance, whose few rags seemed taking leave of each other, "capable of admiring and appreciating these exquisite gems without possessing an obolus."

"These fresh flowers also remain untouched, not a leaf is plucked, not a blossom allowed to wither. They love the beautiful in nature as much as they admire art."

"And yet," said Mardonius, in a low voice, "the people of this city are corrupt, dishonest, avaricious, cruel. It proves that Heathenism, though it admits the highest culture of the intellect, is wholly powerless against the vices of civilization."

"With all their restless activity, their quick perceptions, the love of the ludicrous, as well as of the beautiful, — see there, — there is their temple and their altar to Pity. Has any other people ever erected an altar to pity?" asked Julian.

"Their altar to the unknown God awakens the hope that they may soon learn to know the only God, the Jehovah of all nations," said Mardonius.

CHAPTER VII.

ATHENS.

The next morning Julian awoke in Athens; his eye sought for the first time the deep blue sky of Greece, and his eager ear drank in the melody of the Attic tongue. He left to Mardonius the care of providing a dwelling, commodious for himself and servants, and hastened out to breathe the air of Athens, taking the street to the Cerameicus. He would first pay his homage to the tomb of Plato, who was buried beneath its enclosure. The bell for market had just ceased ringing, and his way led through that liveliest of all scenes in the very hour of its greatest activity. The traders had set up their stalls, and the venders were crying their wares. Here female bakers had piled up their rolls; there simmered the kettles of women boiling peas and other vegetables. Piles of frail crockery were hard by, and the shrill tongues of women, vociferating curses, lost their Attic grace, when the frail wares and the slippery rolls were thrown to the ground together, by an unlucky passenger.

Here were the greatest variety of dainty fish, — fish was the greatest luxury of the table of the Athenians, — the purest oil, transparent as ether; fresh-made cheeses; fragrant honey from the bees of Hymettus. A little way farther on was the flower-market, where were displayed, all fresh, the treasures of Flora. Young women and old stood ready to receive orders for flowers, to adorn the evening feast. Here were garlands for the heads of young men and old, who were on their way to the symposium; — for in Athens, men, even more than women, adorned themselves with flowers. Here were the freshest wreaths for the altars and statues of the Gods; beautiful garlands for the domestic altar, and for the doors of houses when a child was born; — fresh flowers being always in Athens the sign of rejoicing. Public criers crossed every moment, crying the sale of a house, or of a slave, or the loss of articles of value. In another part of the market-place stood cooks, laborers, slaves, runners, down to the lowest menials, waiting to be hired by those in want. Julian had left this care to Mardonius, and hastened on through the arcade occupied by the money-changers. Here were usurers and their victims, bankers and receivers of pledges. On their tables beside them lay their scales, with piles of silver and copper money. Crowds had already collected around them, disputing as to the sums and the interest, in their shrill voices, and with all the gesticulation of Greek vivacity. Julian, as yet, had nothing to do with these affairs, and, hastening on, passed the Cerameicus, between which and the garden of the Academy is the monument to Plato.

Here was the tomb of the great man he reverenced above all others. It might almost be said that Plato held in the mind of Julian the place which devoted Christians accord to their Master. After paying the tribute of his devout homage, he followed reluctantly the path to the Lyceum gardens, regretting that he also could not have been fed with wisdom from the lips of Plato.

The Ilissus flowed through the gardens of the Lyceum, bordered by groves of plane-trees and filled with thickets of the agnus cactus, that shrub whose blossoms are so white and fragrant. Julian threw himself upon the grass and listened to the musical flow of the fountains, following with his eye the winding paths, bordered by trees and flowers, among which the nightingales dwelt unscared. It was not the hour when the gardens were fullest, yet there were many graceful Athenians wearing their robes of soft white wool, bordered with stripes of various vivid colors, and embroidered with golden grasshoppers, to indicate that they were the native Athenians, descended like the grasshopper from its sacred soil and fed by its dew.

Crowds were hurrying to the Gymnasium, and thence to the baths, a luxury indispensable to the Greeks as well as the Romans. The Gymnasium was very full. In the arcades surrounding the peristyle were groups of men of all ages, discussing animating subjects, gesticulating, jesting, and betting.

The grounds for exercise were so full that there was scarcely room for the foot-races, the wrestling, and those exercises of strength which were stimulated by the loud acclamations of spectators. A dense throng had gathered around a pair of wrestlers; but a weak point had just been descried, and one of them came to the ground with a shout, just as the ring opened for Julian to pass through.

The hour for the Gymnasium had passed, and now all who had taken part, the spectators also, began to disperse, and to rush on to the baths. This was a luxury, which, together with the practice of anointing the limbs with pure oil, perfuming, and dressing the hair, demanded much time. Julian despised the last effeminacy, but the bath was necessary for the healthful action of mind and body; he therefore mingled with the crowd and passed on, noticed only as a young man of noble bearing and a stranger.

Julian returned through the Agora. The market was now over, and he could observe at leisure its precious works of art. Porticos or cloisters of marble surrounded the square, and these were adorned with altars and fountains and statues of the great men of Athens. In the centre was the altar to the twelve gods, which was to Athens what the golden mile-stone was to Rome, as from it all distances were counted to the extremities of the land. Here, also, was that unique altar to Pity, the Athenians being the only people who recognized the divinity of that holiest emotion, and built an altar for its worship.

When Julian returned from the bath, he found his apartments, under the care of Mardonius, already arranged for him. The private houses of the Athenians were never large, and as he needed no second suite for women, Julian's consisted of a single house, with apartments for himself and his friends. Mardonius had arranged the house, in as far as a temporary residence would allow him to do, in reference to the retirement, quietness, and earnest study so dear to his master. Between it and the street was a small court filled with trees and flowering shrubs. This court removed the peristyle, the common entrance to Grecian houses, from the noise and bustle of the street, and gave it almost the retirement of the country. Around three sides of the peristyle ran a double arcade of Doric columns, furnished with seats and couches and intended for walking or for refreshment in the open air. In the centre a fountain threw a perpetual shower of diamond drops into the air, and soothed with its musical sound, or led to contemplation by its murmured flow. A border of moss was kept of an emerald green by the perpetual spray of the fountain, and beyond this moss were narrow beds of flowers, carefully watered and weeded, and renewed as soon as they faded. On the right hand of the entrance was an exquisite Apollo, uniting "the ideal of youthful beauty with the ideal of manly strength," and on the left, Julian's tutelary goddess, Minerva, his celestial protectress, to whom he constantly looked for counsel, and whose eyes cast down seemed ever to regard him with favor. These statues, from the chisel of Polycletus, were exquisite works of art, and scarcely inferior to any in the Grecian temples. On the fourth side was a recess leading into the library; before the door, or rather before the purple curtain which served the purpose of a door, stood an altar to Helios, upon which incense was perpetually burning, and where Julian daily offered his prayers.

This precious room, the library or study, opened directly behind the altar to Helios, so that when the Prince was reading or writing, he had only to draw aside the curtain, to know that the incense was burning; to add more, or fresh flowers to the altar. Julian's passion for the works of the poets, philosophers, and tragedians, in short, for all works of genius, has often been mentioned. In procuring them he spared neither expense nor trouble, and perhaps it was the only thing, except in generosity to his friends, in which he was really lavish of his money.

Broad shelves ran all around the room, lighted from the top, upon which were deposited the precious rolls of parchment, each in its scrinium or case. The titles of the books were suspended in ornamental tablets from the outward end, or engraved on the outside. An ancient library must have presented a very different appearance from one of modern days; but beside the books, tablets of various sizes covered with a thin coating of wax were everywhere lying around, that Julian might have every facility for writing his thoughts as they occurred.

The most precious part of this room has not been mentioned. This was the portion near the hearth, emphatically the sacred sanctuary of home in every Grecian house, where the Lares and Penates had their place. These were usually small statues of guardian deities, or images of honored ancestors or of departed friends, cherished with the utmost reverence, and regarded as the guardian angels of the family. In this sanctuary of Julian, they were small images in gold and ivory of his favorite divinities, to whom he addressed his daily and hourly private devotions, and sought their direction in every hour of his occupation, and in every change of his life. Fresh flowers were renewed upon their shrines every morning, and when their sweetness was a little exhaled, perfumes were added to imitate their sweetest odors.

All through the midnight hours Julian's lamp, suspended above his writing-table, was fed with oil by a slave who remained awake for the purpose, and as the clepsydra, or water-clock, ran out, through the slow hours of night, his ardor in study increased, till the first ray of eastern light, striking upon the awning suspended over his roof, threw a crimson flush, which paled the midnight lamps upon his table; then he cast himself upon his couch for a few hours of sleep.

CHAPTER VIII.

THE LECTURES.

JULIAN'S sleeping-room was lighted only through the adjoining library; it had admitted therefore but a faint and doubtful light when Mardonius drew aside the curtain, and the Prince asked him what was the hour.

"The gnomon casts a shadow almost to the extremity of its length," said Mardonius.

"The sun then is not very high, and I am not too late to choose my teachers before the lectures begin."

Gregory of Nazianzen, who was a student in Athens at the time when Julian was also a student there, says: "Every sophist in Athens had his own school and party, who were devoted to him with incredible zeal, while there prevailed in the young students a complete sophistic *furor*. They canvassed and struggled for their masters; and it was not the custom to attend different lectures at the same time, but each one, as a rule, attached himself to one master. The poorer students lent themselves to the business of recruiting, and thus got exemption from class payment. An ingenuous youth could scarcely set his foot upon Attic ground without being claimed as an adherent of a party. They wrangled, they struggled, they threw themselves upon him, and it might easily happen that a young man was drawn quite away from the very teacher he had come expressly to attend."

Julian had been informed of these strange customs of the students, and prepared himself for a struggle. At the same time he put on the simple dress of a private Roman citizen, in order to slip quietly along, and attract as little attention as possible. He bade Mardonius follow him, and, taking the street which led to the Academy, he found it easy, without being observed, to mingle with the crowd already pressing on to the same quarter.

How seductive were the lectures of the sophists to the youth of this age, presented as they were in the attractive garb of poetry and philosophy, especially those of Proharæsius, to whom Rome erected a silver statue as large as life, — "The queen of cities to the king of orators." The old myths, expounded and idealized, were wreathed with the flowers of eloquence, while around, on the heights and in the valleys, stood the serene temples of the Gods, where their eternal youth or perfect manhood was consecrated by exquisite art, adorned by the profuse gifts of nature in groves, flowers, and perfumes, like incense. It was easy to be a Heathen here. It was not easy to continue a Christian, and many who came as Christian youth were seduced to embrace again the old faith.

As soon as it was perceived that Julian was a stranger, a hundred hands were thrust out and a hundred programmes of lectures were pressed upon him. He knew that any inquiry as to the audience-benches, or even the locality of any lecture he wished to hear, would be answered by a practical joke, or an epigram, putting him completely in the wrong. He therefore allowed himself to be borne passively on, while Greeks, Armenians, Cappadocians, Ionians, Asiatics, even Jews from Palestine, vociferated, struggled, and contended for him. These young men were full of exuberant spirits, and ready for every practical joke within the limits of that generosity which belonged to their age.

In the midst of the Babel of tongues, one cried out in Greek, "By Pallas Athena, here is your place with the sons of Attica." Another cried,

"Venus and the Graces forgive you! he is a Syrian, or I am a Jew." This was followed by a shout; and another cried out, "Vulcan was by at the making of those broad shoulders." "By all the Gods," shouted another, "I espy on his face the owl of Minerva." "Old father Time has lent him his forelock for a beard," said one. "His father was a vender of old clothes," said another, "and left him his trading stock." "Venus save us! you may see by his beard that he belongs to the children of Israel," shouted one of them.

Julian now said aloud, that, if the gentlemen would permit him to proceed, he wished to listen to a lecture of Proharæsius. This was received by cheers and clapping of hands from one party, and by hisses and groans from the other. The crowd became every moment more dense, and Julian was pressed upon every side, and nearly taken off his feet; voices were rising higher and higher, and the throng continually augmenting, and as none of the lecturers had yet appeared, Mardonius pressed nearer, in order that, if the Prince should be borne down, he might be able to assist him. This was perceived, and immediately greeted with loud hisses, and one cried out, "Make room for the dry nurse of the young giant." Another said, "Make room for the mummy from the Catacombs."

The Prince had hitherto merely indicated the lecture he wished to hear ; but at this crisis he raised his voice and said, " Gentlemen, I am a Roman from the city of Constantine, and I wish to be permitted to join your noble company in listening to your most eloquent sophists." A tremendous shout of applause followed, and the various parties cried out, some one name, and some another; and as they did so, some of them were received with clapping of hands, others with hisses, and one or two with execrations.

The tumult was now at its height. Julian's cloak was leaving him in shreds, when at this moment two persons entered the grove of the Academy arm in arm, upon whose countenances were impressed the serenity and sweetness which come from inward peace. These were two Christian students, who were afterwards celebrated in the Church and canonized as saints, — St. Basil and St. Gregory of Nazianzen. They were pursuing their studies in the midst of the seductions of Athens, and though one of them became afterwards the bitter enemy of Julian, they now met him with the frankness and generosity which belong to the ingenuous period of youth. Gregory had studied with the Prince in Constantinople, and instantly knew his person. His noble bearing and flashing eye could not be mistaken, although he was somewhat changed by the unfashionable appendage of a thick curling beard.

Gregory whispered Julian's name to Basil, and he, perceiving how hard the Prince was pressed by the differing fraternities of students, cried in a loud voice, "Make way, gentlemen, for Prince Julian, the cousin and heir of the Emperor!" There was an instant of deep silence, and then all broke out with a shout of welcome, a huzza of triumph.

Immediately the fraternity of students calling themselves Romans, including those from Rome and Constantinople, gathered around the Prince, insisting that, according to invariable custom, he belonged to them, and must be their guest for the day. They formed themselves into a procession, two and two, with Julian in the midst, and marched through the olive groves of the Lyceum to the door of the public baths. Here they halted, and those in front raised a wild cry as though they were refused admittance, then threw themselves upon the doors, broke them down, and forced an entrance. Julian remained perfectly quiet; he had heard of this custom, and knew that it was done in order to frighten the novice. The candidate is afterwards initiated with ludicrous ceremonies, and subsequently received in the most friendly manner, as one who is now their equal, and invested with all their privileges. Still the day, or rather the night, was not over. Julian belonged to them for the supper, or principal meal of the Greeks. This was taken about sundown, and consisted of various courses, the description of which shall be left to another chapter.

CHAPTER IX.

THE SYMPOSIUM.

The supper given by the young man to honor Julian's introduction into their fraternity was prepared in the house of a wealthy student, the son of a Roman family which had long been resident in Athens. Ctesiphon, the young man, about the age of his guest, had put in requisition all his zeal to give the Prince a sumptuous repast. Since noon the slaves had been busily employed preparing for the *cœna*. The rooms had been hung with fresh garlands of exquisite taste; fresh perfumes had been scattered and fresh incense upon the shrines, while the curtains drawn back from the door opened a view of the fountain in the atrium, sending forth a perpetual shower of diamond drops, whose sound was both enlivening and soothing.

The gnomon cast a long shadow towards the east, when the young men entered the triclinium, or dining-hall. Three couches were placed at three sides of a sumptuous table of carved ivory. The seats were decked with embroidered hangings, while the cushions upon which the guests reclined were covered with purple silk. Each couch admitted three persons in a reclining posture, and each was furnished with a silken cushion upon which to rest the left elbow, while the right hand remained free. The poetical Greeks proscribed the number of their guests to the number of the Muses, and the instinct of courtesy gave the place of honor next the master of the house to the stranger, while upon ordinary occasions the one most loved reclined upon his breast.

Julian, in his most festive garment, which was plainer, and not in such exquisite taste as the Athenians', had joined Gregory and Basil as they entered the atrium. Slaves met them bringing silver basins with beautifully formed ewers of the same metal. They unfastened the thongs of their sandals, and, taking them off, poured over their feet water mixed with golden wine; after drying them they were anointed with fragrant balsam, which filled the room with its exquisite odor, and then there were placed upon their feet soft embroidered slippers.

The brow of each guest was now wreathed with a garland of fresh green leaves, and the first course was placed silently upon the table, while delicate bread of the finest quality was handed round in tiny baskets formed of ivory. Amid gossip, and gay laughter, and witty conceits, the principal meal, that which satisfied hunger, was brought to a close. At a sign from the master, slaves brought perfumed water for the hands, while others bore off the viands, and swept up all the crumbs.

Fresh garlands, woven of myrtle and roses, were now brought in, tied with ribbons of various colors. While the guests were placing their garlands, two beautiful children, flute girls, entered the room with flutes. These children had light, transparent, but perfectly imitated wings, attached to their shoulders and ankles. Butterflies of silver and precious stones were worn upon their foreheads, and wreaths of fresh flowers were so entwined, as to bind them together in graceful, fanciful forms.

No wine had yet been tasted, but now a slave came forward with a golden bowl and pitcher of beautiful shape. Ctesiphon, pouring from it undiluted wine, raised it on high, and cried aloud, "To the good Gods!" then, casting a few drops on the ground, he handed the bowl to Julian, who reclined upon his right hand, in order to pass it around the table. The flute girls accompanied this ceremony with solemn and subdued tones of exquisite melody, until the last guest had returned the cup, when they ended with a hymn of praise to all the Gods.

Meantime it had been silently observed by most of the guests, that neither Basil nor Gregory had tasted the cup of libation, and that they had furtively made the sign of the cross as it passed. Christianity was now the religion of the Empire, and although there were few Christians in Athens, the very centre of the most gorgeous Heathenism, the place where the Gods received unimpaired reverence, the avowal of Christianity subjected one to no feeling stronger than contempt, and no persecution more afflicting than ridicule. These Christians silently declining the libation occasioned only a slight lifting of the eyebrows of their host, and a slight curl of the lip of Julian.

Beautiful boys, in close-fitting tunics, wreathed with vine-leaves and crowned with roses, now brought in goblets of gold and silver, and a large vessel filled with water, called a crater, through the centre of which ran a cylinder filled with glowing coals in order to keep the water boiling; another vase of elegant form was filled with snow. The amphoras of wine, still uncorked, were placed before Ctesiphon, and slaves under his direction proceeded to extract the corks. This ceremony was performed to the sound of measured music by the flute girls.

As soon as this was done, Ctesiphon cried, "Gentlemen, what shall be the rule, *three* or *five* ?" at which there was a clamor of voices, some crying "*Three*," others "*Five*."

"The wine is old Chian and very potent," said Ctesiphon, looking at Julian.

"If I am permitted to choose," said the Prince, "my voice is for five parts water to two of wine."

Applause followed, but it was not hearty, as some of the guests wished for a carouse.

There was now a conflict of voices which lasted for some time; but Julian observed that Basil and Gregory remained silent. At length one of the company said, "To settle the rule of drinking to-night we must choose an archon."

"Yes, by Jove! we must have an archon," said another.

"No, by the grapes of Bacchus," cried one of the company, "liberty for me. Let us have no archon."

"O, but Minerva forbid! without an archon we shall all go reeling home."

"The dice, the dice! Let us decide by the dice!" interposed one of the company.

The dice were brought. The throw was in favor of an archon, and after seven casts of the dice, the lot fell upon a young man of modest appearance, from Ionia, as archon of the evening.

Theonen, the archon, then proceeded to mix the wine, three parts water to two of wine, to which snow was added as it was poured into small cups; a larger goblet being provided in case any guest should be compelled to drink fines. Fresh chaplets were now brought in, of dark-green ivy-leaves, with fresh-blooming roses.

"The ornament of winter for me," said Julian, as he placed an ivy wreath upon his thick curling locks. Some of the other guests imitated the Prince, saying, "We will leave the roses to the fairer roses, the women."

The young men now began to pledge each other in full cups, and afterwards to celebrate or rather pay secret homage to the ladies of their love, by drinking the number of *cyatha*, or measures, according to the number of letters which comprised their names.

"I drink four cups to the goddess of my idolatry," said a young Athenian, holding out a golden cup for the first measure.

"I always choose a mistress with the longest name," said another; "one that shall reach from the altar of the twelve gods to the land of the benighted Britons."

"How honest must be your homage!" they cried.

The name was sometimes guessed by the others, but it was considered unmannerly to pronounce the loved name aloud.

Ctesiphon cried, "Nine cups to her whom all Athenians reverence."

Another said, "That name is too pure for our cups and too long, — and, Ctesiphon, are we to have no amusement but drinking? Do you honor no god but Dionysos?"

"Terpsichore and all the Graces forbid!" he cried, and gave a hint to one of the slaves in attendance.

The slave admitted two grown-up children, a boy and girl, whose graceful forms and agile movements indicated at once the purpose for which they were introduced. They were dressed in short rose-colored tunics reaching to the knees, and wore wreaths of flowers, the end of which they held in their hands. They began a dance to the flutes' softest melody, which was full of grace and expression. This dance did not consist of mere senseless evolutions; it was the outward expression of an inward sentiment; it was poetry expressed by motion, in which all the limbs, the arms, the hands, took their part. Now, the flowers were thrown above their heads and towards the guests; then, again, they were wreathed about the dancers; then, both were enclosed gracefully in the folds of the flowers. This being ended, hoops covered with flowers were introduced, and the girl whirled them into the air and caught them again with quickest dexterity, dancing all the while and keeping measured step to the sound of the lute and cithara, which the boy struck from time to time.

The young men applauded and clapped their hands at every feat of dexterity, till their enthusiasm increased so greatly that flowers, rings, and trinkets of value were showered upon the happy girl.

Now was introduced a dance which excited almost a fearful interest. Sharp-pointed blades of knives were inserted in symmetrical order into the floor, and these children performed an intricate dance in the midst, with most rapid precision, passing between the sharp blades, making the most graceful evolutions, without touching hand or foot, or receiving a single scratch.

The most fastidious could have objected little to these dances, which, out of respect to Julian's well-known purity of taste, had been selected by Ctesiphon as the most chaste. These entertainments, however, frequently more than bordered on the licentious, and were abhorrent to Christians.

It was observed that, as soon as the dancers were introduced, Basil and Gregory silently withdrew, and, calling for their sandals, left the house.

"Ah," said Julian, "your Galileans have gone to fast and pray elsewhere for our conversion."

"No," said one of the youngest guests, "they have left us to finish their supper on a young and tender child."

Julian, although he hated the Christians, was always just, and would not allow that which he knew to be false to pass unopposed. He saw that the young Greek ingenuously believed what he had asserted, and, looking at him, he said, "That, my young friend, is a calumny invented by their enemies; a Christian would no sooner hurt a child than would a woman; on the contrary, they are extremely tender to young children."

"Yes," cried another,—"Venus, whose worship they abhor, forgive them for it!—they are also very loving to women."

"Ah yes!" said Ctesiphon, "if they are not slandered in this also, it is said they have revived the old, exploded dogma, that women have souls."

"By Jupiter," said another, "they not only

assert that women have souls, but that all men are brethren."

"And that our slaves are *men!*" shouted another, "*ergo* our brethren." This was answered with a scornful laugh of utter incredulity.

"What they call the *Church* of the Nazarenes is the Olympus of old women, of the cripple, of the leper, — even the hetæræ have a place there."

"Congenial company for the celestial Goddesses!" was said in an aside.

"This feigned adherence of the Emperor to the new superstition," said a young man from Rome, "has spoiled our best sports; we are no longer allowed a Christian or two to throw to the wild beasts in the arena."

"By Jupiter," said another from the same city, "a giant gladiator is far less exciting, or even amusing, than a beautiful young Christian maiden, contending with a ferocious lion."

The refined Athenians turned slightly pale, and Julian, dreading to hear a repetition of the horrors of the arena, cried out, "Enough! it is enough that they refuse to worship the immortal Gods! Let them pass!"

The conversation took again a light and graceful turn; and the Athenians sat late into the night. Julian had been longing for the quiet of his study and his books, and he now called for his sandals. This was a signal for the others to retire; all except two or three friends, who sat with Ctesiphon over the dice and wine, until the morning light shone upon the faded wreaths on their brows.

CHAPTER X.

THE ACROPOLIS.

THE Athenian awoke every morning to that glorious combination of art and nature, in transcendent beauty, which was spread out before him; how much more enchanting was it to Julian, to whom it was all new! He had not yet ascended the Acropolis, nor stood before that statue of ivory and gold from the chisel of Phidias, one of the wonders of the world. In this statue the eyes were so carefully inserted in the ivory, and so exquisitely colored, as perfectly to represent the living eye; and as it was gazed upon, it seemed to return the glance with one as living as your own.

Julian passed through the Agora before the hour of market, and having paused a moment before the temple of Aphrodite, he ascended to the Propylæa, or portico, which formed the grand entrance into the area of the Acropolis. It was approached by a gradual ascent for carriages, and then divided into two flights of magnificent marble stairs, one on each side of the splendid portico. A little on the right, as he stood upon the upper step of this glorious avenue, the Parthenon, or "house of the virgin," of pure Pentelic marble, shone like the star of memory. Beyond all conception chaste and simple in its beauty, solemn in its repose, and divine in its serenity.

Julian sat down upon the steps of the Parthenon. At this time, although the political importance of Athens had passed away, the glory of her public buildings continued in undiminished splendor. Philosophy still maintained her seat there. Although she had lost freedom, she had become the great university of the world, the dearest spot on earth to Julian, as the protectress of those studies which made the joy of his life. Below him lay the city, with all its wealth, its taste, its luxury; its varied occupations, and amusements; the eminent intelligence of its people, great, even in its decline. As he looked around, light flashed from the snowy heights of the mountains, and deep shadows rested in the dells of Hymettus. Bright villages, reposing in all their rural beauty, shaded with olive groves, were scattered around, while upon every height and every promontory rose, in perfect beauty, the shining temples of the Gods. The august shades of the great men of Greece seemed to pass before him,— Socrates and Pericles, poets, sculptors, philosophers; but where now were their descendants? He could not conceal from himself that all human greatness was taking new forms and a wholly different meaning. If Julian's sagacity had not been obscured by his pride of intellect, he must have perceived that from Christianity was springing the new, fresh, living principle which was creating all things anew. How, he asked himself, can a crucified Jew and a few fishermen create a principle which shall be stronger than all this glorious spectacle? And stretching his hand towards the statue of Pallas Athena, he swore to consecrate himself to her service.

This action seemed to attract towards him a youth of prepossessing appearance, who drew near, and stood a few steps below him. There was an expression of melancholy resignation in his countenance, so much in contrast with the beautiful charm of his youth, that it excited the curiosity of Julian, who soon perceived by external marks that he was a slave. The youth had also perceived that the Prince was a stranger, and, drawing nearer, he said, "I perceive that thou art not an Athenian, and as my services belong to the temple, perhaps I can aid or guide you, noble stranger."

Julian thanked him, and motioned him to take a seat beside him. An immense throng of people began to press up the broad steps of the portico, preceding and announcing the august ceremonies of one of the days of the festival of the Goddess, the Panathenæa. The multitude passed on to wait for the true procession, which consisted first of hundreds of people, bearing olive-branches, the tree sacred to Pallas Athena. Then came a train of the noblest matrons in Athens, clothed in magnificent robes, each attended by a female slave. Then came the most beautiful youths, wearing the armor of Athena, helmets and shields of gold, which flashed back the dazzling sunlight.

"The two venerable persons who now follow," said the youth to Julian, "are the bearers of the sacred garments of the Goddess. They have been woven with matchless skill, of threads of white and gold, by virgins selected for that purpose. Now, observe, follow the flower-bearers, the noblest virgins of Athens, bearing light baskets upon their heads filled with the freshest and fairest of Flora's gifts."

These were followed by a group of musicians, female flute and cithara players, "for it must be observed," said the youth, "that all the servants of the Goddess are women."

"But now, lose not an instant, for here follows the most interesting part of the procession, the priestesses of the Goddess, six in number. They are selected," continued the youth, "from the most beautiful virgins in Greece. And see how exquisitely noble and composed is their bearing, and how gracefully they wear their robes." These robes were of the finest wool, soft and white, and bordered by a broad stripe of purple. Their hair was bound closely around the head, and crowns of olive-leaves of molten silver rested lightly upon their tresses. Aged men, with white flowing locks, followed their steps; afterwards came the foreigners in Athens, bearing small, exquisitely wrought boats to symbolize their foreign origin.

I have mentioned but a very small part of the procession. The reader would be fatigued by the description, far more than was the Prince by the thing itself. His attention was arrested by the virgin priestesses, who bore their offerings to the altar of the Goddess, consisting of the fruit of the olive, sheaves of wheat, and the first fruits of the summer. They were all beautiful women; but Julian's rare perception of harmony in all things fixed his attention upon *one*, whose beauty was peculiar, and greatly surpassing all the others.

This priestess seemed unconscious that she possessed that beauty so rare, but so absolute, that the child and the philosopher, the sage and the idiot, never differ about it. In these modern times, when the claims of universal humanity are acknowledged, a certain idealized expression takes the place of symmetrical beauty; we do not demand those exceptional forms, whose perfect organization has ever been the standard of beauty. The beauty here spoken of has been the same, from the Niobe and the Helen to Raphael's celestial Madonna. Homer's description of Helen might be taken for that of a beautiful Saxon woman. The softly rounded form; the complexion like ivory, "fresh from the hands of the turner," or, to borrow a modern expression, like the petal of the camellia just opened to the light; the eyes a divine and matchless blue, like the deepest blue of the summer heaven; the whole form the expression of strength and firmness, tenderness and grace, the result of a complete harmony in the moral and physical organization.

Young, vigorous, and healthful as the beautiful priestess appeared, when Julian observed more closely her full eye veiled by the transparent lid, it seemed trembling with suppressed tears, and indicated a veiled sorrow, not softened by resignation, but conquered by the supremacy of will.

Thedorus, the youth at his side, startled Julian's fixed attention by saying, "Pardon me, noble stranger; perhaps you are unacquainted with the beautiful priestess who thus commands your attention? She is distinguished in Athens not more for her beauty than for her independent mode of life."

Julian was thought to regard women with contempt, as vain and frivolous beings, but he said to Theodorus, "Are mind and person then harmonious in that beautiful creature, or, as so often happens, is beauty united to folly? the lustre of the exterior, does it hide a dark soul?"

"I am so happy as to know something of Parthenia," said Theodorus; "my young sister dwells with her as her own attendant, and I believe in her as I do in the angels; her heart is as pure as the ivory of her cheek. Her father, Philotus, has been Archon in Athens, but he passed many years in Rome, and from her Roman mother Parthenia has received much instruction which is never given to Athenian women; and since she dwelt in Athens she has claimed for herself a more independent mode of life than unmarried, or even married, women enjoy here. She receives the noble youths of Athens at her house, and goes to the tragic theatre, veiled only, and without a mask; yet the least breath of scandal has never tarnished her fair fame."

"And does she live alone?" asked Julian.

"Her father is banished from Athens at present, and her mother is dead. It is her intention to follow him; but a certain revenue is attached to her office of priestess, which her father wishes her to retain at present."

"But," said Julian, "as a priestess of Pallas Athena, she is a privileged character, and is protected by her office."

Theodorus shook his head. "Her heart is not much in it, I imagine, and she only waits for her father's permission to follow him to Antioch."

"Let her be faithful to the Goddess," said the Prince, "she will reward her." But he added, half to himself, "Why that expression of sorrow upon her beautiful countenance? Sorrow is indeed sometimes but the shadow of too much joy, and the outward expression the sacrament of the soul's inward beauty."

"Her heart is not wholly in the service of the Goddess; it is even whispered that she inclines towards the opinions of the Galileans."

"Now all the Gods forbid," cried Julian, "that such cursed heresy should ever penetrate that virgin heart!"

Theodorus, secretly, as he thought, made the sign of the cross. Julian observed him more closely, and saw that upon his blonde and ruddy face there was a querulous expression, quite foreign to his temperament, and unusual with the heathen youth, which indicated that the pleasures of his age did not satisfy the cravings of his heart.

"And do you see the fair Parthenia, and does she impart her opinions to you?" he asked.

"God forbid!" answered the youth.

Julian smiled. "Why not *the* Gods? But proceed, tell me all you know of the lovely priestess."

"I learn only through my sister, that she is the gentlest, the kindest, and most indulgent of mistresses; that she admits all, even those who have no claim, to the happiness of conversing with her; and that she is in this like the Nazarenes, — all the unhappy and the unfortunate go to her for relief and comfort."

Julian was excited and interested. He felt, although he would not openly acknowledge, the influence of a beautiful woman upon the opinions of the youth of a city. He remembered how many the baptism of the beautiful Empress Eusebia had converted to Christianity. Certain far-off visions were floating in his mind of the future influence of woman in establishing a pure Heathenism; he forgot that Christianity was necessary to elevate woman to her true place in the *family*, — how much more to make her the purifying and refining influence diffused through society!

The procession had now entered the Parthenon. Julian asked the youth at his side, if he did not join in the sacrifices.

Theodorus shook his head. "I pray only to one God," he said.

"To one! and which of the Gods is your Divinity?"

"One alone, the Great Jehovah!"

"You are then of the race of Israel?" said Julian.

Theodorus seemed reluctant to speak of his religious faith, and Julian did not press him. They descended the steps of the Acropolis together. Theodorus, to enter a place of private Christian worship, — as yet there was no church in Athens, — and Julian to pass through the Cerameicus to the groves of the Academy, where, beneath its deepest foliage and beside its limpid stream, he loved to wander. His nights, which were not spent alone with his student's lamp, were given to the study of astrology and magic, together with his friend Libanius, who, through true attachment to his person, had followed him to Athens. For Julian possessed that magnetic influence which, without will of his own, drew many persons irresistibly towards him, and riveted them for ever unconsciously to his fortunes.

CHAPTER XI.

PARTHENIA.

THE private houses in Athens, as we have said, displayed little of the wealth so lavishly expended upon its temples. They were plain and small. But the residence of Parthenia presented a somewhat different appearance. Her parents having spent many years in Rome, they had learned to unite with the simple elegance of Greece many of the refined luxuries of that capital. The impluvium of her entrance-hall was ornamented by a fountain of singular beauty of form, and the pillars supporting the arcades were of the most precious marbles; the rarest flowers, forming the borders, were constantly refreshed by the spray from the fountain. A Flora of ivory, exquisitely carved, and a small golden statue of Diana, stood on each side of the door which led into Parthenia's own room. Immediately opposite its entrance was a small statue of Athena, and an altar for the offerings to the Goddess. Excepting this, and the usual domestic Lares, the room itself presented, in its purity, a Christian, rather than a Heathen appearance.

The room was wainscoted with panels of delicately carved ivory, divided by a moulding of gold; and above these, upon the different compartments, were paintings of brilliant colors, alternating with wreaths of flowers, fashioned to the life, and formed of imperishable materials. Roses, lilies, and all the smaller gifts of Flora, hung in lifelike forms, while through their stems dropped the most precious perfumes into small vases of gold, formed for their reception. The paintings upon the panels, executed by Grecian artists, were the successive incidents in the life of Psyche, represented with a vividness of art which made the whole history a living reality before the spectator.

Parthenia, one of the occupants of this room, was dressed in the simple fashion of a Grecian maiden. A robe woven of the softest white wool, in texture like the cashmeres of the present day, was worn without ornament, except the jewelled clasps that fastened together the upper part of the sleeves. A purple scarf gathered and confined the robe at the waist, and hung down in front as low as the feet; this scarf or shawl was of fine, transparent materials, so that when opened or expanded it would completely veil the whole person. The hair was bound closely, leaving the beautiful form of the head entirely defined, and the line of the exquisitely formed arm and hand was left unbroken by ornament of any kind. The Greeks were too well acquainted with the laws of beauty to impair the graceful outline of the arm by a senseless ornament. The ornaments of the Grecian women of an earlier time, like the clasps of the *chiton* upon the arm, had the appearance of being worn for use, and Parthenia, as priestess of Athena, was permitted to retain the ancient dress.

Certainly this dress possessed little resemblance to the costumes of the present time, and a Greek girl would have been pronounced, by a Paris or an American belle, without tournure or fashion, but the Greek women imagined their own dress the only one that could be worn with any pretension to elegance. There is a story that certain Ionian women, being suspected of favoring the Persian faction, were condemned to wear the Persian dress. Such was their horror, that they entreated to be sold as slaves, or to be cast into the sea, rather than to be subjected to such barbarism.

Parthenia's parents had spent their married life in Rome. Nature had endowed this only child with singular beauty, and, as a safeguard from its seductions, her parents had given her almost a masculine education. She had been instructed in the philosophy and poetry of earlier times, and had also been taught the accomplishments of the period in which she lived. Her father thought thus to furnish her with the armor of a strong soul, with the shield of an instructed mind, against the terrible corruptions of Patrician society. But nature, as though in defiance of all worldly wisdom, had given Parthenia a most feminine soul, a fine susceptibility, not only to all external beauty and to all expression of suffering, to joy and sorrow, but a deep yearning, an intense longing for something which the instructions of philosophy could not impart, and which she could not find in the rich life by which she was surrounded.

After the death of Parthenia's mother, the attractions of Rome faded from the horizon of her father's life, and he returned to Greece, where he had large estates, and entered into political life; that is, he filled successive offices which satisfied his ambition. Gladly would he have had his daughter adopt his own Epicurean philosophy, and steel her heart against all pain, as anxiety for her happiness was the sole care which disturbed the smooth surface of his life.

When his various employments led him to distant parts of the Empire, he deprived himself of her sweet company, and, contrary to the usages of Grecian society, gave her a separate establishment, where she could lead the independent life often led by ladies in Rome. A life so at variance with that of the Greek women could not but subject her to severe censure on the part of the wise, and to cruel misrepresentations from the malicious. Respectable Athenian women rarely quitted the seclusion of home, except on special occasions, to be the spectators of festal processions or to swell their pomp. The tortoise was considered the symbol of the condition of women in Athens. In Rome, on the contrary, education and custom fitted women to become the companions and advisers of men, and their influence in society for good and for evil was felt and feared.

The office of priestess, indeed, gave her a species of public life, and could Parthenia have been content with being only priestess, she would perhaps have been happy; but those very dispositions and qualities which make a woman interesting, and are the sources of her inspiration, carry with them the destiny of disappointment and sorrow. "The iron chain of conventionalities" can alone protect a woman who is endowed with rare gifts, which excite the jealousy of one sex and the envy of the other. If she break down that chain, her position is still more unhappy; for the plant that by its nature is clinging, and puts out its tendrils for support, can never attain the hardihood of a tree, destined to contend with wind and storms.

It was the day after the procession described in the last chapter. Near the door of the atrium in Parthenia's bower, a woman occupied a low seat. She had reached that age when the sluggishness of the blood and the dimness of the senses render the sun and the warm air and perfume of flowers delightful to existence. This ancient attendant, or nurse, who had reared the beautiful child from her infancy, and now in her old age enjoyed the privilege of scolding, petting, loving, and governing the young woman, sat in the sun, alternately twirling the distaff and falling into brief moments of sleep. The sun, as it shone full upon her head, heightened the brilliant color of her head-dress, and sharpened the outline of her features, which was somewhat harsh, although softened away to tender love when she looked upon her darling.

"Dear child," she said, "your cheek to-day is as pale as the lily that hangs over your head. Those eternal processions and ceremonies will make you old before your youth even has taken the place of childhood."

"Ah Guta! I am more afraid they will make my heart as cold as the marble of my mistress's statue. A lip service without the devotion of the soul is —"

"It would have been wiser, then, to have trundled hoop or gathered crocuses, than to have crammed your poor head with all that learning," interrupted the old woman.

"Alas! my dear mother, — she wished me to become another Corinne; and my father's ambition was to fit me to be the bride of an emperor. Were they happy, the brides? or she, Corinne?"

"And has not my darling everything here to make a queen happy? All but the king," she added with a smile.

"Guta! I would rather fly away to some lone valley and there serve one loving soul; work for him while he worked, and watch him while he slept."

"That is always the fancy of those who are surrounded by adorers, — solitude and *one* loving, doting heart."

"But I would dote, and I would serve," said the young girl.

"What! my bird! exchange your tender plumage and downy nest for naked rafters or the shelterless sky?"

"These gorgeous rooms are only the trappings of idleness and vanity. I wish to learn something of the rough paths of life."

"Ah, teach those feet of pearl to walk the iron path, fit only for horny hoofs!"

"In those narrow, iron paths, where the poor grind, are learned the facts of life. We have too much room, and learn only self-deception, Guta!"

"Where has my darling learned all this wisdom, or rather this folly? Surely not from these surroundings, or from her poor old Guta!" and she looked around with a proud smile.

"That is the secret, Guta; the heart craves a happiness which these surroundings only mock."

"What shall I do to please the eyeball of my heart? You would not stay tortoise-like in your shell, as do the Greek ladies? Shall we go again to the Dionysia? You remember when you went in boy's clothes, and I went to take care of you? Then the young dandies stared at the pretty boy! Now that you go in no disguise thicker than your veil, they stare no longer, — they respectfully adore my little Thena."

"Guta, do not treat me like a spoiled child, who wants a new plaything. I am only wearied by yesterday's labors"; and Parthenia rose, and, scattering some incense upon the altar of Pallas, knelt an instant before it.

At this moment there entered a young girl, who, from her dress, was evidently a slave; but the youthful dignity and refinement of her whole bearing showed that slavery could not have been her original destination, — that accident or misfortune had reduced her to this abject state. She bore a basket of flowers, with the dew fresh upon them, and, placing the basket at the feet of her mistress, began to weave a chaplet for her hair.

"No," said Parthenia, "no wreath to-day"; and selecting a single white rose, she told Areta, the child, to place it in her hair. "With the others," she said, "adorn the shrines and altars."

"Pardon me, mistress dear," said the young girl, "the flowers are all too faded. Let me take them to the fountain, and to-morrow, at the first touch of the flower-market bell, I will procure fresh ones.

There was a loving humility in the manner of this young girl that was irresistibly winning, and Parthenia, although Guta grumbled out, that there was an awful waste of flowers, consented that they should be scattered around the fountain.

How came this fair-haired Northern girl to be the slave of the beautiful Athenian? Her father was one of the Christians condemned to be burnt under the cruel edict of Galerius. His punishment was afterwards commuted into slavery for himself and his whole family. These two children were singularly attractive, and, after suffering various vicissitudes, they were purchased by Parthenia's father. The young girl was given to her as an attendant, or rather as an ornament of her bower, and the boy, Theodorus, was placed as an assistant at the sacrifices at the temple of Pallas. The lot of the girl, although that of servitude, was not unhappy.

It was the hour when the young Athenians and Romans paid the homage of their admiration to beauty; Parthenia's surprise was great, however, when she saw Julian enter with them.

Since the day he saw her at the Parthenon, his thoughts had dwelt upon her more than became one who called himself a philosopher. It was not as a worshipper of beauty, nor as an admirer of that inexpressible grace of manner which belonged to her, that he remembered Parthenia; still less did he think of her as instructed and educated, for he was not above the weakness of disliking "a woman more wise than woman ought to be"; but the beautiful Athenian was a priestess, devoted to the service of a heathen Goddess, and although he had not yet declared himself, yet every one capable of aiding him in giving new life and beauty to the decaying service of the Gods found favor in his eyes. He recollected that Christianity had no real hold upon the higher classes till it had taken deep root in the devotion of woman; that the Patrician women first made Christianity dear to the inmates of their domestic circle. Would it not therefore aid the cause of Heathenism, if a beautiful and educated woman would assist in bringing back the pure beauty of the Greek worship? It was not therefore to bow down before the shrine of her loveliness, as did the other young Athenians, that Julian entered her bower. He looked around, charmed by the elegance of the room; but he observed immediately the absence of flowers upon the shrines and altars. There were no offerings of any description, and no wreaths upon the statues.

"Fair Parthenia," he said, "your apartment is charming; but there is one thing so unusual in a lady's room that you must forgive me for remarking it, — the absence of Flora's gifts."

Parthenia blushed slightly, and pointed to the artificial wreaths now dropping perfumes.

"Yes, exquisite as they are," said the Prince, "they cannot take the place of their living sisters, and Flora, surely, should receive a return for her own rich gifts," — and he broke off a branch of laburnum, which hung near the door, and placed it upon the small golden altar of the Goddess.

"I enjoy the flowers in their second life," said Parthenia, "and bless the man who invented the art of preserving their perfumes. They seem to give us their love after their beauty has departed."

"Like all beautiful things," said the Prince, "music leaves its echo, flowers their perfumes, and when destiny compels us to leave Parthenia, we carry her memory in the heart."

Just at this moment, the petals of the rose which Parthenia had placed in her hair, being over full, and too ripe, fell, and were scattered on the ground. There was a saying in Greece, that, if the petals fell from the flower presented by a stranger, it was to be taken as a warning of the insincerity of the person presenting it. Although Julian did not give her the rose, the coincidence, together with the flattery just from his tongue, called a slight color to the cheek of the Athenian. The Prince shrugged his shoulders, a motion habitual to him, and began picking up the petals from the ground.

"Let us not begin our acquaintance with insincerity," said Parthenia.

"Nor with superstition," said Julian. "The Athenians are said to be the most superstitious people in the world. I saw your altar dedicated to the Unknown God; that is, I suppose, fair priestess, from the excessive care of your countrymen lest any in ignorance should be omitted."

"There are, even among the Athenians," said Parthenia, "some few who would reconsecrate that altar to the new Christian Divinity."

"The Gods forbid! Soil not your beautiful lips by the mention of the Galilean. Faith in him could no more take root in the soul of Parthenia, than I could gather up these fallen leaves and re-insert them into another bud. No, fair priestess, with time and a new era, the full bloom and beauty of the ancient worship shall be restored."

He paused suddenly, for he saw a cloud gather over the countenance of his listener, and he feared he had disclosed too abruptly the thought always foremost. It was too early, also, to declare his decided hostility to Christianity. He changed the subject of discussion, and after a visit of half an hour, at the entrance of three or four young men more elegant than himself, Julian took most respectful leave and withdrew.

These young courtiers had never found Parthenia so absent, although for some weeks they had been saying to each other that she was growing stupid, losing her gayety and wit, &c. She, on her part, had never perceived them so frivolous. Their trifling loquacity was like the chirping of the Attic grasshopper compared with the song of the nightingale in the garden of Plato, to which she likened Julian. And yet there was little, in this first interview, to captivate her imagination, and certainly there was not much in the exterior of Julian that women love to look upon; but when he was interested in conversation, he was transfigured and glorified by the vividness of his perceptions; friends and enemies alike speak of the irresistible power of his eye, and his countenance, not otherwise attractive, was irradiated by the intenseness of his feelings and the flashings of his genius.

As soon as Parthenia was alone, she went to seek chaplets for Pallas and Flora, and scattered incense upon their altars.

Julian had nearly implied that the fair Athenian was guilty of impiety to the Gods, because he found no flowers or offerings upon their altars. The next morning, therefore, she rose and entered early, and found her little attendant busy in the decoration of her apartment; but she perceived with surprise, that the shrines and altars, as well as the Lares of the hearth, were all without flowers; but that wherever there was a possibility of hanging a wreath, all cups, vases, pillars, were most tastefully adorned with the most delicate gifts of Flora.

"What fancy is this," she asked of her little slave; "you must have culled everything delicate and lovely from the flower-market; but you have not given one to the shrines. Have you not gratitude sufficient to give back one of her beautiful gifts to Flora herself?" she said, pointing to the statue of that Divinity.

"Ah yes! my dear mistress, I *am* very thankful. Forgive me — another time," — and she stopped, confused.

"These are so beautifully wreathed," said her mistress, with indulgence, "that I will not change them. Go to the atrium, — you may find something there for the shrines."

"Pardon me, dear mistress," and she sank on her knee; "but all the flowers must be for one God, — our Father in Heaven."

"Is Jupiter, then, your only Deity?"

"God forbid!" cried Areta; and as she kissed the hand of her mistress, she made, as she thought unobserved, the sign of the cross.

Parthenia had observed the sign. "You are then a Galilean," she said.

"Dear mistress, I am a Christian, and I cannot offer anything to the images of the heathen Gods, for we do not believe that they are true Gods."

"Ah yes! I know. But you make a god of that crucified Galilean, the Christ!"

"Oh! do not speak of him with that scornful voice. Did you but know his history, and that it is the sweetest thing to think of his life, and to remember his precious words—"

"Who then has taught you his words? You are but a child, and he lived, as I think, more than three hundred years ago, and even your father's father could not have known him."

"Ah no! but we have the book of his life, the Gospels. My mother read them all, and cherished his precious words in her heart of hearts; and when she gathered us around her knees, she was never weary of repeating, or we of hearing them"; and Areta's eyes filled with tears at the recollection of her mother and her childhood's home.

"But your Christ," said Parthenia, "cursed the Gods of our country, and would destroy our religion and our beautiful temples."

"No, dear mistress! forgive me that I contradict you. The Christ cursed nothing; he was all love and forgiveness. Christians cannot sacrifice to your Gods without denying him, who died for them. And so they have been scourged, and burnt, and sold into slavery."

"Were your parents the victims of persecution?

was it their only crime that they worshipped the Nazarene ?"

"My father was prefect of the guards; he was ordered to burn incense to Jupiter, but rather than do that, he took off his sword and gave it to the officer. To punish him, he was sold, and my mother also. They offered liberty to my brother if he would leave them, but we all clung together and were all sold for slaves. We suffered great misery, till your noble father, seeing how superior was this slave to all others, appointed him to a confidential office under himself, and gave me to you. Dearest mistress, I will obey you in all things else, but do not command me to bring flowers to the shrines, or to burn incense upon the altars. It is not wrong for you, because you believe in your Gods, but oh! I cannot so offend the dear and blessed Saviour."

"Your Saviour, as you call him, is no longer on earth; how then can you offend him?"

"O, he lives! he lives in heaven, and looks down with love upon all who believe in him!" And Areta, embracing the knees of her mistress, burst into tears.

Ah, thought Parthenia, that I could have such faith in the Deity whose altars I serve, as this child has in her Christ! And raising her, she kissed her cheek, and asked her why she wept.

"I cannot help weeping, because you do not believe in the Christ."

"Dear child, you shall in future be spared from adorning the shrines and altars. You shall only bring me the flowers, I will wreathe them. Go now to Guta. I wish to be alone."

In the fourth century, Christianity had made little progress in Athens. There was no Christian church there. Parthenia had regarded it only as a new and vulgar superstition; it had never been presented to her mind united with the charm of natural goodness. Neither had Paganism become so corrupt as in other cities of the Empire. She had had no opportunity to contrast the debasing influence of the worship of some of the Deities with the purity of life enjoined by Christianity. Unlike Julian, she cherished no hatred towards the sect, but she felt no wish to approach them nearer, or to acquaint herself with their principles. And yet there were peculiarities in the mind of the beautiful Greek, through which she would inevitably become a Christian; with all her pride of intellect, and her restless desire after knowledge, she felt a distrust of self, a painful timidity, a want of confidence in her powers, which often made her fall short of what was expected of her, and even of what she expected of herself. Self-esteem, self-confidence, seemed to have been left out of her mental gifts. Endowed as she was with a heart of the tenderest emotions, she had never known a true equal affection. Orphaned so early, and without a sister, her heart had clung only to those inferior to herself; and as her mind expanded, they lost their hold upon her intellect. Still she possessed that quickness of sympathy which is always an original gift to the heart, depending neither upon race, nor climate, nor religion. It is a balsam for the wounds of life, and like those balsams, diffused through many unsightly plants, often also of an ungenial climate, it is the precious gift of Nature to her favorite children.

The gift of the little slave-girl to Parthenia was one of the most beneficent that could be offered to her. A superficial observer would have said that upon Areta alone was conferred the benefit when destiny placed her under the care of her mistress. But when the sweet natural piety and trusting faith of the younger mind was opened to that of Parthenia, so full of uncertainty and of baffled aspiration, her loftier mind rested upon it, as the wearied eye finds repose in the homelike green of the common field. Could she have descended from her ideal height, and permitted that divine sympathy with which God had endowed her to gush out upon all who suffered, upon all less happy than herself, the fair brow of the Greek would have worn a crown of joy. But that all men were brothers and entitled to love, was an idea that never had entered the heathen mind; and Parthenia in the midst of her worshippers, prouder of her intellect than of her beauty, would often turn to the little slave Areta and envy her quiet happiness.

CHAPTER XII.

THE FRIENDS.

LIBANIUS, the Asiatic and the sophist, had followed Julian to Athens. We may also call him a philosopher; for in the midst of a corrupt age, he preserved, together with firm adherence to the old Heathenism, purity of taste, of manners, and of life.

These friends were worthy of each other; their friendship was founded upon the esteem of each for the great qualities of the other, and it was free from adulation on the one side, and condescension on the other. After Julian ascended the throne, Libanius taught him that, although he could command a subject, he must deserve a friend. Both opposed Christianity with might; Julian with intense hatred, his friend with indifference to Christianity, but from love to Julian, and for the philosophy of the ancients, spiritualized by the idealism of Plato. Neither of them could appreciate the new ideas which Christianity was everywhere infusing into the corrupt society of their age. As these divine ideas were first proclaimed by fishermen and Galileans, the proud minds of Julian and Libanius could see no beauty in them. Thus it is ever. The God-like must be lowly born. While the proud and wordly-wise are looking at the stars, the light which illumines all around comes, like that in the "Night" of Correggio, from the humble and rustic manger.

"Let us sit in the atrium," said Libanius. "After the excessive heat of the day, the night is sultry; but how exquisitely does this heat bring out the perfume of your flowers!"

"And how soothing is the murmur of the fountain, and this fresh breeze which finds its way through the marble pillars of the court!" said Julian.

"And the blue of the sky seems deepened by these shadows. Is that the constellation of the Lyre which we see just above the plane-tree?" asked Libanius.

"Ah, this Grecian sky! these Attic nights!" said Julian, sighing. "See, how silently the marble statues of the Gods, gleaming pale in the night, consecrate this place to thought!"

"The dropping of the water-clock alone breaks the silence," said his friend.

"As it measures the hours, it is often my lullaby, when it should be my monitor," said Julian.

After a pause, Libanius said, "Thou art silent, my Julian; art thou thinking of adding another to these Divinities? Aphrodite has surely been of late propitious to thee."

"Jest not! I am thinking that this Athens is the only place for me; this Athenian atmosphere, where we breathe the inspiration of Gods and poets, is the only one where we can live a true life. Here, with these divine companions, would I live for ever."

"My Julian, I think, would add a truly tender heart to these hearts of stone! But seriously, would you be satisfied with the fame of poet and philosopher, and leave the world to Cæsar?"

"What can be better than tranquillity in the gardens of Athens, or in the myrtles around the cottage of Socrates? Shall I exchange my gold for brass, — what cost me a *hundred* beeves, for the low price of *nine?*"

"Jupiter has placed you in the same active path with Hercules and Bacchus, who philosophized, and, at the same time, freed the earth from monsters of vice and crime."

"And yet Hercules was set to spinning. I would rather sing their adventures, as porters do in the streets," said Julian.

Libanius lifted his eyebrows as though he would say, "We shall see." "What then is to become of your reign of Saturn, — *your* golden age?"

"Ah! my friend, our undertakings and our happiness depend not so much on our dispositions as on Fortune, the God who governs all things; besides, I am conscious of no superior talents, natural or acquired —"

"Pardon me, true happiness by no means depends on fortune. But let that pass. Julian! you are not a man to sit down beneath your myrtles and listen to your Attic bees, and that you are dreaming of this effeminate life assures me that some Grecian *muse* has crossed the light of your Helios."

"To govern well," said Julian, blushing slightly, "seems to me more than human. The trade which he has learned, let each man practise. I have learnt to sing."

"But you must be the architect of illustrious *deeds*. It is your right! Your birthright to right the world."

"Might is greater than right. Constantius has it now, and he is capable of every crime."

"My Prince, your position makes you exaggerate your danger."

"Exaggerate! up to this very hour, has not my life been but the permitted boon of the jealous tyrant, who murdered my father, and has inflicted every species of degradation upon me?"

"There has indeed been little of the beautiful spirit of gentleness which Christians assert govern their sect in the treatment of their enemies," said Libanius.

"Alas! what is there in the future for me but ignominious obscurity, or fatal distinction such as poor Gallus met? Ah! could I dwell secure in Athens beneath the protection of Pallas and a softer divinity!"

"Hush! Jupiter is greater than either!" said Libanius. "But he will not protect us from spies. Every time, my Prince, that you cross the atrium of the beautiful Greek, a missive goes on to Milan. At the first kiss, a bowstring will be around your throat, or you will drink together a poisoned cup."

Julian turned pale as death. "Ah, what is the design of the Emperor?" he whispered.

"Has he not a sister, Helena, the sister also of that cruel fiend poor Gallus was compelled to marry?"

Libanius knew well that Julian must marry one of the imperial family, and though he wished to warn him, he was not unwilling to see him charmed by Parthenia. He had always believed Julian insensible to the attractions of woman, and as his ideas of love were not much more refined than those of other Heathens, although his Prince could not *marry* the beautiful Athenian, he was willing the philosopher should obey the leading of the winged boy.

Both friends were silent. Libanius was afraid to recur again to the subject of which he was thinking. He looked at the water-clock. "By all the Graces and the Loves! the hour is not too late. Let us to the divine Parthenia!"

"It *is* too late," said Julian, rising and looking also. "I stir not to-night." He preferred also making the visit without his friend.

"If lovers," as the poet says, "in one day grow old, you have trebled your age; then waste no more days, my Prince."

The color rushed to Julian's brow. "Do I look like a lover," he said, "with this curling beard and this coarse tunic?"

"I know you affect the cynic, but so did Pericles; yet Aspasia loved him."

Julian's eyes flashed, hardly in much anger. He liked to be compared with Pericles; but as a shade had been cast upon Aspasia's fair fame, he would not have her name connected with that of the divine Parthenia.

Anger with him was momentary; and as he

turned to his sleeping apartment, he held out his hand,—"Good night! dearest, best beloved brother." *

Every movement of Julian was observed and reported by spies secretly employed by the sycophants of the Emperor; Julian therefore guarded his acquaintance with Parthenia as much as possible from observation. His visits were made, not at the usual reception hours, but when the crowd of her worshippers had left the beautiful idol alone. That he was admitted at such unusual hours was not because he was heir to the Empire, but because he possessed a magnetic influence which opened all doors, I had almost said, all hearts. Not so,—he had a bitter enemy, as well as spies, in Athens. Of this very time, Saint Gregory of Nazianzen said, "Prince Julian, of all mortals, is surely the most wonderful; an enigma of contradictions; an object of intense love, of intense hatred; enticing, yet repulsive; sought after with wild admiration, yet equally to be feared." If an enemy thus felt his influence, it is not to be wondered at that, where he sought to make himself beloved, he should reign supreme.

The Prince entered the apartment already de-

---

* The phrase with which he closes his letters to Libanius.

scribed, at an hour when he thought he should find Parthenia alone with Guta only, her old nurse. He had in his hand a small basket of fretted silver, in which there were a few of the superb long-stemmed figs so prized by the Greeks, and also regarded as an antidote to poison. These figs were borne by a tree which overshadowed the house where Julian dwelt.

"Lovely Parthenia," he said, "I bring you an offering whose beauty far excels its value, except that the fig is consecrated to the Gods, and upon the altar they furnish a sweeter perfume than frankincense."

"The figs of Athens excel all other figs," said Parthenia, "as much as your figs seem to excel those of Athens."

"I wish," he said, "that I could have brought you the tree itself, as by their long stems its fruit hung around it in a circular form, like cups of porphyry, or a necklace of precious stones."

"They are wonderfully beautiful," said Parthenia, placing one of them upon the altar of Pallas Athena, and are worthy to stand beside the olive-tree of Pallas.

"The fig is deemed by Aristotle an antidote against all poison, — and if thou, fairest Greek, hast an enemy —"

Parthenia, laughing, assured him that she counted her friends by hundreds, and her enemies as naught.

"And thy worshippers?" he said, playfully falling on one knee. Instantly neck, cheek, and brow of the fair Greek were crimsoned by a rush of the blood, and, following the direction of Parthenia's eyes, the Prince first perceived that she was not alone.

Immediately the person came forward from the recess which had partly concealed him. He was a man of noble appearance, richly attired in the Oriental fashion, with a beard longer but more silky than Julian's. He looked old, but upon closer observation the marks of age were wholly in the expression, not in the features. These indicated a person of scarcely forty years. His brow, polished like the finest Parian marble, was shaded by hair of a beautiful brown color, without a thread of white. The most striking of his features were the eyes, which seemed to pierce through and through one like a flash of lightning; but when the countenance was in repose, it was like a mask which concealed a profound depth of sorrowful experience. There was an expression of ill-concealed contempt about the lips in repose, but his smile was inexpressibly fascinating. He seemed like a man to be avoided, and yet there was an individuality so attractive, that it was almost impossible to resist it.

"The figs are superb, worthy to be offered to the Goddess of Love and to her most beautiful minister," he said, bowing low to Parthenia. "Such I have seen only once before, in the garden of Zenobia in Palmyra, where everything attained a beauty unknown elsewhere."

Julian turned his eyes upon him with surprise. "If I recollect aright," he said, "Zenobia has been dead more than half a century."

The stranger colored deeply; but he instantly added: "The Queen has indeed been dead as long, but her garden and the fig-tree have, alas! a longer existence upon this earth, than she who was the most precious of its jewels."

"Homer praises other fruits for their size, but to the fig alone he gives the epithet of sweetness," said Julian.

"Homer adds," said the stranger,

"The same mild season gives the blooms to blow,
The buds to harden, and the fruits to grow."

"That is only in Damascus," said Julian, supposing the stranger to be a Syrian, that true city of Jupiter, unrivalled in the excellence of all its productions.

"Ah!" said Cartophilus, for it was the Jew, "and

are not Palestine and Jerusalem famed for this precious tree, whose shadow protects from its too burning sun, and overtops its ruined walls?"

The Jew's sorrowful thoughts seemed to have wandered back to his country, to the fallen temple, and the stones of Zion; and while Julian was exclusively occupied with Parthenia, he remained silent.

Meanwhile another person had entered, who soon, however, drew to himself the attention of the Prince. His appearance was as striking as that of Cartophilus, although of an opposite type of beauty. His blue eyes, and hair approaching a golden hue, gave him the appearance of a Saxon, and strikingly contrasted with the Jew, whose inky beard, and complexion browned by a Syrian sun, and eyes capable of expressing the most opposite and violent passions, exercised a fascination that made him as fearful as he was at times attractive.

Julian, although talking with a woman, could not long avoid introducing his favorite themes, Homer and his commentators, or rather Homer as explained and illustrated by Plato, who thus comprised, as he thought, all the wisdom and all the poetry of the world.

"Of what value," continued the Prince, "are these schools of Alexandria? They make tragedies, hymns, even Epic poems, things which bear the same names as did the sublime productions of ancient Greece; but how empty, how cold, what mere skeletons of dry bones, are all these works, compared with the surging, rushing, living life of Homer!"

"Prince! your busy life has not allowed you time to study the Prophets and Odes of the Hebrew Scriptures," said the Jew.

"I have read them as I have the Odes of Pindar. They are noble hymns to be sung in the temples of the Gods; but Homer we take to our bosom, as the companion, the teacher, the friend. The blind old man comes in to our tent, sings to us when we are gay, weeps with us when we are sad, works with us, plays with us, and when we sleep lays his gray temples on the same pillow by our side, and does not leave us even in our dreams."

"Noble Prince, we admit all that," said the fair-haired stranger, "but are we never to have anything but Homer and Plato? Shall we for ever gather up the fallen leaves from the trees of our ancient forest, to bind them into garlands and chaplets, and not perceive the fresh-springing verdure and flowers, whose perfumes we tread under foot?"

"Most worthy discoverer," said Julian, with his habitual shrug of the shoulders, "where have you found this fresh soil and this garden of fresh-springing flowers?"

"Commenting upon Homer," continued the other, "will never create another Homer. We must look to the new ideas of the Christian orators for a new poem. Their burning enthusiasm, their new passions of suffering and martyrdom, will create new poets of a new religion."

Julian's lip curled. "Think you that your contemptible superstition will ever inspire men's souls as the Gods and Heroes of our mythology? Leaving our Homer, look at our sublime tragedies, every one of which is a religious festival, in which the whole of the assembled world, were there room, would unite."

"My Prince," said the other, "they are past as religious festivals! As surely hope the tree that has been felled and withered to wreathe itself again with fresh leaves and flowers, as your old superstitions to bear fruit for the people."

"If you would be inspired by religious poetry, and have your whole heart stirred with enthusiasm," said the Jew, turning to the Prince, "read the song of Deborah, and the chant of Moses after passing the Red Sea."

"It is only when the soul is moved and trembling like the chords of a lyre, as in the hymns of the

Christians," said Cesarien, "that the most exalted and purest inspiration of the poet is found."

Julian was silent. There was a charm in the whole appearance and character of Cesarien, the brother of Gregory, which had taken complete hold of him. And although he was a Christian, Julian sought and attached him to his person, and when he became Emperor, made him one of the physicians of his household.

He now continued, undaunted by a frown on the brow of the Prince, and repeated some verses of a Christian hymn. "Yes," he said, "in returning to prayer to the Universal Father, and to prayer more exalted and pure than any other, the Christians have found the true lyric inspiration."

Julian was not inclined to continue the conversation, and soon after he took leave and left the apartment.

CHAPTER XIII.

ADIEU TO ATHENS.

PARTHENIA was completely subdued by the fascination of Julian's character and conversation. Her own powers of wit, of lively repartee, of gay frivolity, which she wielded so well with the young Athenians, seemed to sleep in his presence. And yet, had she been conscious of her power, her own intellect was not so very inferior to his, and in some respects superior, because she was free from vanity. He was rich in every form of instruction, and she had been taught only what a few women are so happy as to learn. In his presence she wished only to listen, for every accent of his classic Greek was melody, and every word seemed to drop from Apollo's lips. While she listened, a transparent paleness overspread her cheek, which gave her an ideal beauty; and Julian began to feel for her a sentiment of more than admiration, of deepest tenderness and passion, from which he knew he must fly.

A monitor was constantly at his ear and his heart, whispering to him that a chain of iron bound his destiny to the will of the Emperor; that at any moment he might recall him to the court, or send him to the remotest corner of the Empire; to connect the destiny of the beautiful Greek with his by marriage, would perhaps have been destruction to both, and when he looked upon the pure pale cheek of Parthenia, he felt that any other union would have been impossible.

Historians have written that Julian never loved any woman; what means had they of knowing? He might, as we have imagined, have subdued passion by an iron will. He was almost ready, as we have seen, to sacrifice his ambition for his love of letters and of Homer; he was not ready to sacrifice his future for love. He did not believe in Christianity, perhaps he did not believe in love! and therefore was not ready for that one priceless jewel to give up the trappings and the gauds of life, much less his great ambition. Besides, he had not yet learnt much of the character of the beautiful Athenian; he had not penetrated beyond its surface. He thought her happy in her light duties as priestess of Athena, and he knew nothing of the longing of a soul for ever seeking what for ever seems unattainable. Did he find it easy to shut her out of his ambitious dreams? Had he known the value of the pure diamond, would he have given up *all* to make it his own? These questions we cannot answer. One thing we know, he feared that the next messenger who returned to the court of Constantius would bear back his empty slippers, and perhaps his heart, as proof of his assassination.

Julian sought, in his conversation with Parthenia, to increase her reverence for the beautiful fables or myths of Paganism, and asked once if she had studied the meaning of the exquisite painting on the walls of her apartment.

Parthenia said, that she supposed the divine Psyche represented the progress of the soul as she passed through her earthly trials.

"The soul, in the first moment of her existence, is represented of such ideal beauty that she might have passed for one of the Immortals, as the soul is indeed immortal. This purity of beauty excites the hatred of Aphrodite, the Goddess of sensual love, and she sends her son to excite in her a passion for some unworthy object."

"But," said Parthenia, "this magnificent palace into which we see her entering, seems not the abode of a soul."

"In this palace," the Prince continued, "she is placed in circumstances of happiness, but of trial.

Eros, her invisible lover, subjects her to the severe privation of not beholding his face. All within the palace is hers; but it is not sufficient to satisfy the boundless aspirations of a soul; she is charmed by invisible music and addressed in the sweetest accents of love, but, overcome by melancholy and curiosity, she approaches her invisible husband with a lighted lamp."

"Ah," said Parthenia, "how beautiful she is, as she bends with the lamp over the sleeping boy, and we tremble, because we see that the oil must overflow!"

"Yes, that burning drop and that start of terror awake the God of love. He flies, and Psyche stretches her arms imploringly and in vain after him."

"She seems to say, 'Take me with thee; I am also immortal!'" said Parthenia.

"Yes, but before the soul is prepared for immortal happiness, it must pass through many trials of sorrow and repentance; through many severe experiences of this human life, represented in various forms upon the panels by these servile labors. At length, through submissive sorrow, and after trial and purification, she recovers a more celestial beauty, but falls into a deep sleep. Eros, her husband, awakes her by sweet music, and the touch of his arrow."

"And," said Parthenia, "as she is received again into the Olympian heaven, how lovely are the Graces and the Hours, as, in their mystic dance together, they shed roses through the sky, and we seem to hear the music of Apollo's lyre as they sing in chorus!"

"Thus, fairest Parthenia, the soul is victorious over all trial, and enters Olympus with the Immortals."

"Yes, the soul itself. But Elysium admits no female soul."

"We must believe with Plato, that each soul is but a fragment, but half a soul, till he meets the feminine part which makes his perfect; then they become one, and enter Elysium together."

"But what becomes of those who never find the soul with which they could unite?"

"Fairest! they do not seek aright. To the desire and pursuit of the complement of ourselves, Plato gives the name of love. When we have found it, we shall become one again, and Elysium is made up of such."

Parthenia could not keep down a burning blush, but she hastened to say, "But what an Elysium! what a melancholy immortality! O, who would wish to descend into those dismal fields of which Homer sings? The pale ghosts are for ever weeping their lost human life, and the joyous light of the sun!" And she turned her large sad eyes upon Julian.

"We must admit," he said, "that the divine Homer does not describe so happy an immortality as Plato hopes for the good and wise.

Julian had taken in his hand a small golden lamp in the form of Eros, or celestial love, holding a butterfly suspended above the flame. "See," said he, "beautiful Parthenia, the profound meaning of this simple emblem. It represents the soilure of matter, and the suffering of the soul, purified by love, through fire or the deepest sorrow."

Parthenia trembled from head to foot. Was this fiery trial preparing for herself? Must she pass through the fire? She knew not.

Another day, the Prince turned to an exquisite ivory statue of the youth Narcissus reclining upon the margin of the river Cephissos. "See, fairest," he said, "the fable of the seductions of beauty. Intoxicated by his own loveliness, the youth forgets the truer beauty of the soul. A cold egotism takes possession of him, till he at length dissolves into a river of tears, and on its margin springs the Narcissus, which is called the flower of Hades."

"And is this the reason Sophocles crowns the Furies, the Divinities of hell, with this mournful flower? I have never woven it into any chaplet. It seemed to me to bring sorrow connected with its sculptured cup. But," continued Parthenia, "is it not fabled that Narcissus, when flying from the Nymph Echo, who pursued him with her love, was turned into a river, and the forsaken Nymph wasted away till naught was left but her voice, which may even now be heard among the hills."

But their talk was not always of myths and fables. Julian's mind was like a many-sided prism; he could throw at pleasure a coloring of joy or of sadness, of genial humor or gayety, upon every topic, and as music was one of his passions, he sometimes brought with him a master of the lyre, and they sat silent while the Athenian moon cast a more religious light upon the statues of the Gods.

Thus costly hours were given to the beautiful Athenian,—hours which he redeemed by whole nights of study; ah! too costly for the peace of Parthenia, for she gave in exchange the rich treasures of her virgin heart.

With hours and days too swiftly winged, the Prince had counted six months in the city of Pallas. They were the happiest of his life. For besides his admiration of the character of the Athenians,—"they were the only people," he said, "who in word and deed practised justice,"—he lived openly under the protection of his Heathen Deities. It was true that he was surrounded with spies, notwithstanding the secret efforts of the Empress to change these spies into concealed friends, who would warn rather than betray.

She had endeavored to keep awake in the mind of her husband a favorable recollection of Julian, persuading him that the Prince was a youth of an unambitious temper, whose allegiance and gratitude might be secured by the gift of the purple; that he would be content to fill a subordinate station, without aspiring to overshadow the glories of his benefactor; and as Constantius for the first time sincerely acknowledged that his single strength was unequal to such an extent of care and dominion, it was resolved that the Prince should be recalled from Athens, and that, after celebrating his marriage with the sister of the Emperor, he should be appointed, with the title of Cæsar, to rule over the countries beyond the Alps.

After an obstinate, but secret, struggle with the favorite eunuch, the Empress succeeded in having a small guard of honor appointed to conduct him to Milan.

"Now all the Gods come to our aid!" said Libanius, when this guard, which had secretly arrived in Athens, made itself known to him; "for how will his great spirit meet and conquer this cruel contradiction of all his cherished hopes?"

Julian himself says, years afterwards, that "he groaned, and sobbed, and wept." These tears do not convict him of cowardice or weakness. Athens had become to him what Rome has been to so many others, in later years, the home of orphaned hearts. It was also his bitterest enemy, the assassin of his whole family, who had recalled him, and to what a destiny! — to dwell with informers, slanderers, and enemies, thirsting for his destruction, and, cruellest of all, to wed Helena, the sister of the wife of Gallus, who is described by historians as like one of the infernal Furies, thirsting for blood.

It was the morning of the day on which Julian was to leave Athens. The steps of the Acropolis were yet wet with dew, and the hyacinths sent up, from their freshly opened calyces, the perfume of the early dawn, when the Prince ascended the hill and stretched his arms towards his own Pallas Athena. He prayed, but he dared not look towards the dwelling of Parthenia. Ah! was he not leaving there in that little spot, scarcely discerned in the morning twilight, the wine of his life, the lovely muse who had left her sisters to be the inspiration of his being? Had she not woven for him a wreath of joy richer than all others, and, as the flowers fell away, would not the thorn remain for ever with him?

He turned towards Hymettus, which lay hushed beneath the transparent sky; he traced the winding course of the Ilissus, and, beyond the walls, the olive groves of Plato's Academy, where all but the most precious hours of his life in Athens had been spent; then he looked along the sacred way to Eleusis, where a few days before he had been initiated into the most holy of the mysteries of his religion; and as he turned again towards Athens, he saw the spray of the fountain rising above the shrubs in Parthenia's little court. This drew a sharp cry from his heart, — he had no more tears to weep.

Slowly the Prince took the path to Parthenia's dwelling. Guta met him at the door. "By all the Infernal Gods!" she cried, "what has happened?"

"Has the shield fallen from the arm of Athena?" asked Parthenia. "You wear the color of misfortune, Prince. Minerva protect you from calamity!"

"It has already come," he said; "this day I must leave Athens!"

Parthenia felt her knees sink under her, the pale ivory of her cheek became a deathly white, and she shook in every limb. She did not attempt to speak. She did not feign.

Julian turned away, and a pang, like the thrust of a poignard, shot through his heart. It was one of the strokes of their Nemesis, in which both believed. Blind fate had smitten them both; what could they do but be silent and submit? The Prince turned to her again, — and the expression of his face remained for ever in her memory. "All is past now," he said. "The immortal Gods for ever bless you!"

Guta came near, and, placing her arms around Parthenia, drew her head down upon her breast. "Weep," she whispered, "weep, my darling! tears will do you good; the burden of silent grief is too heavy for you to bear."

Parthenia was roused; pride, which never fails a woman, came to her aid; she held out her hand to the Prince; he knelt on one knee, and pressed it between both of his. Neither dared to speak. And thus they parted.

CHAPTER XIV.

THE COURT OF CONSTANTIUS.

JULIAN with his escort had completed their voyage, and landed at one of the ports of the Adriatic. The rest of the journey was by land. At Milan the Emperor still held his gorgeous but effeminate court. It was an afternoon in autumn, when the little cortege of guards, few in number, and without splendor, preceding the carriage of the Prince, approached the gates of Milan. A strict incognito had been preserved throughout the journey, and Julian's fretful spirit was continually chafed by the locking of the carriage door by the leader of the guard, thus making prisoners of himself, of his physician, and his faithful Mardonius.

The setting sun shone upon the towers of Milan, and the whole plain of Lombardy was bathed in that magic light which, in the climate of Italy, and rarely in our own, precedes its withdrawal. Julian, a lover of nature, felt the hour; his heart was softened. He recalled the same hour in Athens, when he had so often watched from the rock of the Acropolis the tender veil of darkness silently drawn over the landscape. His abstraction prevented him from seeing that a carriage approached, escorted by only two servants. It was plain and *open*, and a lady in an easy attitude reclined within.

As it drew nearer, Julian knew that it was the Empress, and that she had obtained leave to meet him thus publicly, was an assurance that no open hostility was intended towards him. He kissed respectfully the hand of his benefactress. "Now Minerva protect you!" he cried. "What God or Goddess has put it into your heart to come thus to bless an outcast —"

"Hush!" said Eusebia, "we owe nothing to God or Goddess. The good Being who watches over us has put it into my heart to love you. Come into my carriage, and we will enter the palace in the face of the whole court."

"And shall I see the Emperor?" asked Julian, turning pale, not with fear, but with emotion at the recollection of Gallus.

"The saints forbid that he should see you in this garb!" said the Empress, looking at his cloak of dark cloth, his long beard, and sandals of leather.

"The philosopher's robe is certainly becoming," said Julian.

"The courtiers, with their heavy embroidery, their jewels, their perfumes and flowers, their gaudy colors, would deride and ridicule the dark robe of my philosopher; and these hands," said the Empress, with a smile, "must wash away their ink-stains before they don their jewelled rings."

"Pshaw! are these hands made for jewels?" he cried "But, noble Princess, by all the Gods, I adjure you to tell me what is the meaning of this mandate of recall. Thus was Gallus summoned; and his image, bleeding and slain, is ever present with me."

"Banish it, Prince! We have conquered the eunuch. Beside, Constantius needs your help. The Empire is too unwieldy for the brain or the hands of one man. The Barbarians are pressing upon the North. The Emperor will give you the purple, and attach you to himself by every bond."

"Now the Gods forbid! How can there be peace or union between the assassin and myself?" and Julian rose, as though he would throw himself from the carriage.

The Empress caught his arm. "Madman!" she cried, "is this your philosophy? Will you expose yourself to these talebearers around us? Listen!" and the Empress detailed the plan of the Emperor, of sending him with an army to Gaul and the Danube. "But first," she said, and she turned her penetrating eyes full upon him, "he will bind you to himself by a bond stronger and more enduring than the purple robe of the Cæsars."

Julian cast down his eyes. He trembled.

"In short, it must come, Prince!" the Empress continued. "Nemesis is stronger than you or I. The Emperor will give you his sister Helena for a companion!"

Julian crimsoned, and then became pale as death. "Never!" he cried. "O Immortal Gods! forbid that the sister of the fiend he gave to poor Gallus should ever be companion of mine!"

The Empress took his hand and pressed it kindly. "There is only one course for you, my cousin; that of absolute submission. You are alone! The only friend who adheres to you in the court of the Emperor, is sitting by your side; what other course can you take with the smallest hope of safety?"

Julian pressed his lips upon the hand of the Empress. "Only friend; ah! yes, I know thou art. Obtain for me, then, through thy blessed influence, that I may retreat into obscurity, — that I may return to the city of Pallas, to the study of philosophy, to the ever fresh delight the poets give, with Homer as their leader, — and I will gladly leave the world to Constantius."

The Empress turned a half-melancholy, half-suspicious glance upon him, beneath which his eyes sank. There were indeed obstacles to unreserved confidence between them; the Empress was a sincere, though not a fanatical Christian, and Julian in Athens had turned openly from Christianity, and waited only a more favorable moment to make his apostasy known elsewhere. They were both silent during the rest of the drive. Eusebia's beautiful brow wore a shade of care, and the Prince seemed not yet assured, but sat calm, gathering his fortitude for some terrible encounter.

They turned aside from the palace, and Julian's brow cleared when he found he was not taken to the prison he had occupied before he was sent to Greece, but that a spacious suit of rooms had been prepared for him. Eusebia left him at the door. He kissed her hand with fervent gratitude, which was inexpressibly augmented, when, examining his room, he found that she had selected with her own exquisite taste a superb library for him, consisting of all the most celebrated philosophers and poets of Greece. His own librarian was already there, taking the beautiful rolls from their cases, so that Julian at a glance might admire the costly copies. Oribasius, his physician, who enjoyed his entire confidence, was also there, and Mardonius would soon follow.

No attendants were allowed him except two young boys, who served as pages, and were the medium of communication between the Empress and himself. He had not been permitted to see the Emperor. The eunuchs well knew that an interview would be a guarantee of safety; they therefore exerted every artifice to prevent the Emperor from granting him an audience.

He was left to contend alone with the difficulties of his position. In the solitude and darkness of night he traversed the apartment, and the longer he thought upon his position, the more terrible was the aspect it assumed. Should he surrender himself to the will of his enemy, form a closer union with him by taking the wife he offered him, and crush for ever the fair hope of the future which he had formed in Athens? He yearned for that home of the soul, as it arose again in memory touched with deeper hues from distance and uncertainty.

Eusebia had bidden him to write to her when his decision was made. He placed the waxen tablets before him, and as he paced the apartment, from the statue of Minerva to the place where the stylus invited him, he murmured forth his prayers. After a while he began and finished his letter, in which he besought the Empress to obtain leave for him to return to Greece, or to private life upon his own estate, which he had inherited from his mother. "As you comply with my wishes," he said, "may the Immortal Gods bless you with the fruition of all yours. May they give you children and heirs to take the place you would bestow upon me, and, noble friend, send me immediately from you."

When Julian had finished his letter, he felt for some moments a degree of calmness; but soon the struggle renewed itself in his soul. "Shall I oppose the Gods," he said, "or imagine I can judge for myself better than they, who know all things?" He turned to the statue of Minerva, and besought an answer to his prayer. To his excited mind he seemed to hear a whispered voice which said, "It is enough for human wisdom to discern the trivial events of the present moment. The counsels of the Gods embrace the whole. To them the most distant future, as well as the most remote past, is now *present*. As they are the cause of both past and future, must they not necessarily be acquainted with the present?"

"Counsel me, then," said Julian, "O ye august Deities! who behold my divided mind. Blessed Minerva, send one of the angels of the sun, or the moon, to declare thy will."

Again he seemed to hear a whispered voice which said, "And thou! thou who pretendest to be a man and wouldst steal thyself away from the Gods, who have great designs through thee for that future to which thou refusest to give thyself! This is folly! This is cowardice!"

Julian, confounded, said, "Shall I then cringe and yield to avoid this death, or, like Socrates, commit everything to the Gods, possessing, wishing nothing, but cheerfully *casting my care upon them.*" *

Having brought himself to this state of complete acquiescence, trusting in the Gods, borrowing a phrase from the Christian Scriptures, which had become familiar to him when he was a reader in the Church, he felt a singular degree of calmness descending into his soul. Under its influence he destroyed the letter he had written to the Empress, and, throwing himself upon the couch, he slept till morning.

The next morning, the 6th of November, was the birthday of the Prince. He entered upon his twenty-fifth year. He hailed it as a good omen that the sun rose clear and beautiful, for the short autumn day was to be filled by a brilliant pageantry.

Constantius, who no longer consulted the Senate in the choice of his colleague, had appointed this day to present Julian to the court and the army as

* 1 Peter v. 7.

his chosen partner in the cares of the Empire, and in the presence of the multitude to array him in the purple robe of the Cæsars.

Julian was scarcely awake when a crowd, assembled on the outside of his apartment, claimed entrance in the name of the Emperor. The Prince ordered his pages to throw open the doors, and immediately the court-barber presented himself; a small, effeminate-looking African, in his silken embroidered robes, his gorgeous turban, and jewelled slippers. He was followed by servants with perfumes, unguents, scented waters, and all the exquisite aids for a complete toilette, which this luxurious court exacted of those who would enjoy the favor of Constantius. The room was soon filled with a crowd which excited in the philosophic Prince only contempt.

The officer next under the chief barber displayed his golden basin, his razors and embroidered napkin. "What," said Julian, "are you ordered to present me with the mark of the tonsure? I have decided objections to all the insignia of monkism."

"No, noble Prince, Venus forbid that we should touch the flowing honors of your head, except to make them more graceful and becoming; but no one can enter the court with that outward sign of the philosopher," indicating Julian's thick beard.

"The sign of wisdom is not, as formerly, worn on the chin, but on the head."

"As the sign of folly is sometimes worn there, in lengthened ears," said Julian.

"Folly has many signs, and none more striking than the affectation of singularity in dress," said the barber.

Julian had resigned himself to all; he therefore submitted without another word. Soon were the shaggy honors of his chin removed, and the winning expression of his lips, so long concealed beneath the moustache, rendered his physiognomy far more attractive to every lover of the human countenance. His hair was then curled and perfumed; the inky stains effaced from his hands with scented water, and precious jewels, the gift of Constantius, placed upon his fingers. Now he was requested to put on a complete suit of armor, of burnished metal, which flashed back the sunbeams that entered the high windows of the apartment.

Thus arrayed, Julian went forth to meet, for the first time, the man whom he had ever regarded as his deadliest enemy. He had never before worn armor, for his pursuits had been peaceful and literary; he felt, therefore, an invincible awkwardness, an instinctive modesty, which made him cast his eyes to the ground, instead of taking upon himself those court airs and that insolent bearing, the fashion of the time.

As the Prince passed through the antechambers crowded with the satellites, the eunuchs, the effeminate loungers, clad in silken robes, whose every motion sent out a perfume which sickened the healthy senses of Julian, he became the mark of covert sneers and sarcasms.

"Are we to have a masquerade to-day," said one, "that Apollo appears in the armor of Hercules?"

"Apollo has met with the fate of Vulcan," said another, "and his fall from Heaven has robbed him of grace."

"Now, by Venus! our hero of to-day is too much an anchorite to represent the Divinity of Lemnos."

Their idle sarcasms were soon checked by the appearance of the Emperor and Empress to mount their chariot.

The public square was filled with an excited crowd. The troops were drawn out in front of a gorgeous tent, in which stood a throne for the Emperor and Empress, guarded by the Roman eagles. The brilliant sun of Italy flashed back from the burnished armor of the troops, touched with light the golden eagles, and heightened the brilliant colors of the tent, while the impatient multitude swayed forwards and backwards, trying in vain to encroach upon the open area in front of the throne.

At length the trumpets gave note of the slow approach of the Emperor, whose impatient horses were kept back to a slow pace, that the multitude might enjoy the gorgeous array of Constantius, his robes heavy and stiff with embroidery and jewels. By his side sat the Empress, whose beauty was scarcely heightened by the priceless jewels of her dress. In a plain chariot drawn by two horses, with his two young pages, who sat at his feet, Julian followed. He was pale as death. In his inmost soul was concealed the thought that this pageant would end, not in his honor, but in his death. He sat mentally repeating the verses of his favorite Homer.

When the tent was reached, the Emperor and Empress ascended the throne, and Julian, descending from his chariot, knelt before them. Constantius, taking him by the hand, presented him to the army. "Behold," he said, "I present you my well-beloved cousin, the son of my adoption, the partner of my cares, the colleague to whom I intrust a share of the interests of this Empire. Threatened as we are with dangers on every side, the weight of responsibility is too heavy for one grown old in your service. The presence of the Emperor is required, both in the east and in the west; the single strength of a man is unequal to such an extent of dominion."

A respectful murmur ran through the army and among the multitude. The Emperor understood it as a more sincere expression of opinion than that voice of flattery which continued to assure him that his all-powerful virtues, and his celestial fortunes, would for ever triumph over every obstacle.

Presenting Julian anew, he asked, "Is it your pleasure that the Prince should receive the purple, the title of Cæsar, and a partition of the cares of the Empire?" Immediately a shout rent the air. The soldiers dashed their shields against their armed knees, then raised them on high, uttering prolonged shouts of joy and exultation. For the first time Julian looked up: his countenance lightened, joy flashed from his dark eye, and a noble pride glowed from his cheek; his height seemed greater, and his whole bearing majestic.

The purple robe was now brought, and Constantius himself placed it upon his shoulders. He was invited to return to the palace in the same chariot with the Emperor, and amid the shouts and rejoicing of the excited multitude they left the field together. The crowd was so dense that their progress was very slow, and, as Julian sat side by side with his deadliest foe, those lines of Homer again recurred to him, —

> "The purple hand of death closed his dim eyes,
> And fate suppressed his breath."

His apprehensions were increased, when, instead of returning by the grand staircase of the palace, where the imperial guards were drawn up, he was conducted to a distant wing, where a suit of rooms had been prepared for the Cæsar very remote from her whom he regarded as his only friend in the palace of the Emperor.

Julian threw himself upon the divan, excited by the crowding and changing emotions through which he had passed. In moments of high exaltation or of sudden good fortune he believed himself the special favorite of the Immortals. Now they had opened a career for him, and there dawned upon his mind visions of the future, in which he saw, through his wise rule, and throughout his whole government, justice made supreme; rapacity should cease; the rich should no longer oppress the poor; the golden age should return upon earth. Then fairer visions rose. The temples of the heathen Gods were to be restored to more magnificent perfection; a purely refined worship established. The glorious arts of Greece should adorn the processions, crowding and thronging the temples; music, dancing, and the Olympic games should be revived. There should be a temple to Helios, or the sun, where no beast should bleed, but fruits and flowers, songs and music, and the productions of human genius, should be collected as offerings to the vivifying and life-giving God.

He started from his couch and paced the apartment. "Grant me, O Immortal Gods!" he cried, "but ten years of life, and every temple shall be restored. Upon every height shall rise new, immortal structures; in every valley shall bloom the gardens of Plato, the groves of the Muses. Lyric hymns, processions of virgins, of noble youths and white-haired old men, all shall hymn thy praises. In gold, in ivory, and in whitest marble, the Gods shall stand, looking with serene eyes over the deep blue waters and the rejoicing land."

As he thus paced his apartment, where stood the statues of the great men of every age, his steps were arrested by that of Christ, which was common in Christian houses. The Prince stopped and gazed upon it,—the serene brow, the meek and patient lip, the downcast eye, whose lid seemed swelled with pitying tears. "Ah!" he cried, "the Galilean! the abject one! the crucified! shall he dare to place Calvary above Olympus, and conquer by the cross?" Doubt, like an ice-bolt, passed through his mind; for the moment he recognized the strength there is in meekness, the patient endurance and the exalted faith of the lowly.

On the following morning, the Prince's devotions

to Helios and the lesser Divinities being duly performed, he attempted an egress from his luxurious apartment, but found himself still a prisoner. At this moment Oribasius, his physician, entered, with his usually serene countenance somewhat overclouded.

"Noble friend," said Julian, "let no discontent come near us. Let us bring Athens and Olympus into our smaller compass."

"Ah! but we can carry nothing out. As I attempted to go forth, I was arrested by the guard, and searched; no letter, no note or message, may go out from you to friends."

"Friends! Alas! they do but just admit the plural number, and are contained in this apartment; for there is the noble Euemerus delighting himself with the Empress's splendid gifts. But my learned seer, prophet, interpreter of dreams, listen to mine. Does not the divine Homer tell us there are two portals from which issue dreams? Tell me, you whose prophetic insight is clear, which is the true."

"Did your dream proceed from the ivory gate, whence issues the light, fantastic train of winged lies?"

"Ah, no! the images of truth come from the opaque horny portal. But you shall hear, and Minerva give you wisdom to interpret."

"Æsculapius rather," said Oribasius, "the interpreter of dreams."

"Listen," said the Prince. "A lofty tree grew, as I thought, in a spacious hall, with its branches bending down to touch the ground. From its root sprouted another, small and young and very flourishing. For this small plant I felt intensely anxious lest it should be uprooted, together with the tree. Approaching nearer, I saw the large tree already fallen to the earth."

"And how was it with the smaller one?"

"Ah! I feared it was destroyed also. But it stood aloft, green and flourishing. Then I exclaimed, What a downfall is this! and will not all, root and branch, perish together? But a stranger stood near, who said to me, Be not afraid; observe it with attention; the root remains in the ground; the plant is yet unhurt, and will spread itself around and flourish more firmly.'"

"He who stood near you was not a stranger. It was rather the faithful friend who now stands by you, and thus interprets your dream," said Oribasius.

"Then what mean these guards, and this strict imprisonment?" asked the Prince.

"Rather this luxurious apartment, and this sumptuous repast," said the physician; for slaves began to prepare, with golden covers, and jewelled cups, and the luxury which the Emperors had borrowed from the East, a repast for Julian and his two friends.

"Will Constantius make me an effeminate minion of his court by feasting and wine? Jupiter forbid!"

"He has already shorn you of the outward insignia of a man," said Oribasius, touching his beard.

"By the Gods!" said Julian, "I will be a man, not only in brain, but in cheeks and chin."

"Enjoy the good things the Gods send you at this hour," said Oribasius, turning to the repast, and inviting Julian to join him.

"Bah! I have always hated luxury, as much as a debtor hates the Forum," said Julian.

"Let us not neglect this pure ruby blood of the grape," said the temperate Oribasius. "Apollo himself would not despise this pure nectar."

Julian had fallen into a reverie.

"Let not Minerva wait," said Oribasius, "till Momus opens the portal—"

"Ah! how happy should I have been," said the Prince, "to have sung for the Muses and myself alone; but now it will be as dishonorable to cultivate poetry, as it was in former times to be unjustly rich."

"Remember your dream. A life of action is now your destiny! You have no longer a choice."

"I would have brought again the pure Castalian fountains to the lips of the faithful —".

"Let us rather carry our own lips to these generous wines, and make them fountains of wisdom."

"True," said Julian, "the beautiful cannot die, and wisdom is as immortal as Athena."

They placed themselves upon the couches at the luxurious table, and were served by the two pages.

Julian hated all superfluous luxury, as much as he loved choice spirits and congenial friends around his board. A few moments sufficed for his repast, which consisted of fruit or pulse, and water. He now took only a portion of bread and a cup of wine, and looked upon the whole with anger. "Here have I," said he, "been preaching abstemiousness for twenty years, to be shut up at last and fed, as though I were to be exhibited for my obesity. There is but one more degradation —"

At this moment Euemerus, the librarian, entered. He was pale with anger, and strove in vain to appear unconcerned.

"What has disturbed the serenity of my learned friend?" asked Julian.

"We are treated like thieves or conspirators," he cried, "searched at the door, and compelled to give over to slaves all but the bare robe from our back. It is the work of the imbecile eunuchs; they are mad with rage and envy; they have filled every office of this house with their spies and traitors. Their perfumes are sickening, their viands disgusting, their luxury enervating. There is only one thing here that is welcome, Nature's precious offering of flowers," — and he took a vase of costly flowers from the hands of the page who was presenting them.

"If the Prince pleases," said the boy, "the Empress desires him to wear this chaplet at supper."

Julian started, and examined the flowers closely; he found that Eusebia had resorted to this expedient to inform him that his betrothal with the Princess Helena would take place the following day.

"Truly, noble friend," he said, "you see the disciple of Zeno transformed into the Roman exquisite, and a garland must finish the masquerade." And after secretly withdrawing the note from the wreath, he placed it on his brow.

Julian now became pale and silent.

"Here," said Oribasius, taking up the flowers again, "are not merely the Sybarite rose-leaves; here is laurel to weave a crown. Take the sweet omen that Minerva sends, to reconcile you to your destiny, my Prince."

"The Gods have answered my prayer. I leave my fate in their hands," said the Prince.

"Let us weave a crown, then, for our hero's brow," said Euemerus.

"Not, my friend, till he has earned that crown," said Julian.

CHAPTER XV.

HELENA.

CONSTANTIUS had exchanged his gorgeous purple for a robe of sables; and as the November night was chilly, he sat with closed doors and windows.

"How shall we now dispose of our philosopher?" he said. "Shall we send our new Diogenes to search for a man among the Barbarians?"

"Your Majesty intends giving him a wife," answered Eusebius, the chief eunuch, to whom this question was addressed; "surround him then with luxury, steep him to the lips in pleasure, and he will soon become like all the other young Sybarites of the Empire, less than a man."

"I doubt the success of your experiment. Julian is of sterner nature; like Ulysses, he would bind himself to the mast and let the songs of the Sirens pass."

"If he cannot be ruined by luxury, or by woman," said Eusebius, "let us send him to be knocked on the head by the Goths and the Allemanni."

"Or to talk Greek to the Barbarians, and philosophy to the Northern Bears."

"Send him to the Gallic frontier, with an escort of two or three hundred men, and your Majesty will be troubled with little news of him or of his philosophy."

"Poor fool!" said Constantius; "he thinks he can read the secrets of nature through his converse with the stars."

"Does your Majesty really wish to be rid of the Prince? There is a surer way. Your law forbidding Pagan sacrifices is in force. It is well known that Julian prays to Helios, and sacrifices in secret to the Gods. The precious foreign birds he imports so prodigally, are not to delight him with their music. With all their glittering plumage, they are cast upon his secret altars."

"Fool! have I not winked at these things? Have you forgotten the sacrifice at the mouth of the Tiber to allay the storm, while the Emperor himself was in Rome?"

"Ah, your Majesty had sufficient reasons for ignoring all that folly. But there is a fact which, if known, is sufficient to insure and excuse the destruction of the Prince. I have certain information, that Maximus, by incantations and magical rites, assured to Julian the undivided rule of the Empire."

"The saints forbid! Do you not see that the destruction of the Prince by any other than the most obvious means, that is, the sword of an enemy, would be, not only a political crime, but the most fatal of mistakes? The blood of Gallus has not yet sunk into the dust."

The eunuch bowed, and for the present concealed his hatred of the Prince.

In another apartment of the same palace, and nearly at the same hour, two women were in earnest conversation. They were apparently not very far from each other in age, although she who seemed to hold the first place in rank and dignity had numbered fewer years than her companion. The beauty of her high-cut features, and the noble proportions of her form, showed her Greek descent. The Empress, who had been three years married to Constantius, had from conviction become a Christian, and there were traces revealing an inward life of deep emotion upon her countenance. That perfect repose which her classical beauty demanded, had been marred by the struggles of a sensitive nature to preserve its purity and Christian faith, in a court so corrupt, and in the midst of creatures so sensual.

Her companion was Helena, the destined wife of Julian. She was less beautiful than the Empress, and had reached that period in life when the freshness of departing youth is wooed to remain by all the appliances of art, and at a time, also, when all the aids of beauty were carried to the utmost perfection. Helena's brow was overclouded, and little in her attitude or expression indicated the anticipations of a happy bride.

"Julian is no common man," said the Empress; "if he were not Cæsar, if he were not heir to the Emperor, he would yet be most noble, and beautiful as Apollo."

"Beautiful! yes, but how ridiculously awkward, with that perpetual shrugging of the shoulders, and hurrying breath."

"That is from the rapidity and intensity of his conceptions; words afford him no adequate conveyance of his thoughts. They rush and crowd and tumble over each other."

"Think too of that wilderness of beard and its savage inhabitants."

"This last ridiculous falsehood we know is a calumny, invented by Gregory or Basil. Besides, has not the razor passed over those lips, and revealed the exquisite expression of his beautiful mouth?"

"Look at his inky fingers."

"Look rather at his godlike brow, upon which honor sits like a king, and then at those constantly varying eyes, now flashing fire, and now, again, melting into tenderness."

"Yes, his eyes betray the real tenderness of his nature; but to know one's self to be merely a political necessity, — to know that all his truth and faith are left with that Muse in Athens!"

"That also is a falsehood of the Athenian students," said Eusebia. "Besides, is another heart quite pure and single? The first stone should part from stainless hands."

Helena blushed, and her eyes filled with tears. "Ah! how willingly would I have given myself to Julian, had I been sought for myself; but to know that I am merely one of the base links of the chain with which Constantius binds the Prince to his interests —"

"Not to himself alone, but to the Empire. Think of being the mother of a new line of Emperors."

"Whether I bear a son or not, I am merely a sham, a puppet of Constantius's state policy. And with what indecent haste is this marriage consummated! If I had not watched Julian from my litter, the day when he was invested with the purple, and when he so far outshone the meaner multitude— "

" Ah, yes ! " interrupted the Empress, " it is only to see him with other men, and when his noble brow kindles with enthusiasm, and his eyes flash intelligence, and his whole person is transfigured, to know how immeasurably he surpasses all other men."

The Empress remained silent for some moments, and Helena dared not disturb her sad reverie. She had gone back in thought to her Grecian home in Macedonia, where, as the daughter and sister of Prefects, she had received every homage, and been sought by many suitors. One alone had not sought her, Julian; but him she could have honored and loved above all men, when she was chosen by Constantius, and neither her own nor her father's ambition could refuse the diadem; the gorgeous, heavy honor, while love's inner shrine was cold and empty.

At length she raised her eyes, heavy with unshed tears. " It has ever been thus," she said. Woman has ever been the slave of circumstance. Men who have denied her the possession of a soul, have sacrificed her, body and soul, to cement their iniquitous contracts, or to carry out their cruel wrongs. In all the long ages of history *one* only has been just to woman, because he knew the heart of woman. The Nazarene, the Crucified, placed her upon the same level with man. 'Let him who is without sin cast the first stone at her'; demanding from her accusers and judges the same purity as from her. He knew the heart of woman; he said, 'She is forgiven, for she loved much,' thus making her frailties bud from the root of her highest virtues; showing that the excess of good, her capacity for loving, becomes the excess of evil. When women are really Christian in heart and in truth, they will attain their true position, and take their part in the great events which change society."

"Women have already done that," said Helena; "yet I cannot imagine a Cleopatra or a Zenobia watching at the couch of a leper, or binding up the wounds of a common soldier."

"Those are not the acts which make a Christian, but the disposition from which they flow; the forgetfulness of self, the disinterested care for others. Expanded views of the whole of humanity, arising from the first, and tender care for all, flowing from the other; when women are thoroughly Christian, they will be the mothers of princes worthy to reign; until then, ah — "

"Until then," said Helena, "they will continue to divorce and repudiate, murder and poison wives, alas! half heathen and half Christian, like myself."

CHAPTER XVI.

THE BARBARIANS.

Julian left Milan, the first of December, to cross the Alps, with an army composed of only three hundred and sixty men. The streets were thronged with the people in holiday attire, for in this pleasure-loving age every occasion was made a festival, and as Julian's marriage, through the influence of Eusebia, had been nearly private, the people would indemnify themselves for the loss of the public games by making his departure a holiday. In the midst of legions of gaily caparisoned troops, the chosen number which were to accompany Julian marched out of their barracks, with their heavy knapsacks and their winter clothing, prepared to cross the Alps in December.

It was the custom at all public celebrations, and at the departure or arrival of troops, to suspend crowns of laurel, and of flowers, throughout the streets; and as Julian placed himself at the head of his troops, whose small numbers had called forth a shout of derision, one of these crowns became detached from its hold, and fell directly upon his head; the shout of derision was exchanged for one of joy and triumph.

As he passed at the head of his small troop, upon a well-trained charger, through one of the gates, there started up before him an apparition of an infirm and blind old woman, who cried out, "Behold him who cometh in the name of the old Gods, to rebuild their fallen temples, and re-establish their worship." Julian trembled, for she had given utterance to his own secret thought at the very moment.

Before the end of December the Prince made his entry into Vienna. He was received with the utmost joy by all ranks of people; all ages and both sexes poured out to meet him. They had longed for Julian as for a public benefactor, a tutelary angel, whose presence was to alleviate all public burdens, and put an end to all public griefs. It is difficult to understand upon what foundation they could build such extravagant hopes. What could they expect from the presence of a young Prince educated, like Julian, under the shadow of the schools, who had never seen a naked sword, or known anything of war except from books?

The Germans, who had passed undisturbed across the Rhine, had, at the time Julian was sent out, destroyed forty-five cities, without counting chateaus and villages. They occupied the whole length of the Rhine, and ravaged with impunity the whole country. The Gauls who had escaped death or servitude, suffered all the horrors of captivity in their own cities. The enemy took from beneath their eyes their flocks and their harvests, and the little wheat which they could sow within the circuit of their walls alone fed their families.

What could they expect from a young Prince, upon whose head only twenty-four winters had shed their wisdom? Besides, Constantius, the very day he left Milan, secretly despatched, in all haste, a courier to Marcellus, his general of cavalry, with orders to distrust and mislead Julian, and also to withhold from him all assistance. At the same time secret emissaries were sent, with orders to endeavor to detect him in some crime or rebellion which would cause his destruction.

The winter has past since the beginning of this chapter. It was now the summer solstice, and couriers had arrived from all parts of the Empire. The heat was excessive, but, notwithstanding, the Empress was present in the audience-chamber, not concealing the deep interest she felt in the despatches received from Julian. The burning rays of the sun were excluded from the lofty room; immense fans, ingeniously suspended from the ceiling, were waved perpetually to and fro by pages, and cooling waters and costly perfumes were constantly diffused through the heated atmosphere.

The Emperor, clad in the thinnest garments, but not without costly jewels and embroidery, reclined upon a low couch, surrounded by the various ministers of his luxury.

Constantius, too indolent for business, had left the whole arrangement to his chamberlain, carelessly interposing when any peculiar circumstances caught his ear. The despatches from Gaul had just been read.

"They have not succeeded then," he said, "in inspiring that foolish boy with a love of pleasure, or of dice, or of—"

"Ah, no, Sire! his days and nights have been spent in study and in business. Even before he left Vienna to seek the Germans, who had just raised the siege of Autun, he evinced the wisdom of an old, experienced general—"

"That was no great mark of wisdom, but the most egregious folly, to take the most dangerous road because it was the shortest," said the Emperor.

"That folly cost him his arriere guard," said one of the courtiers. "His enemies were in ambush, and deprived him of this essential part of his army."

"But this accident," interposed the Empress, gently, "has taught him that a wise suspicion is a most essential quality, even indispensable in a good general."

"By the mere terror his success has inspired," said one friendly to Julian, "he has compelled some of the Barbarian kings to make treaties with us, and this before he came to pass the winter at Sens."

"But there the boy was besieged. Do not the despatches say so?" asked the Emperor, languidly.

"And deserted by Marcellus," said the chamberlain; "who dared to say that he received secret orders to suspect the Prince, and to withhold from him all assistance."

"The traitor!" cried the Emperor, apparently in violent anger. "Let him be instantly arrested."

Furtive smiles passed round the courtiers, and some of the enemies of Julian trembled.

"Well, but the pedantic boy consumes the midnight oil," said the Emperor, "learning the art of war in Cæsar's Commentaries?"

"No, Sire! Every day, and long past midnight,

the Prince was upon the ramparts at Sens, with his own hands repairing the walls, and encouraging the troops; filled with anger, indeed, to find himself deserted by Marcellus, but always ready to repulse the enemy. All resort to him. He is adored by the soldiers. Every soldier there would sacrifice his life for the Prince."

"We shall see," said the Emperor, "when anything decisive is attempted."

"As for the battle of Strasbourg,"* said one of the courtiers, "it was mere child's play, a bagatelle, — to give the Prince a pretence for boasting."

"It was some little cause for exultation," said the Empress, "when the whole Roman cavalry wavered, to place himself as a barrier which they must leap over, or stand firm."

"Ah, your Majesty, we will baptize him, good Christian that he is, Monsieur Victorine."

"Rather pray to your Gods," said the Empress, "that they afford you such a cause for boasting."

The courtiers saw that the Emperor received all this with complacency, and one ventured to add, "This monkey clothed with the purple, this imperial buffoon, will soon be extinguished. Let your Majesty send a real warrior, an experienced

---

* Argentoratum.

general there, and his glories will melt away like frost-work in the sun."

"But this hairy pedant, all thorny with Greek, has not studied the art of rhetoric in vain," said another. "His simple soldiers believe him greater even than the Emperor himself; it takes no conjurer to predict to what height he aspires."

"It is not by his rhetoric that he wins the hearts of Germans," said the Empress, "for I am certain the pure classic Greek alone flows from his tongue. True, your Majesty," the Empress continued, "it is not the evanescent power of language alone. It is his inflexible justice, his impartial clemency, his dauntless bravery. The soldiers admire his intrepidity and contempt of death; and when they see the Prince sharing the coarse fare which must content them, sleeping without fire, rising in the coldest midnight to make the rounds of the ramparts, and to speak a kind word of encouragement to every, even the lowest soldier among them, they worship him, and they would die, every one of them, would die for him."

"It must be confessed," said a courtier, bowing low to the Empress, and thinking he was gaining her favor, "it must be confessed that it was no easy task to win both the soldiers and the oppressed inhabitants of the Provinces, so many years trodden down and robbed by grasping prefects and cruel generals."

"Ah yes!" said the Empress, "it was a new and astounding thing when Julian told a man that his own wife belonged to himself; that his children should not be thrown into the flames which had already consumed his granaries and his barns."

"Instead of burning the wheat, he pays for it. It is no longer the law of the strongest," said one of them.

"Tush! the pedant has become a Solon as well as an Alexander. Let us vote him an ovation, and be done with him. I am tired of hearing Aristides called the Just."

"What will you say when I tell you he has ordered his soldiers to respect the honor of women?"

"Yes! but it raised a mutiny, and it was only after he had ordered some of his soldiers to be crucified that he was obeyed," said another.

"And a woman may pass unmolested through the country," said one of them.

"Julian would not look at the beautiful captives brought from the remotest parts of Gaul or Britain, where their complexions are like ivory."

"The Prince has always been a woman-hater," drawled an effeminate courtier.

Eusebia would have annihilated him with a look.

Thus the first campaigns of Julian, brilliant though they were, drew towards him no favor at the court. They would have been much more glorious, had not the Emperor placed around him secret enemies and false friends. At length, however, by the intervention of the Empress, the whole command of the army was given to the Prince. Through her influence, also, Severus, the officer next in command, was sent out to him. He was a man full of honor and disinterestedness, and though many years the senior of Julian, he executed his plans with the skill of an experienced captain, and the obedience of a good soldier, and with as entire good faith as though himself had been their author.

CHAPTER XVII.

THE CHRISTIAN.

PARTHENIA remained still in Athens. Her father had gone to his Prefecture in Antioch, but she remained to complete her year's service in the temple of Pallas Athena. Athens was now associated with the memory of Julian. He had thrown the magic light of his genius upon the common day, and gilded every moment as it passed with joy. His presence had made the world rich to her; the morning and the evening hours were winged with love and happiness. There is, in the life of many of the most fortunate of the earth, a golden age, or hours and moments of gold, that take the place in life which the golden age holds in history. Then nature is kinder, the skies are of a more tender blue, the air is more balmy, the flowers are tinted with richer colors, the world is more beautiful, the countenances of our friends are lovelier, we are ourselves better; and oh! so happy! In our hearts the lamb leads the lion, and they both lie down in peace together. Parthenia had lived in this age of gold while Julian was in Athens. Had it altogether passed away? Ah no! memory lingered, and hope shed a light like the morning planet that precedes the return of the sun.

The retired avenues of the Academy, beneath the plane-trees, where the nightingales sang, and the Cephissus murmured, were her favorite walks. Towards the evening of one of those serene days, she was leaning upon the statue of Ariadne, when she heard the name of Julian proclaimed by messengers just arrived from the Piræus. These messengers held the place of newspapers, and proclaimed the news from street to street. The burden of their present message was the recent elevation of Julian to the purple, his marriage with the Emperor's sister, and his departure with a small army for the Rhine. Parthenia heard no more. She sank down by the statue which supported her, and all vitality for a moment seemed lost. It was but for a moment; the natural vigor of her health restored her to consciousness, and to the sense of an intolerable pain. As she recovered, the whole of that enchanted period of her life when Julian made its light and joy, appeared to her like a point of time, a moment, for ever past. And the future? There was no future for her, — there could be none. Her life was closed, and a dark shadow stood weeping over it!

Ah, it was not so! She was only on the threshold of the long solitude, — that solitude of the heart which God appoints for all true souls. All true greatness is wrought out in deep inward solitude, and God gives this solitude to his beloved as the sternest trial of life.

As from moment to moment Parthenia recovered possession of her reason, and was able to look steadily upon the ruin which had overtaken her, she asked, "Why have I thought myself superior to others? Why have I been proud of my intellect, if thus my hope is destroyed, and the fountain of my life for ever dry? I believed myself favored of the Gods, — that Pallas was my friend, — and shall this leaden death, this icy grief, for ever shroud me?" Then, with the thought of Julian, a softer sorrow returned. Destiny, the cruel heathen Fate, had separated them for ever; but she had known the bliss of love; she had known what it was to love a noble, a real soul; and she asked, "Had I a right to hold back when this godlike gift was presented to me? Should I have turned away from this consecration? Ah no!" Julian, so truly noble in himself, was yet transfigured in the eyes of Parthenia. She remembered every sentence he had ever spoken. The half-murmured words of love, rare and low as they had been, were burnt into her soul and for ever ineffaceable there.

She rose now to go to the altar of Athena, which stood in a retired walk, where in happy days she had been used to pray; but the cold marble image of the Goddess, looking down upon her with its human eye, in which there was no pity, struck a coldness upon her heart as of marble itself. She tried to pray. She tried to recall the emotions which all the worship of the beautiful had inspired in Julian's presence; but she found that love had been the key which had unlocked for her the mysteries of the beautiful in the worship of the heathen Gods. There was no sympathy in those cold, stony eyes, there was no pity in that marble breast, for the crushed and bleeding heart.

Despair was fast gathering over this deserted soul, when she saw approaching her the brother of her little slave, Areta. Theodorus would have immediately withdrawn, but in blank despair Parthenia longed for the sound of a human voice. Theodorus was also touched, he knew not why; but he saw there was sorrow in that prostrate form, irremediable by him, and he said, "Beloved priestess, would you only see my grandfather; he would comfort you —"

"And who is your grandfather?" she asked.

"He is an aged man, who has often seen the priestess in the temple," he answered.

"And why can he serve me?" she asked.

"Because he knows all the avenues that lead to the heart, and those of sorrow he has oftenest passed through."

Parthenia blushed faintly to find that her sorrow was so legibly written upon her brow that a child could read it. "How has he learnt the secret ailments of the heart, and the art to heal them?"

"He is a Christian! He worships the Crucified."

Parthenia motioned him to be silent. She remembered Julian's aversion, and shrank inwardly from all contact with those he called Galileans.

The stars now began to appear in the violet-tinted sky, and the dewy air brought out the fragrance of the gum cistus, whose scattered petals were wafted by the evening breeze. The tumult of the city was hushed, and the Athenian maiden prepared to return to her home. Theodore, who walked a very little behind her, observed the complete *abandon* of her manner, the noble drooping form, the starry eyes cast down and veiled with unshed tears. He longed to speak to her to try to comfort her. At length he heard her murmur, "How mysterious, how insoluble, is the enigma of this life, how strange this love, so late found, so soon lost!"

"Sorrow," dearest mistress, he ventured to say, "is that inexpressible mystery in which God's love is hidden. Believe me, this is only a bud of sorrow which will blossom into ineffable joy. I do believe it is God's purpose to lead you thus to the Crucified, who consecrated all sorrow by making it his path through life."

As Parthenia entered her own dwelling, the moon had risen, and its soft light touched the statues of the Deities around, cold and silent like ghosts, who would not, who could not, return an answer to the thirsting soul. "O," she cried, "for some loving witness, for some sure and certain conviction that this is not all of life; that, bereft as I am of love and joy, this is not the fading away for ever of happiness! O for a whisper, a sound, an assurance that there is something beyond; that there is an Immortal soul to survive; that there is a God to grant; that there is a world after this; that beyond these starry points — beyond, O somewhere beyond — where love shall live again — where the parted shall meet — where Fate, Destiny, the dreadful sisters, shall lose their power to sever hearts, and life shall begin again!"

Exhausted by her emotion, with this sharp cry upon her lips, she sank down upon her couch. She sobbed herself away to calm, and seemed to sleep, and awoke again, as she thought, at the sound of music, — a single voice unlike any she had ever heard. It was tender and childish, but very sweet, and as Parthenia listened, she recognized the voice of her little slave, Areta.

"Angel Jesus, who dost lie
Far above the stormy sky,
In thy mother's pure caress,
Stoop, and save the motherless.
At thy threshold low I bend,
Who have neither kin nor friend;
Let me here a shelter find,
Shield the shorn lamb from the wind.
Jesus, Lord, my heart will break!
Save me, for thy great love's sake!"

The hymn ceased, but not the soothing influence upon Parthenia. She called the slaves and told them to throw away the chaplets prepared for the evening guests, to-night she would admit no visitors.

"Come," she said to Areta, "bring thy lyre and sing to me those simple hymns learnt in thy infancy."

As Parthenia reclined upon her couch, the young slave sat at her feet, and sang in her sweetest child-like voice the hymns learnt at that earliest Christian church, the knee of the mother, the earliest and the last; for, in the words of one who felt their truth, "if Christianity were to be compelled to flee from the throng of busy men, its last altar would be the mother's heart, its last audience the children gathered round the knees of a mother, its last sacrifice the prayer breathed in silence from her lips, and heard only at the throne of God."

The vineyard of Albinus, which Parthenia had promised her little slave to visit, was not far outside the eastern wall of Athens, and lay in the shadow of the mountain around whose base wound the sacred way to Eleusis. Rising above the heights, the exquisite color and form of the Acropolis, with all its matchless temples and statues, began to be touched with the morning beams of the sun, when Parthenia left the city.

Albinus, the grandfather of Areta, was a vine-dresser, and also what we should call a market-gardener. His cottage was covered by vines and flowers, and overhung by large fig-trees, that cast down upon the court beneath the quivering shadow of their indented leaves. Since the dawn of day, the old man had been clipping away the vine-leaves where they too much overshaded the clusters of purple and amber grapes, the most luscious of which he put aside for the tables of the rich, they bearing a high price in Athens, while the smaller grapes could be bought very cheap indeed; grapes, fruit, and honey, and the most delicate kinds of fish forming the diet of the Athenians.

The hale old man was wiping his brow, for the morning sun was hot, when the *lectica* of Parthenia was set down at the vineyard by the Syrian slaves, who had borne its light burden from the gate of Athens.

Parthenia, graceful in every action, apologized for her early visit, through the wish to give pleasure to her little handmaiden, who was, excepting Theodorus, whom we have seen in the temple, the eldest of the family. The pale cheek of the mother flushed a little, at seeing the priestess of Minerva beneath her roof; but, with humble courtesy, she said she hoped it would not offend her belief in another faith to witness their morning worship. You could not look upon the face of Areta, for the mother bore the same name as the daughter, without feeling that hers was a nature which would have ripened on the sunny side of life, and in the climate of happiness; instead of which, she had climbed the rocky path where her own bleeding feet had kept her from slipping, for hers had been the martyr's path, and all but the martyr's crown. Even at this early age there began to appear a superior order of women, formed through the influence of Christianity. The glowing zeal and suffering virtues of such men as Basil and Gregory and St. Augustine are said to have been formed by the tender care of their Christian mothers.

Parthenia expressed her strong wish to witness their morning worship; while she was charmed to see that the personal purity and elegance which the Platonists insist upon as essential to true worship were preserved in this Christian family. The little bustle which their entrance occasioned had ceased, when the mother unrolled a portion of the sacred manuscript. Parthenia knew that it was one of the Gospels, although, in her pride of Athenian culture and Grecian learning, she had never imagined they were worthy of her attention. But as Areta read, "Come unto me, all ye who sorrow and are heavy laden," she thought she had never heard words so tender, uttered in a tone of such deep sympathy, from a voice musical, but full of tears. Her own tears were also on her cheeks. The reading over, all knelt, except the old man, who had taken the children upon his knees; they were caressing his brow and temples, and, not to disturb them, he uttered the short prayer sitting, and with the little girls on his lap.

She had never seen worship thus adapted to accommodate the simple and the weak. She expressed her surprise.

"Our Master," said Albinus, "called little children to him, and said, Of such is the kingdom of Heaven; and we only imitate him when we make the church consist of those who will form it hereafter; we can become children again only in simplicity and innocence, and thus must we become disciples of Jesus."

The Athenian maiden had often listened to stories of Christian cruelty; she blushed at her own levity of belief, and, as they drew around the morning meal, she felt the genuine polish and true courtesy of the heart which served it.

"Is my second Areta," asked the old man, "worthy of her who bore her? Does she never disobey so kind a mistress?"

"In one thing only have I found her reluctant, and in that particular, by obeying me, she would offend you Galileans."

"Grandpa is not a Galilean, he loves to be called a Christian," said one of the little girls, taking the witness of his faith, his dislocated wrist, in her fair little hands and kissing it.

"We are Christians," whispered the other, "we are never Galileans."

Parthenia smiled. "I see," she said, "that even your babes are zealous for the honor of your sect."

"Yes, the tear-drops of *our* love for Christ have baptized them into love for him also. I rejoice, noble Athenian," continued the old man, "that all except one of my children are daughters. A new influence is coming into the world through Christian mothers. How blest will be their influence upon their young sons, when — not like the Spartan mother, as she binds the shield upon the tender arm of her boy, and says, 'With it, or upon it,' or like the Roman mother, making him swear hatred to his enemies — the Christian mother baptizes her son into love and pity, and says, 'Love your enemies, do good to those who hate you, pray for those who wish you evil!'"

Parthenia was a Greek, and these humble and long-suffering precepts sounded abject to her Athenian ear; but her woman's heart softened at the picture of the Christian mother, the guardian and inspirer of her sons! It was the Athenian custom to give the young boys into the charge of a pedant to be instructed in warlike and manly usages. They were taught to revenge injuries, to look down with a haughty assumption of the superiority of manhood upon woman, and upon everything weaker than themselves.

Tears gathered in the eyes of the maiden. She was thinking of her past life, a vestal in the temple of Pallas, her life arid and desolate, and of the beautiful picture presented by the daily duties of the humble and feminine Areta; at the same moment, a contrasted and repulsive vision of those ascetic Christian recluses, the monks and nuns, who fancy themselves to have reached the very summit of Christian perfection, rose before her.

"How," she asked, "do you reconcile your Christian mother, encumbered with her sweet cares, with that other flowerless and leafless growth of your religion, the ascetic monks and nuns, who bury themselves in the reedy islands of the Nile, or in the sunburnt deserts."

"Noble lady, Jesus, our Master, gave us no example of recluse life, and left no command for ascetic self-denial. *We* do not read his lessons thus. God has made the world so wonderfully fair, that pious hearts may love it. Proud withdrawal from all human passion, is no part of the religion of him who entered with sympathy into every human relation. These extremes of ascetism will be punished, I fear, alas! by a return to lowest degradation."

Parthenia expressed her surprise, for at that moment the practice of asceticism was thought the truest worship, or the world was so corrupt, that, to be religious at all, they were compelled to go out of the world."

"Certainly," said Albinus, "we would allow to those who feel the need of contemplative repose, or who seek seasons of repentance, to retire from the world, but the highest attainment of the Christian life is to live for the good of others, to do the duty which lies nearest to you, and leave the rest to God."

A bright color flashed into Parthenia's cheek. "O precious words!" she said; "I may then hope that my life has not been all in vain."

"Your life, noble lady, must reflect much that is good, much which one who looks beyond mere forms would accept, even in the worship of your Gods, but which we Christians reject."

"Alas! it is like a broken mirror," said Parthenia; "some few of the scattered fragments may be sparkling and brilliant, but it can never again reflect a perfect image."

"I would ask for you but one change, dearest

lady, to make your life like the priceless jewel, which all the possessions of the world could not outvalue. Give your heart to the Son of God! He looks with the same love and pity upon the bewildered mind, as upon the sinning life. He turns only from the haughty and false of heart."

CHAPTER XVIII.

LUTETIA, OR PARIS.

JULIAN had finished his third campaign in Gaul. He had re-conquered and re-established the cities destroyed by Barbarians along the course of the Rhine. He had formed peaceful colonies, governed by just laws, regulating the amount of tribute, and diminishing the taxes. He sought to administer justice, not exactly according to the rules of Roman usage, but after his own views, which were, "that a prince was a living *law* who should temper by his own clemency that which the dead law had made too rigorous." Governing, in the name of the Emperor, with these views, yielding nothing to favor or riches, he had made himself beloved by the inhabitants, adored by the army, and approved by the wise and impartial, who were not the courtiers of Constantius.

In the midst of winter, the Prince had returned from his campaign on the Rhine to his beloved

Lutetia, or Paris. Paris, at this time, extended little beyond the island enclosed by the Seine, which was connected with the opposite shores by two wooden bridges, from one end of which stretched a noble Roman road to the heart of the Empire. Here, in an ancient palace, surrounded by gardens and spacious Roman baths, Julian and Helena held their frugal and unostentatious court. Remains of massive walls even now attest the grandeur of these ancient structures, whose simple architecture presented few ornaments. Pillars enclosed long rows of arcades, where the stern soldier, encased in his armor of steel, kept his monotonous tread through the long nights of the Paris winter.

Julian loved these wintry nights and the gloom of these Northern skies; he felt also a sense of security here, away from the treachery of Constantius's court, and the fawning insincerity of the chamberlain. Here was no amphitheatre or arena for gladiators, so abhorred by the purer tastes of the Prince; he could spend his nights in study; and together with his learned physician, Oribasius, he established an Academy in the little city.

He loved the frank and genial character of the Parisians. They worshipped Venus and Bacchus, but not with the insolence and obscenity of the old cities of Greece and Rome, and Julian, had he been ready *publicly* to declare himself a Pagan, would not have been offended with the impurity of their worship in this Northern city.

Let us return for a moment to the court of Milan, where the courtiers and eunuchs are assembled. The deep red angry spot still burnt upon the cheeks of the Emperor; couriers had arrived from Gaul, and from the Prince, but the watchful Empress was no longer there to unveil the secret malice of his enemies. She had died suddenly, and not without suspicion of poison, and now another wife gave the Emperor the promise of an heir.

The populace had learned the news, and the angry courtiers, as they sat in the presence-chamber, heard the victories of Julian proclaimed through the streets, and listened to by the excited populace.

"Thirty thousand of the people of Gaul, with their wives and their children, who had been made prisoners, are restored to their homes!" cried a man who stood upon the highest steps of a temple. The populace threw up their caps and shouted.

"The whole Rhine is now at peace, and subject to Rome," cried another.

"Let us go to the Rhine, the Rhine, the Rhine!" they shouted.

"Silence!" cried a hundred voices, "let us hear more."

"The cities which had been destroyed have been rebuilt at the expense of those who destroyed them," proclaimed the same man from the steps of the temple.

"Houses must be dirt cheap," they cried; "let the houseless in Milan move off, and Julian will give them shelter," — and they sent up a tremendous shout of "Julian, Julian for ever!"

"Silence! hear what the Prince has done. He has built immense granaries all along the Rhine to store the corn to feed his armies."

"Yes, and he brought this corn from Britain, a country where the sun never shines, in ships built at his own expense," cried another.

"And all for the love of his army," they shouted.

"And all this before he is thirty years old."

"Thirty!" screamed a woman, "he is not yet twenty-eight. He was born the very day with my own blessed son, who is now in Hades."

While the people exulted in the success of Julian, and proclaimed his victories through the streets of Milan, Constantius had the meanness to appropriate the glory, and take the merit to himself. Sending letters crowned with laurel to all the provinces, he put his own name in the place Julian's should have filled. By this artifice no one was deceived, and contempt only fell upon himself.

The enemies of the Prince now took a more subtle method; instead of depreciating his merits, they exaggerated his fame, his talents, his important services, but insinuated that, with the army so devotedly attached to his interests, he could mould them to his will, and soon place himself in opposition to the Emperor. "Deprive him of his army," said one, "and he will be powerless."

"He is no true Roman," said another, "should he deny his best troops to serve the exigencies of the state."

"By this he can prove his loyalty," said the eunuch. "Should he refuse, he is a traitor to Rome and to your Majesty."

"So let it be," said the Emperor.

A tribune and other officers were instantly despatched to Julian, with orders for him to send to the Emperor four entire legions; and also that from each of the remaining bands three hundred of the best and bravest youths should be selected for the service of the Emperor in Milan. No treachery or injustice towards the Prince could be greater; as these, the best of his soldiers, had been enlisted with the express condition that they should never leave their wives and children, nor be compelled to cross the Alps into Italy. The attachment of the Gaul to the small circle of his home was riveted by the simple pleasures of his life and the few but intense objects of his interest, and to compel him to leave them was like tearing soul from body.

Julian had gone up to his observatory; the night was starless, and no planetary influence could be relied on. He was already absorbed in his midnight studies, when he was startled by the horns of the couriers breaking upon the silence of night. He ordered the messengers to be brought into his presence. He was now informed that the commands of the Emperor were not addressed to him, but to the Grand Ecuyer, and conceived in terms outrageously insulting to the Cæsar.

Never was situation more embarrassing. If he refused the demand of the Emperor, he would subject himself to the imputation of treason, and there were many already watching to accuse him; if he complied, he would leave himself and the Gauls at the mercy of the Barbarians; besides, he had given his sacred word to the troops enlisted in Gaul, that they should not be sent beyond the Alps; many of them, who had wives and children, had entered the army relying upon that promise.

As the morning advanced the tumult increased, and as Julian descended the steps of his palace, he found the avenues thronged by the people and the soldiers. The soldiers' wives pressed around him, holding up their infants and crying aloud, repeating his promise that they should not be sent across the Alps, and beseeching him not to abandon them.

He ascended an eminence, and with all his fluent eloquence and impassioned manner addressed a few words to them. He said, there was only one course for him, and for them, — they must obey the Emperor; not to do so would be sedition, nay treason. "For myself," he added, "I shall resign all command, and never act more in public. I wait only for the return of my officers to do so."

Consternation kept the soldiers silent, and Julian, finding the tumult subsiding, promised the soldiers an extra subsidy, and to provide wagons to carry their wives and children across the Alps.

CHAPTER XIX.

THE CONSPIRACY.

THE halls of the palace were brilliantly illuminated, and the light of countless lamps reflected in the silent river as it flowed softly beneath the windows. The Prince gave a banquet to the officers of the troops which were to leave him on the morrow. Two officers closely disguised were walking stealthily along the margin of the river, evidently seeking concealment. "Are all things ready?" whispered one.

"The tablets are prepared and ready to be placed on the couches of the leading men at the right moment, and each has his cue."

"Nothing must be hinted till the Prince has left the room," said the first.

"Then we must take care that the leaders do not drink too much."

"The boys are charged to put double measures of Neptune's element into the more generous gift of Bacchus."

"Julian has been questioning the augurs and astrologers again. I swear by the terrible sisters, the *first* will give him all he wants."

"And he will interpret the others just as his wishes tend."

"It is astonishing how these occult powers agree with the wishes of those who consult them."

"Hush! Do you then think he seeks what we are determined he shall have?"

"Was there ever an eye like his, and ambition did not hide beneath?" said the first speaker.

"We shall see," said the other. "Cæsar thrice refused the crown."

"Our Cæsar will refuse it but once. A divine voice, he says, accompanies him. Let him hear that voice whispering, and he is ours."

The second officer laughed incredulously, and soon after both entered the banqueting-room.

It was past midnight. Julian did not leave the banquet till he had spoken to every officer, even of the lowest grade; he had promised the soldiers that, as they defiled by the palace next day, he would appear and receive their final adieus.

As he returned to his own apartment, he met one of the handmaids of Helena, and inquired for his wife, who was ill. She had retired to their sleeping-chamber, and he betook himself to another apartment, which looked out upon the altar of Jupiter, standing near the Seine. Julian endeavored to pierce the murky night, through whose gloom the flame upon the altar could hardly struggle. A few faint stars were seen through the openings of the clouds, and the sounds of revelry from the hall reached dully upon his ears. The rushing, hurrying clouds were a fit emblem of the thoughts casting alternate gloom and glow upon the mind of Julian. Should he submit to the loss of his best soldiers, and so undo all the good he had effected in Gaul, or should he disobey the Emperor, and kindle a civil war between them?

"What had there ever been but war between them?" asked Julian.

He called a page, and sent for his physician Oribasius.

"Not yet in bed, my Prince?" he asked as he entered.

"No, Oribasius; you see a man whose nights henceforth will be his own, to give to sweet Poesy, and her sterner sister Philosophy. I have done with the cares of the state."

"He who is sure of the purity of his motives of action can scarcely go wrong, whatever path he takes," said the physician.

"I have no foothold left. Bereft of my best soldiers, all I have done falls into ruin."

"Honor and conscience are left, my Prince, and with wisdom and courage you can meet every event."

"Most learned Joseph! interpreter of dreams! give me the solution of this night's vigil," said the Prince.

"A waking dream! But must I give both dream and interpretation, my Prince?"

"Ah! I forget. To your other gifts you add that of divination. Methought the Genius of the Empire stood before me, arrayed in pure white with wings of purple. His form was that of a beautiful youth, like Apollo, or that favored being, the companion of Psyche, and he offered me the crown; thrice I retreated, and thrice he pressed it upon me. Then in a tone of reproach he said, 'It is a long time, Julian, that I have stood concealed at thy portal desiring alone thy elevation. Thou hast forced me many times to retire. If now thou shouldst refuse to receive me, grieving, I shall leave thee. Remember, it is but a little time that we can be together!' Fearful of myself, I turned to fly, and met those dreaded forms, the three sisters who control the destiny of mortals. She who held the fatal shears stood with them open to cut my thread of life! I awoke. Interpret, most learned among the wise!"

A shade of sorrow passed over the brow of the physician, but at length he said: "That power to which we give the name of Destiny, my Prince, is but the secret, long-cherished desire, moulding the character, and at length giving a direction to events."

"Ah no!" said the Prince, impatiently. "'The light car of our destiny is borne on by the sun-steeds of time, and lashed by invisible spirits,—we run our course, and whether the goal be death or glory, the mortal hand cannot hold the reins to see.'* What now does it concern either Gods or men, that I have spent the best years of my life in moulding this wild people into a civilized nation? The Emperor withdraws my troops, and we are again overwhelmed by these wild Barbarians. Thus we strive, and a breath from our overruling destiny sinks the scale, and all is over. Were I a true Nazarene, the wildest monastery, a thousand miles above Alexandria, should be my retreat."

"What a splendid opportunity to study Plato and Plotinus!" said Oribasius; "but, the Gods be thanked, the heroism of self-abnegation does not belong to my Prince."

Julian threw open the window towards the east, where a small temple to Helios had been erected by himself. Faint streaks of light began to divide the

* Goethe.

clouds as he stood ready for his prayer at the first darted sunbeam. He started, and turned to Oribasius. "Were the guards at their posts when you entered?" But before he could be answered, Nebridius, the Prætorian Prefect, rushed pale and breathless into the apartment. "Prince!" he cried, "stand firm, and refuse what they demand, or fly! Fly for your honor, before hesitation becomes treason! We will protect your retreat!" Fire, and a noble scorn, flashed from the eyes of Julian. "Still this tumult," he cried to the guard, "and bar the doors."

"Singly, in the midst of that armed and angry multitude, have I opposed the troops, who, driven to madness by the demand of the Emperor, swear to devote themselves to the Prince alone," said Nebridius. "Unseconded, I asserted the right of Constantius, and cried out, Sedition and treason!"

Oribasius turned coldly from him. "*You* alone," he said, "deserted the Prince!"

"He was right," said Julian; "if the Prefect was alone there, he is not alone here. I stand on his side, and assert the right of Constantius. But what has happened? Answer, Nebridius!"

"At the moment when the officers were most heated with wine, skilfully worded tablets were thrown among them, crying out against the tyranny of Constantius, lauding the virtues of Julian, who, they said, was betrayed by the Emperor. Just then a loud voice exclaimed, 'Soldiers! brothers in arms! let us swear by the Immortal Gods to stand by the Prince; he alone is worthy to reign." At that moment the helmet of the Cæsar, with its laurel wreath, which he had accidentally left in the banquet-hall, was raised on high, the officers thronged around it, and swore homage upon their knees, and, rising, drew their swords and crossed them; the Christians swearing, upon the cross thus formed, eternal fidelity to the Prince. Hark! I hear them approaching! hundreds of feet are beating the pavement of the atrium!"

"The doors are barred!" cried Julian, pale as death, not from fear, but from the momentous importance of the hour. But now he gave orders to open them to admit the soldiers.

Julian saw, as they entered, his well-tried, veteran soldiers, and there was that in their aspect which said there was no retreat; they had ventured their *all* upon this cast, and whatever the result as to Julian, for them there was no going back. The Prince began an oration, the soldiers clashed their swords upon their shields and cried out, that they wanted no Greek, no philosophy, they wanted him at their head!

The Prefect, Nebridius, ordered the guards who remained loyal to attach the ringleaders, and take them off to prison, or to instant execution. Upon this order a hundred swords were flashing in the eyes of the Prefect, and one of the most audacious struck his hand, and severed it from his arm. "Hold! Barbarians!" cried Julian. "Let every sword be instantly returned to its scabbard. Is this the way to gain my consent, by wounding my friends in my presence?" and he took off his mantle and threw it over the Prefect, who had embraced his knees for protection.

"Nebridius is no friend," they cried; "he is the friend of Constantius, but he is sacred under the mantle of the Cæsar," — and, still protecting him, Julian sent him with a guard to his own house.

The Prince, finding they would neither listen to him nor his friends, said he would retire and consult the will of the Gods. But not without an oath that he would return before the water-clock had dropped out the hour, would they allow him to leave them. Julian declares, in his letter to the Athenians, that he did not consent to the wishes of the soldiers till he received an answer from the Gods; that they, the Gods, commanded him no longer to oppose the wishes of the army, but to assume the imperial power.

The tumult increased, and seemed prevailing throughout the palace; they therefore hastened the return of the Prince to his soldiers. They saw instantly from his aspect that the answer of the Gods had been propitious, and they cried out for a diadem!

"A crown! a crown!" was uttered by a hundred voices. "Let the Cæsar Augustus be crowned instantly, and receive our homage, here, upon the spot!"

"Where shall we find a diadem?" "Surely," they cried, "the caskets of the Empress are not empty!"

The jewel-boxes of Helena and of the officers' wives were sought, and an ornament in the form of a tiara, worn by Julian's wife, was produced.

"No," cried the Prince, "no female ornament! The pageantry of vanity shall not encircle my brow!"

"Here," cried an officer, "is a collar studded with jewels, belonging to the caparison of a noble steed." "No vanity can sully this," they said; but the superstitious Emperor shrank from the semblance of a crown, worn by an animal without reason. At length a collar of great value was found upon the neck of Maurus, a spearsman, and offered to Julian. "Ah, this is a brave soldier's ornament," cried the Prince, "and will bring no disgrace to another soldier!" — and he placed it on his head. A deafening shout arose, and the soldiers rushed forth to do him homage upon their knees.

With a majesty he knew well how to assume, the Emperor forbade this act. But something they must do. "A shield! a shield!" they shouted. Instantly he was raised in the air upon a shield borne upon the shoulders of the men, shouting, "Cæsar Augustus! Julian! Emperor!" Thus was he carried around the camp amid the clashing arms and shouts of the army. "O Plato!" cried Julian, "what ignominy for a philosopher!"

When he returned to the palace, his friends and attendants observed the pallor and dejection of his countenance. He desired to be alone, and shut himself into an upper room, that room which looked out upon the altar of Jupiter, where he spent the day in solitude. As the evening twilight gathered, and the trees shut out the crimson glow of the western sky, those who looked for the new Emperor could see that he was pacing the sheltered walk along the margin of the Seine. The murmur of the river as it lapsed along its banks, and the music of Æolian harps formed by the cypress-trees, soothed him into a tranquillity of spirits that he had not felt since the arrival of the Emperor's orders. The mystical element of Julian's character, his faith in overruling influences, in a destiny whose decrees were irresistible, in aid of that vain self-exaltation which made him believe himself a favorite of the Gods, took possesion of his mind, and composed it to tranquil acquiescence. The Gods, whose will it was that he should govern this great Roman Empire, had thus converted, as he believed, the blind instinct of the soldiers into their own instrument to accomplish their purpose.

Now, then, he bound himself anew to re-erect their altars, to repair their temples, to renew their sacrifices, and make their worship the sole religion of this vast Empire.

The next day the new Emperor ascended the throne in his imperial robes, and with all the majesty becoming the true Cæsar Augustus. The fasces and the axe were borne before him, and although he continued to wear the soldier's collar as a diadem, the majesty of his countenance lent to it a glory surpassing the gems of the royal crown.

All those who had been enemies, as well as the friends of the Prince, pressed around him for pardon, employment, and favor. He declared, in the same manner as he who, upon the same spot, imitated him fifteen centuries afterwards, that, without regard to precedent or favor, he should bestow on *merit alone* all employments, both civil and military. This declaration flattered and excited the simple soldiers, who henceforth believed that they had the right to aspire to everything.

Next, he offered pardon to all those who had opposed and conspired against him, even to that eunuch who had pledged himself to his assassination. Nebridius, the Prætorian Prefect, who had openly declared himself the enemy of Julian, now besought him on his knees to give him his hand to kiss, as a pledge of his favor. Julian withdrew his hand, saying, "If I give *you* my hand, what pledge shall I have for those who are really attached to me? But you have nothing to fear, — retire wherever you please."

Having thus despatched his most pressing affairs, the Prince retired to his library to perform the delicate duty of preparing an embassy for Constantius.

The secretaries were summoned, and sat, style in hand, while the Prince, embarrassed and uncertain, walked the apartment.

Oribasius, his physician, was called to aid him, and Mardonius also. Julian was not ashamed to ask this guardian of his infancy in what terms he should write to the Emperor.

"Write to him, my Prince," he said, "in a style

at once firm and modest, as a man who does not fear his anger, but wishes sincerely for his friendship."

"Ah!" said Oribasius, "the friendship of the wolf for the lamb! the sincere friendship he has shown for all his relations."

Julian turned to the secretaries. "Say that I entreat him to believe, that the good of the empire demands that we should be united in friendship, as we are in blood."

"Promise him some Spanish horses, and a legion of barbarians to swell his army," said the librarian.

"I foresee only his rage and violence," said Julian, "and the empire rent again by civil war. But the soldiers without pay, without reward of any kind, half naked, tired of gaining battles, which are a pure loss to them, driven to frenzy at last by the order which tore them from their wives and children to carry them across the Alps, to a country where they surely believed they should die — "

"Let these things be urged as their motive for compelling his unworthy cousin to put on the horse-collar," said Oribasius.

"No," said Julian, taking it off, "it is after all an honest soldier's ornament, not so paltry as the real bawble, for which so many have lost their heads."

"Tell him," said Mardonius, "to thank the Gods for giving him a man to share his empire who has twice the brains, and six times the prudence, which he possesses."

"Tell him, said Julian, "that he may appoint the prefects, but that I claim the right, by the appointment of other officers, to reward those who have shed their blood for me."

In the midst of these contradictory orders the official letter was finished, and inscribed by the modest appellation of "Cæsar," and ambassadors appointed to present it to the Emperor.

Julian and Mardonius were left alone, when the old man approached, threw himself upon his knees, and embraced those of Julian.

"What does this mean?" cried the Prince. "Rise, my father; that posture is not fitting for you or me. Rather should we exchange positions, and I remain at your knees."

"Prince! I read your intention," cried the other. "The humble letter, the letter for the public ear, is sent; but in the other, meant for Constantius alone, you will permit yourself to pour out the bitterness of your soul, in invectives and reproaches which will kindle again these cruel civil wars, sow again the dragon's teeth upon the field you have so nobly reaped."

"What! would you have me, like the abject Galilean, when smitten on the one cheek, turn to him the other also? Whatever we may write, Constantius will find pretext and occasion to destroy us."

"Remember Themistocles and his Athenians," said Mardonius, — "'Nothing can be more advantageous, but nothing more unjust.'"

"Ah! we are not Athenians! Beside, I claim no more than I already possess, not solely by the unanimous voice of the people and the army, but by the permission of Constantius himself. But, my father, your admonition comes too late. Both letters are on their way, and must be left to the speed of my ambassadors, and the disposition in which they may find the Emperor." And Julian, embracing his faithful servant, left the apartment.

CHAPTER XX.

ANTIOCH.

ANTIOCH, the eastern centre of Greek fashion and Roman sensuality, enclosed within its walls more of ancient luxury and ancient corruption than any city of its size. The rapid and rather turbid stream of the Orontes washed the foundations of its palaces, as it rushed by, connecting them with the Mediterranean, through the harbor of Seleucia. Caravans, traversing the open plains on the other side of Lebanon, and passing between the ranges of Lebanon and Taurus, brought all the riches of Arabia, and the merchandise of Mesopotamia, to the doors of the luxurious inhabitants.

The city, rising high upon the basis of the mountains, was environed by gardens, blossoming with the luxuriant vegetation of the South, bringing the fragrance of Arabia to mingle with the cool breezes of the Mediterranean Sea. The streets, intersecting at right angles, were lined with a double colonnade of marble pillars, and at each crossing a gorgeous fountain threw high its refreshing waters. The aqueducts, the baths, and numerous theatres, showed that the Antiochians understood the means of luxury as well as the arts of pleasure; but in their midst arose the noble Christian church, proclaiming, that in the centre of the seducing pleasures of heathenism, "in *Antioch*, were the disciples first called Christians."

Parthenia had left Athens, after three years of service in the temple, to join her father in Antioch. As she passed through the magnificent streets, on her way to her father's house, her eye was arrested by the octagon church, dedicated to Christ. The open door showed the pavement of precious marbles, the walls sparkling with gems and pictures. She contrasted this grandeur with the humble dwelling of Albinus, where she had first witnessed the sweetness and simplicity of Christian worship. She had read the manuscript of the Gospel put into her hand at that time, but, accustomed to Greek elegance, the simplicity of these Scriptures and their lowly subjects offended her taste, and shocked her pride of intellect. She there learnt, that the humble and poor of spirit should enter first into the kingdom of the blessed; that the master and the slave were judged by the same law; that the wicked, and certain women whom from her irreproachable purity she loathed, were admitted to the presence of Jesus, and wept at his feet. She was not yet prepared to receive the humble lessons of Christianity. She was not yet ready to sit at the feet of the Crucified, and to say, "Not I, but *thou*; not as I would, but as thou wilt." The fear of ridicule and of worldly shame was not yet swept out of her heart. But she resolved that she would examine for herself. She would see with her own eyes, and hear with her own ears. She would put aside her Grecian fastidiousness of taste, and enter that temple of the Galilean.

Not many days passed before she entered with the worshippers into the Christian church. Her astonishment was great at the gorgeous ornament of every part. The precious marbles wrought with Grecian art; the pillars encrusted with jewels; Christian symbols gemmed upon the walls; the cross, the palm, the dove, and the serpent as the emblem of sin, were there. It presented a contrast indeed to the severe simplicity of the heathen temples; but the Christian emblems were without meaning to her, as well as the spiritual ideas of Christianity, which had begun to be expressed in its churches. The altar bore the symbolic cups, and the lamb in purest silver; while a wreath of incense rose perpetually, like a voiceless prayer.

Women were kneeling at the steps of the altar. Parthenia threaded her way upwards, led on by the marble form of Christ, which looked down with benignant expression upon the group of suppliants. This statue was wrought with less perfection than those of the Gods she had worshipped upon her own heathen altars, but there was in the face an expression of human love, of tender pity, and divine patience, which made her long to know something more of him it represented. She knelt, and unconsciously a prayer for help was breathed in whispers from her lips.

She was not conscious that her robe (she yet wore her dress of priestess) had swept that of another woman, kneeling by her side, till she saw her carefully remove herself from the contact, and look at her as though defiled by the touch. Parthenia raised her eyes to the face of the other. She was a woman of humble presence but of beautiful features, where there was an expression of stern aversion, which said: "Stand aside, I am holier than thou! thy contact is offensive to me!" They turned from each other in mutual dislike. A stern intolerance began early to incrust the melting heart of Christian love.

Antioch, in comparison with Athens, might be called a Christian city. The bells rung to early prayers. Bishops and presbyters, gorgeously attired, drove their white mules, attached by golden harness to their carriages, through the streets. Crowds of scantily robed monks, with bare heads and sandalled feet, were met by processions of catechumens on their way to receive Christian baptism. Parthenia's attention was arrested by frequent processions of high-born ladies, bearing food and wine and garments outside the city, to place upon the tombs of the martyrs, ready for wandering beggars, for the destitute, the sick, the famished; this class of people being forbidden to enter the already crowded city.

The Grecian maiden no longer enjoyed the calm and tranquil hours that filled her Athenian life with the repose of beautiful forms, varied by the excitement of poetry and soothed by the charm of music. She saw that the Christian woman's life was filled with thought and care for others, and often with complete self-denial, and even abnegation of self. She had not entered the church since she was repulsed at the altar; she resolved, however, to follow the Christian women, to see what constituted their employment outside the walls of the city.

Passing with her attendants beyond the outmost gate, she approached a bare, desolate field, covered with ruinous huts. The field looked as though a rain of fire and brimstone had fallen upon it and consumed every green thing. No tree spread its refreshing shade over the ashes of its soil, no tendril of the vine curtained its blackened roofs. Several Christian women were there, and Parthenia saw the lady who had repulsed her at the steps of the altar enter, carrying food to one of the ruinous huts. She ordered her bearers to allow her to alight from the litter.

"Madam," they said, "no one enters this accursed enclosure."

"Dearest mistress!" cried Areta, "Jesus and the holy angels forbid! none except Christian women enter here."

"And where Christian women go, may not a Greek, an Athenian, enter? Why is it forbidden?"

"God forbid that you should enter that gate! It leads to the accursed field where lepers are banished; none enter except the officers to bury the dead, and Christian women who come to comfort the afflicted."

"If women come here, surely I may enter," and she passed through the gate alone. The little maiden lingered at the gate, but the other frightened attendants fled.

Parthenia had heard of this loathsome Syrian disease, but she had never witnessed it. As she entered the nearest hut, the same lady who had repulsed her at the altar was seated by the hard couch, supporting the crippled victim of disease, while she read in a low, tearful voice the precious words from the Scriptures, — "He hath anointed me to preach the Gospel to the poor; he hath sent me to heal the broken-hearted, to preach deliverance to the captives"; and then those still more precious words, — "Come unto me, all ye who labor," etc. As the tenderness of the voice and of the words fell upon the tortured ear of the sick, repose took the place of anguish upon the emaciated features. The noble Greek listened, and her heart was also soothed. "Am I not weary with thinking?" she said; "Am not I heavy laden with doubt?" and that tender voice touched her inmost soul, and her tears fell unheeded.

The lady rose to perform the same office of Christian love for another, still more loathsome than the last; and as their eyes met, a slight blush colored the pale cheek of the Greek, and deepened to crimson when she found that it was indeed the same who had repulsed her in the church. She could not reconcile the humility of the one action with the hauteur of the other. "Permit me to ask," she said, "is this a cruel penance commanded by your religion, to expiate some unrepented sin?"

Monica, the person addressed, saw by her dress that she was a stranger, and found neither levity nor contempt in the question. "Lady," she said, "how can one who loves the Saviour do otherwise? Has he not said, 'Inasmuch as ye do this unto the least of my disciples, ye do it unto me'?"

"And are Christians in such close personal relations with their God?"

"He whose words I just repeated, whose command we thus obey, is not our God. Although we believe him the first of created beings, he is not the same as the Supreme God, the Father."

"Ah! I cannot comprehend your religion," said Parthenia; "another, calling himself a Christian, has told me that your Christ is 'God of God, light of light, very God of very God, not created but always existing,' and that the last Emperor had decreed severest penalties against all who taught a different doctrine

"Yes, but a simple woman cannot believe what the Council of Nice has ordered us to receive as our faith, and thousands, from the late Empress to the humblest of her subjects, believe that the Son, our Saviour, was a created being, and dwelt among us, and was perfect only because God willed that he should be perfect."

"Ah! this brings your Saviour, as you call him,

nearer to your confidence and love; as our Apollo is nearer to us as the humble shepherd of Admetus than as the glorious God of Light."

"Do not blaspheme," said Monica, turning from her, and making the sign of the cross.

"The Gods forgive me if I blaspheme them, in likening the immortal God of the Lyre to a Jewish malefactor," said Parthenia.

"Can you, then, a worshipper of beauty, see no beauty in that eternal self-sacrifice; thirsting for love, can you see no love in giving himself for us?"

"I am not a Christian," said Parthenia; "and when I see Christians shedding each other's blood like the bitterest enemies, I pray, Jupiter preserve me from such belief. Then, again, when I see delicate Christian women tending the most loathsome subjects of disease, leading their sons and taking their sweet infants to the arms of that benign Jesus whose statue is above the altar, and whose divine countenance sheds upon them a benediction, my thirsting heart longs to lay itself at his feet—"

"Return with me to my house," interrupted Monica, eager to convert a soul; "my lectica stands without, and is sufficient for both."

The Athenian consented, and both ladies ascended one litter, and were borne on the shoulders of men to the dwelling of the matron.

CHAPTER XXI.

PHORION.

MONICA's dwelling was one of the richest in the city. Left early a widow, her husband, a distinguished lawyer, had ordered by his will that the paternal home should remain unaltered till their only son became of age to enter upon his estate. He had been a man of refined culture and artistic taste, and it was his delight to fill his house with exquisite works of art, and to surround himself with every refinement that ingenuity could invent to render even luxury fastidious.

No Christian himself, he had yielded indulgently to his wife's conscientious scruples, and consented that she should renounce all the gayeties of the world. Her life was consumed in labors for the Church, — in pilgrimages to the tombs of the martyrs, where it was the custom of Christians to place food and wine for the destitute. We have seen her at the bedside of the leper, where with other

Christian women she performed the most loathsome offices. If it were a sincere, though mistaken piety, it was certainly a wholly superstitious asceticism which caused the women of that age to divest themselves of all the charm of delicacy, and to consume their beauty and their health in austere self-denial, and in labors too heavy for their strength to endure.

No contrast could be more striking than that of Monica's humble person with the house she occupied. Gliding softly through apartments filled with Grecian statues and Byzantine mosaics, she presented herself only, " that adorning which consisted not in wearing gold or putting on of apparel, but that which was hidden in the heart, even the ornament of a meek and quiet spirit," etc.

The apartments of Monica looked out upon the Orontes and the cultivated opposite shore, where the vine and the fig, the myrtle and the bay, flourished almost without vicissitude of seasons, sheltered by the overhanging mountains. Beneath the windows rose the perfume of every Eastern flower, perpetually freshened by the numerous fountains. So abundant were the springs in this favored region, that it was called the " home of the waters."

Parthenia had become the guest of Monica, who

had striven and prayed for the conversion of the beautiful Athenian, while the latter sympathized deeply in her hostess's anxiety touching her only son, a youth of about twenty years. This young man had been seduced into the errors and follies of the time. His Greek education sharpened an already penetrating intellect; but the lectures of the Sophists had involved him in errors which his mother felt that only the Divine Spirit could tear away. He was therefore the constant subject of her exhortations and prayers, — prayers which the bishops said must finally effect his conversion, not to Christianity, — he was already a nominal Christian, — but from errors of philosophy and conduct.

Phorion, in accordance with the fashion of the time, had an establishment separate from the paternal home, and Parthenia had been some days his mother's guest before she saw this cherished son. On one of these mornings, at entering the apartment of his mother, she was greeted by a young man whose exterior instantly won for him her sympathy and admiration. He was of that slender and beautiful symmetry which had been the model for the sculptors of Athens, while his almost faultless features, and a certain sharpness of outline, showed his Grecian descent. The studied care of his dress combined what was convenient in the costume of the Frank with the lingering fashions of antiquity. The toga had long ceased to be worn by the young exquisites of the time, but the tunic of Phorion was of the richest colors, with jewelled buckles, and a collar enriched with emeralds like those which adorned the clasps of the tunic.

He rose to greet his mother's guest with a silent but genuine indication of sympathy, for his mother had often made her the subject of conversation, as he had so lately himself passed through the same experience of doubt and suffering which had resulted in faith in the Nazarene as a divine teacher; but his mother was not satisfied with this,—she wished to convert him to the stoicism of Christianity. All her exhortations were now directed to induce her son to embrace the monastic life. She longed to sever ties which she considered sinful, and for that purpose she would have banished him to one of the monastic solitudes, too often the refuge, at this period of the Church, of all those who had not strength to meet the temptations or the sorrows of the world.

In the manners of Phorion, especially towards women, there was all the refined courtesy of the man of the world, united with the tender sympathy of human brotherhood which marked the Christians of that early age of the Church.

As was mentioned above, Phorion's home was not with his mother. Not many days had passed since the first interview with her guest, when, with light footsteps and joyous expression, he sprang into her apartment when Parthenia was also present.

"What good news do you bring me?" asked his mother.

"Listen! Do you not hear the heralds, with trumpets, and the soldiers, shouting the name of Julian?"

"I hear only a new tumult," said his mother.

"Listen! Julian, my fellow-student in Athens, my friend, has arrived at Constantinople after the most dangerous march that ever hero achieved. Constantius, who went out with deadly hate to meet him, — thanks to the immortal Gods! they have taken him to themselves!"

Parthenia turned pale as death, and his mother's face flushed deeply to hear her son speak thus of the heathen Deities.

"Never were such victories or such a march as this young hero has achieved. Cæsar's glories are pale to his, and Hannibal's mere boy's play. Think of it, my mother. He is scarcely older than your effeminate, petted son!"

"You do not tell us what he has accomplished," said Parthenia recovering her voice.

"Ah! pardon me, I forgot all, but that he selected the bravest of his troops, and, casting behind them every hope of retreat, he plunged at their head into the pathless depths of the Black Forest, there where the Danube conceals its sources; following their infant streams through deep morasses, swimming rivers, scaling mountains, struggling again through pathless forests, so that for many days the fate of this intrepid hero was unknown."

Parthenia started, and again became pale as death.

"But," continued Phorion, "he surmounted every obstacle; and behold him, my mother, the hero! Not having lost a single follower, he emerged upon the broad-swelling Danube, there where he purposed to do, near Vienna. A fleet of light brigantines was lying at anchor; he seized some food to satisfy his ravenous soldiers, and boldly committed himself to the waves. Ah, how destiny favored him! The blessed winds, sent by Gods or angels, carried this fleet above seven hundred miles in eleven days! Ah, I see my noble friend upon the prow of his vessel, his glorious eye flashing, his noble brow thrown upwards, and onwards where glory beckoned him, and hope, to scatter blessings upon this great Empire! O noble Parthenia! could you have seen Julian when enthusiasm for some great object illumined his features, you would have said he was the most glorious of mortal men."

"And what of Constantius?" she asked, her voice trembling, but keeping back the blinding tears.

"It was now that he heard of the rapid progress of the Prince, and, disguising his anguish under the semblance of contempt, he prepared to meet him and let the fate of war decide which should be master of the Empire. But the Gods, or rather, dear mother, God's providence, interposed, — a fever destroyed the hope of Constantius, and Julian is now sole Emperor and master of the world."

"Forbear, my son! Your joy makes you impious!"

"And where," asked Parthenia, — "where is — where is your friend? How was the Prince received in Constantinople? and did Helena — did the Empress accompany him?"

"Ah, that was the most glorious of all! The whole city went forth to meet him, and at the distance of sixty miles myriads thronged around him, lifting him upon their shoulders, with shouts of the soldiers and the people; the joyful tears of the women; children pressing upon him, kissing his hands and his garments; flowers, perfumes, garlands and crowns of roses, were showered upon him, — on the Emperor alone. The Empress, who was lèft to follow by slow stages, was arrested on the way by fatal illness. She died, — and Julian is again free!" Phorion paused, arrested by his sympathy with Julian, and the rapid changes in the countenance of Parthenia, who had listened breathlessly; and now tears rolled silently over her death-pale cheeks. "But," continued Phorion, "when the senators and officers of the city, who had waited to meet him at the gates, saw the small, simply arrayed hero, clad only in the scanty cloak of the philosopher, with modest expression, unpretending carriage, they could scarcely believe that it was this simple youth who had subdued the Barbarians, reconquered the cities, and traversed, overcoming every obstacle, the whole of Europe, from the waves of the Atlantic to those of the Bosphorus; and more than all this, that he had evinced the wisdom of the philosopher and the experience of the statesman, and had shown clemency and moderation, as well as wisdom."

"Ah!" said Parthenia, "Julian desires more than all else to stand high in the admiration of the world. The Immortal Gods preserve him from the fate of him who wished to guide the coursers of the sun."

"Amen!" cried Phorion; "but listen!"

"Hark!" said Monica, "the heralds are approaching."

With music, trumpets, and measured steps, the heralds came on, preceded by a guard of soldiers, escorting the heathen high-priest in his robes, and a procession of the priests of the various Divinities. By accident or design they paused before the house of Monica. The trumpet sounded three times, and the herald proclaimed aloud: —

"By decree of the Emperor, Julian. The worship of the ancient Divinities is commanded. — The temples of the Gods to be immediately reopened, and restored. — Perpetual incense upon the altars, and daily sacrifice, enjoined. — Every violation of this decree will be punished as sacrilege."

The herald passed on. It was as though a thunderbolt had fallen in the midst of the little circle. Monica threw herself upon her knees, and began praying aloud. Phorion became thoughtful and silent. The decree could not, he thought, affect him. He was striving for truth in his own soul, and cared not much for outward professions of any kind.

Parthenia bent her head, and seemed to be praying silently. She was yet perplexed and groping in darkness. She remembered Julian's enthusiasm and eloquence whenever he mentioned the ancient

Divinities, and she could not for an instant doubt his entire sincerity in proclaiming their worship.

"The Emperor believes," she said, "that he is under the immediate care of the Immortals, and that they have made him the ruler of this great Empire, in order to restore their worship in all its purity. And who can assure us that it is not so?" she added, with a sigh.

"Still," said Phorion, "though he consults the auguries and professes to believe them, he never is influenced by them; he never turns from that which his own wisdom or his passions urge him to follow, whatever the victims' entrails may predict. Julian," he continued, "will never become a persecutor; he believes in argument, not in violence; in reason, more than in power."

"His humane heart will never permit him to become a persecutor," said Parthenia.

"Cease, my children," cried Monica, who had now risen from her knees, — "cease, my son, to glorify the Apostate. Be not so impious as to excuse the enemy of our religion. He has turned his back upon the influences of the Holy Spirit, and he will now be guilty of every wickedness."

"Madam," said Parthenia, "you are unjust to your son, and to the Emperor. Truth is as precious to him as to any follower of the Nazarene.

He believes that every form of religion is but a separate ray of that great central light, the Supreme God, the creator and origin of all worlds."

"I admire and venerate Julian," said Phorion. "The defect of his mind is, that feeling and imagination overweigh clearness of thought. He is wedded to the past, and incapable of appreciating the new ideas which have been poured into humanity by the coming of Christ, the promised one. He would revive the beauty of the ancient myths, but —"

"Do not you admire their beauty?" asked Parthenia.

"Ah yes! but not as I do the sublime and touching history of Jesus. Study the manuscripts in your hands, and your woman's heart cannot fail to feel their truth."

At this moment their attention was arrested by a company of monks from the Euphrates, passing beneath the window, — a sight never yet witnessed in Athens. Parthenia could not help expressing something like disgust at their bare feet and ragged beards, and her Athenian eye was offended at the absence of all grace or beauty in their costume.

"That is the creature," whispered Phorion, "that my mother wishes me to become."

Parthenia looked from one to the other, with the

utmost surprise; and Monica, who had heard what he said, answered, "Because, my son, it is only by taking upon yourself holy vows that you can break those sinful ties that now consume your life."

"O my mother! do not call the pure passion which binds me to one innocent being sinful. Beside, how could I take one vow to sever another which I regard as more sacred?"

"While you are enthralled by an earthly love, you cannot serve God with singleness of heart and pure devotion. Pluck out the right eye, cut off the right hand, is the command of our Lord."

"But," said Parthenia, "I thought it was the boast of your religion that it made woman the equal companion of man, and bound them together in the blessed union of one with one, — the fusion of two hearts into one," — and her cheek glowed with the thought.

"Such was the meaning of the instructions of our Master," said Phorion; "but cold-hearted priests and ambitious prelates, who wish to create for the service of their ambition a militia of monks, have perverted his divine commands, and for their own sinful purposes celibacy and asceticism — "

"My son, do not blaspheme," interrupted Monica.

"Oh," said Parthenia, "I have dreamed of a

lovelier destiny for man and woman,—a home, where wedded hearts might daily find new felicity in their own peace, and in obeying the almost divine precepts of your Nazarene."

"Such is always a woman's heaven," said Monica. "Cannot you raise your imagination above that sensual heaven of mutual love and wedded hearts?"

Parthenia crimsoned, but she went on to say: "I have been almost won to believe in the divine origin of your Christian religion, when I found it admitted woman to equal privileges with man,—gave her a soul, and made her the partner of man's serious occupations, rather than the slave of his passions."

"The religion of the Nazarene demands sacrifices, expiation, repentance; and they can only take place in solitude and retirement," said Monica.

"I do not find," said Parthenia, "in those lovely precepts of your Gospels any scorn of the world or contempt of woman. On the contrary, I find the most loving spirit of condescension, even to the wicked."

"Sacrifice and self-devotion," continued Monica, "are the two angels upon whose wings we must ascend to heaven."

"Pardon me," said Parthenia, "but our heathen religion is marked by sacrifice. The legends are full of it; but that of the innocent virgin Iphigenia stands alone in its loveliness."

"Iphigenia is nerved for sacrifice by the presence of Achilles, in whose memory she wishes to live as a perfect, unflawed diamond," said Phorion.

"Ah, you look upon that single, pure-souled deed like a man, and think it inspired by the wish to live in the memory of a lover."

"Does not Euripides give it that interpretation?"

"Euripides was a man, but I think he assigns higher motives to the heroic maiden; she loves her country with enthusiasm, and is glad to sacrifice herself for it. She would die for her country, but she expresses a truly Grecian idea when she says: 'It is right that she should die, rather than Achilles expose himself to danger, for one man is of more worth than a thousand women.'"

"How can your woman's heart fail to feel the difference when this pure victim's blood flows at the altar of a female Deity who is pleased, the poet says, 'when the blood of *human* victim flows,' and that of our Christ, who places woman on the same level with man, and says also that he will have mercy and not sacrifice, or only the moral sacrifice of a pure heart?"

"We cannot reason," said Parthenia, "about the beautiful myths of our ancient history. Many of them to my Greek mind are touching, including the beauty which is an element almost entirely left out of the history of your Christ."

"Ah, does it seem so to you?" said Phorion. "Where there is love, there is beauty. Love is the key that unlocks the treasury of the beautiful." (Parthenia started. It was the idea, almost in the words, she had once used when Julian left her alone.) "And it seems to me that our Christian idea of sacrifice," and a tender and beautiful expression enlightened his thin features as he repeated, "our Christian idea of sacrifice includes the idea of loving, although not blind to the depths of evil of those for whom we die. It must be a boundless love, like that of Jesus for sinners."

"How strangely changed are all our ideas of sacrifice!" said Parthenia. "In early times we offered upon all our altars fruits, flowers, and the lovely green things of earth; now, blood must flow. Even upon our most tender domestic altars, — to Vesta, the protectress of the hearth, to Venus, the guardian of the heart, — we must sprinkle the blood of lambs or doves."

"Speak not such blasphemous words!" cried Monica. "God alone is the guardian of the hearth and the home."

"Pardon me, dear Monica, I have as yet known only the dead letter of your religion. I feel and know that there is one only Supreme Divinity, but I find it hard to believe in your Christ."

"It is the pride of your intellect which prevents you from embracing the lowly —"

"No, my mother," interrupted Phorion; "the blessed light is dawning in the mind of the noble Parthenia. She waits only a little stronger illumination"; and, turning to the beautiful woman, he said, "I feel, I am sure, that you are not far from entire faith in Christ. Study the Gospels, now that you are free from the gorgeous pageantry and the seductive beauty of the heathen worship, and with a mind so candid, and a heart thirsting for truth, you cannot fail to attain it."

Parthenia saw his pale face glowing with the ardor and deep conviction with which he spoke, and she felt that there was an immeasurable reality of earnest faith never inspired by Heathenism. Tears, sweeter than any she had shed, rolled silently over her face, and she rose and would have left the room, for she felt the need of solitude; but as the slave raised the heavy curtain of the atrium to let her pass, a young woman of singular beauty fell, as she was rushing into the room, almost upon her.

Parthenia stood aside to let her pass, and she could not but pause to look at the young creature, who, in a state of extreme agitation, fell at the knees of the matron, and burst into violent weeping.

Phorion became crimson, and while he trembled with agitation, he hastened to raise the young woman from his mother's knees, and to deprecate by the tenderness with which he treated her the stern and angry frown that gathered upon his mother's face.

"No," she cried, resisting his caress, "I will not rise till I am heard,—till your mother promises that she will not try to turn your heart from me,—that she will not tear you from me,—that she will not divide us."

She spoke with such rapidity and so interrupted by sobs, that, although Phorion took her in his arms, and said tenderly, "Olympia, my mother cannot divide us," it was some moments before she could be soothed and induced to leave the presence of Monica.

To account for the sudden appearance of this young woman we must go back a little. Phorion, as was the custom of the young men of his time, and before he became a convert to the Christian faith, was connected with this beautiful young creature through a sincere attachment of the heart. Unlike other young men, he had been constantly faithful to her; and although they had two children, their union had not received the sanction of the Church, nor was he bound to her by civil laws.

This was partly the fault of his mother, who constantly pleaded pecuniary difficulties, hoping to break off the connection. Monica's religion was tenderly expressed towards the suffering, but it made her sternly unrelenting towards those weaknesses of the heart, which she regarded as sins.

A marriage with Olympia would not, in her view, have redeemed their connection from sin, and all her efforts tended to induce her son to join one of the monastic orders, and thus for ever to sever their union.

Phorion had never dared to present her to his mother. Neither Olympia nor her children had ever before crossed the threshold of Monica. But now the agonizing fear of the former lest his mother should succeed in separating her son from her, had been terribly augmented by learning that a beautiful Greek was dwelling under the same roof. A jealous fear was added to her other terrors, and she could no longer resist the step she had taken.

We shall see in the sequel whether the heart of Monica was softened towards her.

CHAPTER XXII.

JULIAN AS EMPEROR.

Immediately upon the entrance of Julian into his palace at Constantinople, he could not fail to make bitter enemies. He found it filled with hungry mouths and idle hands. Idlers, flatterers, imbeciles, filled every apartment, crowded every avenue. He who dined upon a single vegetable found a *thousand* — literally a thousand — cooks in his kitchen. A water-drinker, he found nearly a thousand cup-bearers in his service. Eunuchs, for whom Julian felt an especial aversion, like venomous toads, lurked in every corner and thronged every avenue. How could it be otherwise, when a small sum of money only was necessary to purchase an office in the Emperor's household, and his palace became the asylum of the imbecile, the shelter of cowards. The revenues of the Prince and the taxes of the people were exhausted to support an army of domestics, which cost more, as Julian found, than an army of soldiers.

The first morning that the Emperor awoke in the palace he found his apartment lined with mirrors, and his long beard reflected in a hundred different angles of perspective. His first order was to summon a barber to execute the necessary curtailment upon his chin. Soon he heard the hoofs of a troop of horse and the noise of a procession of wheels, which drew his attention to the window.

A superb carriage, drawn by six beautiful Thessalian horses, followed by carriages of different forms, each bearing a person of distinction, entered the court.

"What is the meaning of this embassy?" he asked the page in waiting.

"Your Majesty has ordered the chief barber, and his assistants follow him," said the boy.

The Emperor burst into a loud laugh, checked by the opening of the folding-doors.

There entered a man magnificently dressed. His tunic was embroidered with gold, and his mantle, sown with pearls, was bordered by a deep fringe of gold. He was followed by numerous assistants, each bearing some implement of his office; to one was intrusted a golden bowl; another bore the razor, whose handle was incrusted with diamonds.

Julian, who sat in his simple tunic, could scarcely preserve the befitting gravity, when the magnificent chief barber bowed low before him.

"There is surely some mistake," said Julian, rising; "I did not summon a Councillor of the Empire, but simply a barber, to conform my beard to the fashion of the court. Will it please your Excellency to sit?"

"The mistake is your Majesty's," said the other. "I have the honor to fill the office of chief barber. I shall be most proud to exercise my skill upon the lip of your Majesty. Nothing but the moustache of the Emperor passes under my razor; the rest of the sacred beard is left to my assistants."

"And what, may I be permitted to ask, are the appointments of your office?"

"Your Majesty will hardly think them above mediocrity. I have rations for twenty persons, food for twenty horses, and a pension commensurate with these appointments. Besides, I received many gratifications from your indulgent predecessor, which I hope will be doubled by the immortal person that I have the honor to serve."

A smile of derision curled the delicate lips of Julian. "And your nine hundred and ninety-nine assistants," he asked, "do they also live at the expense of the Emperor?"

"They form but a very small part of those requisite for the magnificent service of the Emperor," said the barber, beginning to tremble at the derisive tone of Julian.

"For me they are quite superfluous. A man who cannot shave his own beard does not deserve to have one. One pensioner of your profession will suffice for my frugal household. I am determined to feed no idlers; therefore dismiss your train, if you would remain yourself in my service."

The chief barber raised his eyebrows, but dared not proffer a word. He found that he had to do with a very different person from the effeminate Constantius.

Julian now summoned to his presence the comptroller of the finances, and without ceremony swept from the civil list all except the most indispensable officers of his household. "I shall never probably enter again the troubled state of matrimony; I have therefore no need of eunuchs; let the whole brood be dismissed." Like a herd of noxious animals, for Julian had reason to hate them, they were chased from the palace.

"A man who eats but from necessity, and that standing or walking, has no need of a gorgeous table with menials around it; let all such depart," he said. "Retain only servants necessary to keep my palace in perfect repair and order. I am neither hunter nor racer; I love neither the stadium nor the amphitheatre. I therefore need only the usual guard of princes."

These proceedings of Julian gave occasion to the most opposite judgments. The larger portion of his contemporaries condemned him wholly, or found that he was far too philosophic for a prince. They said that, so far from attaining the just medium between simplicity and ostentation, he outraged the former, as his predecessor had outraged the utmost magnificence. They averred that he rendered the imperial government contemptible, by despoiling it of the exterior which would dazzle the eyes of the people, and that a modesty so extremely displaced was only a refinement of pride, and worse than any ostentation of luxury.

A few only of Julian's admirers declared, that a Prince who knew so well how to govern, who had shown such brilliant as well as such solid and useful talents, could well dispense with the *éclat* borrowed from ostentation; they said also, that he could display his personal elevation by treading under foot all factitious grandeur; and that his subjects should be the last to blame him for dispensing with an ostentatious luxury, which was procured at their own expense.

Regarding him from one point of view, it seems that Julian had studied books in his closet more than he had studied man in daily life. A certain degree of splendor short of ostentation is requisite to strike the imagination and keep up the prestige of royalty. In the eyes of the people, a prince with a plain doublet cannot be pointed at as an object of as much admiration as one clothed in all the splendor of royal robes and jewels. The tangled beard and inky fingers of Julian lost him more admirers than his stern sense of justice gained for him friends.

Urged on by his intrepid and earnest spirit in laboring for the public good, Julian was not sorry also to make his enemies feel his power. He created a chamber of justice for the trial of those who had abused their influence under the former reign. To escape the reproach of condemning his personal enemies, the tribunal was held at Calcedonia, and he gave the judges the power to execute their sentences, without appeal and without delay.

This tribunal did little honor to the judgment or discernment of Julian when it selected Ursulus as a victim of its resentment. This venerable man, who had been Grand Treasurer under Constantius, had become odious to the army, because he had spoken of their cowardice with the indignation it merited. But beside the nobleness and excellence of his character, which should have been his protection in the eyes of Julian, the Prince was under peculiar obligations to him. When sent into Gaul without money, and almost without soldiers, on purpose that he might fail, the Treasurer of the Province received private instructions from the Grand Treasurer Ursulus to furnish the sums necessary for the army, and for the support of the Prince's frugal court.

Ursulus now lived surrounded by his dependents, to whom he was a beneficent providence, and blessed with an only daughter, beautiful and accomplished, who had secretly become a Christian, and lived to practise the lovely precepts of Christianity. He was seized by some creatures of the army, hurried before the tribunal, and condemned to death. His daughter hastened to the presence of the Emperor, and threw herself at his feet, passionately pleading for the life of her father.

Julian raised her, and promised all she asked; but, alas! it was too late. She received in her arms only the lifeless body of him who had filled her young life with happiness. Julian restored to the daughter the confiscated estates of her father, and bitterly wept his too late interposition to save the life of his venerable friend.

The fate of Ursulus and of a few others has drawn upon the Emperor the malediction of partisans, as well as the stain of ingratitude; and it is not a sufficient excuse that he was ignorant of the condemnation of Ursulus, for a good prince should be ignorant of nothing touching the welfare of his subjects.

Julian, like Napoleon and others, was fond of believing himself destined to some great work. Napoleon also believed himself the man of destiny; but in the "Pattern Democrat" there was nothing in common with Julian, the "favorite of the Gods." Julian was an ideologist, Napoleon was the apostle of common sense. Julian believed himself, and a few of the aristocrats of nature, perfect; Napoleon said, "The worst disease that can afflict the human mind is the desire for perfection." Julian believed in necromancy and mystery, the occult sciences, as means for accomplishing his purposes; Napoleon believed in brass and iron, in cannon-balls and money Julian was a lover of the romantic, and was for bringing back the old forms of beauty from which life had fled. Napoleon lived only in the present, and believed in his own iron hand.

Julian's appointed work was the restoration of the old religion. To this he subordinated every other object. But though he believed in this destiny for himself, he had too much intelligence not to feel how extremely delicate and difficult was his mission. The Christian Church, during the three hundred years of its existence, had maintained itself against penal laws and bloody persecutions, from all of which it had come out with new strength and fruitfulness. But to a mind indisposed to receive Christianity, the Church could at no time appear in a less attractive light than in the time of Julian. It was in a state of implacable discord. The chief cities of the Empire had flowed with blood shed in religious quarrels. The great truths revealed by Christ had no longer the charm of novelty. The Church itself had passed through the earlier period of its noble moral enthusiasm. At this moment Christianity and Paganism stood opposed to each other, each owing a portion of its present condition to the other, and balancing their respective forces, the great issue being which should advance and which decline. Christianity had not disdained to adopt some of the external graces and unessential ceremonies of the Pagan worship, and the old religion had received a strong infusion of the elements of the new. The three Graces, incense, flowers, and music, having been the handmaids of Paganism, lent their service to the Christian altar; and Paganism endeavored to adopt the charities of brotherly love and external purity from Christianity.

Julian had not the power to perceive the essential

difference between the two religions; that Paganism had no root in itself; it contained the seeds of death, while Christianity possessed the power of recreating and purifying itself. Its streams, however stained and colored by the channels through which they passed, ran clear again through the infinite purity of the fountain.

The Emperor had no sooner arrived in Constantinople, than he ordered, by a general edict, all the heathen temples to be opened, and those that had fallen into decay to be repaired. The cross, not then the emblem of sorrow and humiliation, but of the triumph of Constantine over Heathenism, was everywhere conspicuous. It floated upon the air in banners, it surmounted the cupolas of the churches; it was carved upon the fronts of houses, and placed as an emblem upon public buildings; it was worn upon the breast as an ornament, and upon the hand as a seal; perhaps there never was a time when the cross was so wholly an emblem of triumph and of power. But now, by the order of the Emperor, the cross was everywhere effaced, and the gold and ivory of the heathen Gods gleamed in every square and in every street. The statue of Christ, calm and serene, blessing the gathered multitudes of the poor and humble, had stood in the centre of the city, upon a golden pedestal; this had disappeared, and was replaced by the winged God, Apollo, gazing at the sun.

Where were the Christians who had yesterday filled the streets, hastening to the churches amid the pealing of bells and the chanting of anthems? They were silent, filled with consternation, for as yet they knew not the temper of the Emperor. Instead of these, processions of Pagan priests and priestesses, in their white robes and myrtle crowns, thronged the streets. Everywhere the blood of sacrifices was flowing, and the mingled smoke of incense and the odor of the burnt-offering infecting the pure air of the Bosphorus. Julian himself assumed the office and the robes of Grand Pontiff, and dedicated in his palace a temple and altar to the sun; or rather his palace itself became one vast temple to the heathen Deities. In his garden every God had his statue and his altar, where the Emperor morning and evening offered his prayers. In the morning, to welcome the return of the sun, he slew his victim; in the evening he bade the sun adieu with a second sacrifice. The same homage was rendered to the moon and stars; his night indeed was almost wholly spent in prayer. The people saw him prostrate before the idols, kissing their feet; going and coming in their service with an anxious mien, bringing wood for the altar, kindling the fires, inspecting the entrails; thus giving to the people an example of piety surpassing the zeal of the Christian Emperors.

After Julian had been a week in Constantinople, he summoned around him his best beloved friends. In the foremost for true attachment were Libanius and Maximus, the sophist and the necromancer who had predicted for him the possession of the Empire. So great was the fame of the latter, that in his journey from Sardis to Constantinople the whole population of Asia put itself in motion to attend him. Magistrates and persons of distinction hastened to render him homage. The streets and public squares were so crowded, that his chariot could hardly pierce through the throng. Applause, incense, and flowers were heaped upon him, and while the philosopher, affecting humility, wrapped in his philosophic cloak, buried himself in the depths of his coach, his wife received the adulation and answered the orations and the felicitations of the populace.

As they entered one of the gates of Constantinople, they were soon astonished at its strange diversity of appearance from every other city. Instead of the chaste and severe beauty of the Grecian temples, extending their horizontal lines and purely simple pillars, the churches rose in gorgeous splendor, adorned with marbles of divers colors, and incrusted with precious stones; with domes hanging in the air, apparently suspended from the sky. This new feature of Christian architecture, beautiful as it is, at first offended the severe taste of the school-taught critics, and until they had seen the masterpieces of Grecian art, brought there by Constantine, they imagined themselves in a city of Barbarians.

"Strange," said the companion of Libanius, one of the numerous lecturers of the time, as they were proceeding to the palace, — "strange that our enlightened Emperor should disdain the restraints of the Gospel, and yet make a voluntary sacrifice of his reason in the temples of the heathen Gods."

"He can secretly withdraw from their altars into the sanctuary of the temple of his conscience," said Libanius, "and refresh himself with the wisdom which is concealed beneath the fables of the Gods."

"Julian has had no ambition to become a martyr," persisted the other. "He dissembled and concealed his religion till it was safe to make it known."

"The beauty of truth was concealed in the mind

of the Prince," said his friend, "and now, like the statues of the Gods, which have been hidden in their temples, it appears again with new conviction and beauty."

"Will not truth itself suffer from such profound dissimulation?"

"The ass in Æsop disguised himself under the lion's hide; but our Julian," said Libanius, "concealed himself beneath the skin of an ass."

The Christians feared Julian's power much more than they did his arguments. Libanius saw the crimson blood rush to the brow of his companion, who was a Christian, and would not resent the insult; but Libanius was a humane and generous man, and he hastened to add: "You have nothing to fear. The Emperor is too careful of his fame to become a persecutor."

"No? His army bless the fat oxen he sacrifices to his Gods. Whole hecatombs have perished, and the soldiers assist with fervent devotion and voracious appetites at the burnt-offerings."

These friends of opposite religious faith were on their way to the palace, and as they entered the court the perfume of a thousand flowers, concentrated by the heavy dews of the night, (for Julian's audiences were held in the early morning, and he who would enjoy his favor must be no sluggard,) the wonderful lucidity of the waters of the Golden Horn, the songs of innumerable birds, the softness of the atmosphere, seemed to prophesy to his friends that here at least the Emperor must relax the stoicism of his manners, and yield to the effeminacy everywhere surrounding him.

No, even here his robe was without embroidery, his hair without perfume, and his unringed fingers bore the marks of the pen he had just been using.

As they entered, Julian rose and embraced Libanius, and conducted him to a seat near himself, surveying him with eyes over-brimming with the tenderness he felt. "Now," said he, "I feel that I am really Emperor, now that I can command the presence of the friends I best love."

Maximus was already present. His dress was not without affectation; for although he retained the coarse cloak of the philosopher, he wore upon his breast that mystic jewel, formed of a single eye of living sapphire, the lashes of which were composed of minute diamonds. This eye flashed light with every motion, and, like that of Maximus himself, it seemed to penetrate the thoughts of mortals.

Having embraced his friends, Julian continued his interrupted remarks, which indicated that he had at this moment in contemplation that measure which was the opprobrium of his short reign, — that of excluding Christians from the instruction of youth, and from all offices of trust and emolument in the Empire. "Professors and masters," he went on to say, "should be distinguished, first by their morals, and next by their talents."

"Greek is by none taught with such purity and elegance as by the Christians, Basil and Gregory," said Libanius.

"The Christians study the eloquent dialectics of antiquity in order to establish what they believe to be truth," said Maximus.

"Ah yes! they intoxicate themselves with the beauty of the Grecian Muse, before they turn to the chaste caresses of the Christian virgins," said Julian, with a sneer.

"They wound us with our own weapons," said the philosopher.

"If they would teach our authors," said Julian, "they must worship our Gods. I will permit them to choose. They must adore the Deities of Homer and Demosthenes, or content themselves with teaching Luke and Matthew in their schools."

"Sire," said one present, supposed to be a Christian, "how large a portion of your best subjects will you condemn to ignorance?"

"By the immortal Gods," said Julian, his eyes flashing as they did when excited, "if they would enjoy our bounty and drink of our libations, they must offer sacrifices and supplicate the Gods."

"It is not with your Homer and Pindar and Æschylus that you can convert your subjects, Sire! The simplicity, the absolute purity, the wonderful beauty, of the sayings of their Christ charm and win their pupils from all your Grecian authors. Their listening ears drink in the words, as the parched earth drinks up the evening rain. Then the power of these simple words that a child can lisp! no thunder of Demosthenes, no winning tenderness of Virgil, has ever wrought such change. The rough become gentle; the cruel, tender; the haughty wins back his enemy to love; the miser unclutches his grasp and scatters his hoards,— mutual forbearance, the love to forgive and bless, rules in every household of Christians, and these are the virtues you must annihilate before you can reconvert your subjects to believe in your Gods."

Julian had several times changed color during this speech. "By those immortal Gods," he said, "I would neither rob them of their virtues nor their learning. They shall neither be scourged unjustly, or by any other means ill-treated; but those who worship the true Gods shall always be preferred to the Galileans, — or I am no longer Emperor."

There was silence for a moment, interrupted by

the entrance of a person who had brought an accusation against a citizen of Ancyra, — an accusation which, in Constantius's time, had been a capital offence. This man, his enemy informed the Emperor, had prepared for himself a purple robe, emulating the color of the imperial garment.

"Well, then," said Julian, laughing, "let him have a pair of purple slippers to complete his costume, and let the informer be scourged barefoot from the palace. I am determined," said the Prince, turning to his friends, "to purge my court of the whole army of spies and informers. They are perfectly odious to me. If I cannot win the confidence of my subjects, and govern without these noxious vermin, I will not reign at all."

The Emperor now turned to one of his secretaries, and took from his hand a homily which he had himself composed upon the duties of the heathen priests, and began to read it aloud. It was very long, and taken for the most part from the Christian Scriptures. The Christians present could not help smiling, as precepts were read which must have clung to the memory of the Prince from the Epistles of Paul, as he formerly read them in the church.

After he had finished, the Christians present found nothing new in it; on the contrary, the

Pagans, especially Libanius, thought it too strict, and that it enjoined upon the priests a virtue and a charity which none of those present would be willing to practise.

"No one has ever before thought of reforming a religion in which morality has always been a stranger," said Libanius.

"It will be of little use," said Julian, "to restore and elevate the temples, if we leave the priesthood unreformed."

"The Christians," said an Arian present, "began with repentance before reformation."

"We will oppose virtue to virtue, discipline to discipline," said Julian. "Even the women shall be subdued to the obedience of our ascetic rule."

"That is not the rule of the Christians, Sire," said one of those present. "The Christians have converted man's home from the anarchy of hell to the bliss of paradise. They have made the fireside an altar to love, where they cherish and guard the purity of woman. Their young women are like angels, their children messengers from heaven."

"Enough, enough," said Julian. "Let those who will, dwell in their paradise of married angels. Our business is with the priesthood. The goodness or the wickedness of the people has its principal source in the good or bad example of its teachers."

"And we are ready to lay upon them a burden which one of us would not touch with the finger," said Libanius.

"No, I do not demand more than I have already done. Not to praise myself, when the estates of my mother, which had been forcibly kept back, were restored to me, I bestowed them upon the needy."

"How can those who, like myself, have been presented with a noble estate, ever forget thy generosity, Sire?" said Ætius, an Arian prelate who was present. "The beautiful park you have given me in the island of Lesbos is a precious reminder that I owe thee eternal gratitude."

"You must cancel the debt with Lesbian odes, surpassing those of your great predecessor, Sappho, unless you prefer canticles in honor of the carpenter's son," said Julian, with a bitter smile.

Julian sometimes robbed his nobleness of its charm by the sarcasms he cast about him. Yet his liberality was boundless. He exhausted his private possessions in gifts to his friends. To one he presented a farm, to another a villa, a house, a park. To his youthful adherents he gave horses, a carriage, a mantle; in his letters there is perpetual mention of smaller gifts, such as precious figs, rare wines, costly jewels. Julian was really generous. The charm of his manners and the influence of the purple, no doubt, magnified his noble deeds beyond their real merit; but he practised secretly a touching form of generosity, in providing for those female attendants in the temples who had been deprived of their living through the closing or destruction of these temples. There are letters of his in which these timid pensioners are mentioned in words of pity and tenderness.

CHAPTER XXIII.

THE CHRISTIAN CHURCH.

PARTHENIA had faithfully read, and had begun to understand, the spirit of the Gospels; her woman's heart felt their sweetness and purity, but her Greek instructed mind revolted at the humility and self-abnegation they enjoined upon those who believed in Him whose life they exhibited. She witnessed the daily duty of Christians, so full of peace and beauty; she saw how easy the severest self-denial was made to them; she observed the fidelity of domestic life, the devotion to each other of the married, the tenderness of parents for their children; she saw how the stern and noble duties of friendship were performed by those who were reproached by the world as base, unfaithful, and criminal.

The form of Christian worship also presented itself to her artistic mind divested of the grace and beauty she had been accustomed to in the pageantry of the Grecian ceremonial; she missed the processions, banners, flowers, and music; the golden and laurel crowns; the games and dramas; the odes chanted by a thousand voices; the incense rising from a thousand different points; — she missed much that was chastely beautiful, as well as that which was gorgeously rich. The Christians in their forms of public worship borrowed from the heathen ceremonial; but to a mind fed upon the pure laws of artistic beauty their worship lacked grace, and appeared homely and formal.

Then also the laws of morality were apparently shaken or changed. In the heathen code, not of Plato, but of common use, humility was base, and pride the source of all greatness; with the Christian, pride was a vice, and humility a precious virtue. "Blessed are the poor in spirit," revolted even her woman's standard. She could not at once admit the different grades and proportions of virtues and vices, when regarded from a Christian or Heathen point of view.

One of the most touching ceremonies of the Christian religion was to take place on the next Sabbath, — the ceremony of confirmation, which the Church in its sagacity has placed just on the threshold of adolescence. At the moment when the heart begins to feel the charm and the peril of the passions, when new sympathy and added succor are needed by the young stranger entering the seductive paths of life, the Church does not forget him; it holds in reserve a support; the confirmation and first communion is the beautiful ceremony of betrothal to Christian duty.

The great church was prepared for the ceremony. The Christians, as I have said, borrowed many lovely decorations from the pagan temples, — flowers, the freshest offerings of nature to the Divinity; and perfumes, a legacy of love from the flowers; and incense as it ascends, the emblem of the aspiring soul. The organ, that gift from the Church, had not yet been invented, but thousands of youthful voices chanted the Hebrew psalms and filled the church with melody.

The church was densely crowded; the esplanade in front was also thronged; for, in addition to the confirmation, a great man, an officer of the government, had sought refuge from his enemies at the sanctuary of the Christian altar.

The church, as I have mentioned before, was in the form of a Greek cross, and surmounted by a dome, as the emblem of eternity, colored blue and powdered with stars, to represent the eternal heavens resting over the earthly worshippers. Parthenia, entering with Monica, did not perceive these spiritual ideas, which were beginning to be expressed in Christian architecture. To her pure Greek taste, the church was too profusely ornamented, and wanting in the simple unity of the pagan temples.

Monica and herself took their places in the gallery, beneath the dome, appropriated to women. How was Parthenia's pure taste offended by the gaudy dresses of the ladies! Upon the robes of some of the most distinguished were embroidered or woven in many colors New Testament histories, such as Lazarus in torment, or the miracles of Jesus. Each was attended by a page or by a young female slave, bearing a large embroidered purse, from which the lady ostentatiously distributed her charity.

"Are they really persons of rank?" she asked Monica. "Do they not hold a less respectable station?"

"Alas!" said Monica, "the Church is as corrupt as the women are vain. Look at those ecclesiastics just entering; see their gorgeous surplices and jewelled capes; and how can we expect women to be exempt from vanity?"

The church was filled to its utmost capacity. There were ten thousand persons present. The Bishop's entrance was greeted with prolonged shouts and clapping of hands, which rose to the dome, and seemed to shake the foundations of the temple. Parthenia turned to her companion. "Is that the man," she asked, "of such power and influence that he sways this great multitude at his will?"

"Yes," said the other; "look at his slender, fragile body, his sunken cheek, pale but for one burning spot, and at those eyes, which, when they turn towards you, seem to reveal depths through which eternity burns in wrath or love. Look, and acknowledge in that frail instrument the intense power of Christianity."

"You forget," said Parthenia, "that to me this pageant, though deeply interesting, is not so significant as to you Christians. I do not know the meaning or significance of that dark figure clinging to the steps of the altar."

There was indeed prostrate upon the steps of the altar a noble figure, clothed wholly in sackcloth, and with his head thickly sprinkled with ashes. This was an officer high in rank, and one of the great men of the city, who had offended the people; and although the bitter enemy of the Bishop, he had fled to the altar, placing himself under the protection of one whom he had deeply injured.

The hymn was read, and now there arose from that vast multitude the music of a thousand voices;

the sea of melody filling the circumference of the immense church, ascending to the dome and circling around it, as it mounted higher and higher; the heavy thundering base, the softer tenor, the exquisite purity of the virgin soprano, the shrill piping of the children, the trembling voice of age, for all united, young and old, slaves with their masters, children with their parents, inspired, as with one divine impulse, to fill the church with the praise of God. The melody of the hymn had scarcely died away, when a great noise was heard without the church; then began the clashing of arms, drawn swords, and the trampling of a great multitude. The officers of justice, with a detachment of soldiers, had entered to demand the fugitive at the altar. A tumult arose, and many persons left the church.

"What will the Bishop do?" asked Parthenia. "Will he deliver his own enemy into the hands of *his* enemies?"

"No!" said Monica. "The Church protects the guilty as well as the innocent. See, the Bishop comes down from the pulpit; he confronts the soldiers."

"Listen! what does he say?" The soldiers have suddenly paused in their march to the altar, and their jewelled swords ring on the pavement.

He has told them that only through his body shall

they approach the altar! He has said to them, that not till they have hewn him down shall they seize that trembling fugitive.

The frail and bending form of the Bishop seemed to expand and enlarge, as he stood before those angry men; but they turned, amazed at the majesty and power of this fragile being. They shrank at his flashing eye and inspired voice. These bold, intrepid men of iron paused, looked at each other, and then left the church.

"It was his bitter enemy that he shielded with his own life," said Monica; "and this enemy could trust in none but him whom he had deeply injured."

"The basest of men turn in extremity of peril to the best," said Parthenia.

"He knows that the Bishop is a follower of Christ, and, like his Master, will return good for evil," said the matron.

"Even without your Christ, men have faith in each other. How many noble friendships are there in our ancient histories!"

"Ah, yes! but these are exceptions. 'If you love those who love you, what merit have ye?' asks Christ. It is only the Crucified who upon the cross cried, 'Father, forgive them!' He only has taught us to forgive and love our deadliest enemy."

Parthenia was in no mood to contend. She thought of Socrates, and continued silent.

After rescuing the fugitive, who still remained covered with sackcloth at the foot of the altar, the Bishop ascended the pulpit. The sermon was addressed to the young; but at every brilliant passage, at every striking thought, exclamations and plaudits broke forth. Parthenia observed that the women were the most conspicuous and eager in clapping their hands, waving their perfumed handkerchiefs, and bending forward to catch every accent that fell from those golden lips; for it was Chrysostom, the eloquent preacher, the almost adored confessor, who received the name of the "Golden-mouthed."*

The beautiful ceremony of confirmation took place after the sermon. Processions of young persons of both sexes, clothed in spotless robes of white, wearing crowns of fresh flowers, each with its catechist at its head, drew near and knelt around the railing of the altar. Parthenia looked on, as hundreds of these young heads bent successively beneath the benediction of the Bishop. She remained in perfect quiet, silently contrasting the purity and beauty of this ceremony with one somewhat analogous in her

* Chrysostom was sixteen years older than Julian, and preached at Antioch, his native city; but Julian died before the most brilliant part of the career of Chrysostom commenced.

own religion, — that in which the young were initiated into the mysteries of the Festival of Adonis, — which, although it began in chaste and lovely ceremonies, ended in dancing, and in orgies corrupting to the purity of both sexes.

Monica had descended to the floor of the church, to be nearer the centre of interest, and hours passed insensibly while the Greek maiden remained in perfect quietude. Her whole life passed before her in living pictures, as it is sometimes said to pass before the mind of the drowning. Was there any part of it since her childhood that she would recall? Had there been an hour when her soul had found its complement of good? She had heard persons say, they would live over their lives without change. Ah! they had sat at a full table. Their souls had never hungered. Had it been so with her? Ah, no! She had had moments of bliss. Once, in Athens, when Julian whispered words of love. But could she stay the wings of that fleeting moment? Had the full cup ever been at her lips? Had she ever held the thread of her destiny in her own hand? Yes, for one moment, when he whispered, "*My* Parthenia!" But she had not had courage to lift the full cup to her lips. Nemesis, smiling, had offered her the thread, but it had slipped away from her hand.

She thought of her Greek life. How little sufficed for happiness in Athens,—nature, beauty, art! But had these ever filled the measure of her soul? Ah, no! She had longed for something beyond; her heart had been empty. With the memory of Athens arose the beautiful forms of their Deities, and the ceremonies of their worship. How simple was that of the Christian now before her! She felt at this moment what she had read in the Gospels; that theirs was an inward principle; that the *motive* was *all*, and the outward act little. Then the spectacle below in the church,—how adverse from all her previously formed ideas of power! The great man, the ruler, lying in sackcloth upon the steps of the altar, and that fragile and lowly being, with only the cross in his hand, turning back the armed strength of the mighty, and conquering by meekness. Surely, she thought, it must be true. He who would be chief among these Christians must be the servant of all.

Christians aver, she said within herself, that they have constant communion with an ever-present heavenly Friend, and that this spiritual communion fills up their capacity of joy, the measure of their bliss! Ah that I could attain that joy! But this religion of the Crucified One is not the religion of joy, but of sorrow. The Christians love their Christ so intensely, that they thank him for pain and sorrow, because it likens them to him. O that I could love him thus! She raised her eyes to the statue of Christ above the altar, already mentioned. The waning light fell upon the face in such manner as to bring out the whole beauty and tenderness of the expression. Divine pity and love seemed to look from those eyes directly upon her. At this moment, a single voice of exquisite purity sang the words:

> "Jesus, hast thou borne the pain,
> And hath it all been borne in vain?"

They seemed addressed to her, spoken to her heart. "Ah, no!" her heart answered, "it has not been in vain. I believe in thee, O thou Divine Jesus!"

It was not through reasoning that Parthenia would receive the Christian faith. Her imagination must be excited,—her heart touched. The fables of her Greek mythology had long since lost their influence. She believed in the one eternal Spirit of Plato, but her heart demanded something more,—a being of more human sympathies for her to trust in, and to love.

She heard approaching footsteps. She rose and looked around. The congregation had left the church, and the officers were approaching to see that all was safe. Still she lingered, and looked again at the countenance of the Saviour. Ah, she sighed for a beam, a look, from that divine countenance such as Mary met at his tomb! She seemed to hear a voice close to her ear which whispered, "I am near thee, even in thy heart." She looked hastily around: there was no one in the church. She needed but this. She sank upon her knees, and tears came to her relief.

When she rose to leave the church, she saw by the long shadows of the pillars that the daylight was departing. The soft flames of the silver lamps, already lighted, were reflected like stars in the polished marble of the pavement. The shadowy beings around, in the pictures on the walls, and the soft gleam of the marble statues, and all the emblems of the Christian faith, the cross, the lamb, and the palm, assumed a mysterious and subduing influence upon the soul of the Grecian maiden, and from that hour she confessed herself a Christian.

CHAPTER XXIV.

THE EMPEROR IN ANTIOCH.

JULIAN had determined to pass the winter in Antioch, that city so full of seductive pleasures. The philosopher, the stoic, the ascetic, feared none of these. He began his journey on the first of June, and at the different cities through which he passed he was met, not, like former Emperors, with gifts of rare animals and birds, exquisite works of art, and presents of gold and jewels; for Julian, a patron of genius and cultivation, had appointed as governors of the provinces men learned and skilled in belles-lettres; he was therefore received with discourses, and speeches full of flattery, which he answered in choice Greek orations, that he had sat up all the previous night to compose.

At Pessinos he paused to consult the Cybeline oracle. Callixine, the priestess, who had suffered from the persecution of the Christians, met him with joy, taking care to give him answers from the oracle which flattered all his designs; he not only confirmed her in her privilege as interpreter of Cybele, but appointed her priestess of the neighboring temple of Ceres.

As he continued his journey, he found himself besieged by all sorts of persons, who came to complain or to ask for favors. He listened to them with exemplary patience, and judged them with equity, punishing severely those who calumniated the innocent, through malice, or to deprive them of possessions which they wished to appropriate to themselves. To those who came trembling before him, lest some old and almost forgotten fault should be remembered, he said, "Go home and tell your neighbors that you live under a prince who follows the maxim of a great philosopher, and seeks with all his heart to diminish the number of his enemies, and increase that of his friends."

Antioch had put on a festive air to meet her Emperor. The long colonnades of marble pillars were wreathed with flowers; the fountains, so profusely gushing in every part of the city, sent the whole of their sparkling waters into the blue vault; and the Pagan priesthood, with statues and music, incense and victims, went out to meet their favorite Emperor; and even the Christian population, hoping from Julian's clemency and his reputed generosity of character a wise, if not a perfect toleration, also joined the wide jubilee.

The Christians, however, soon fled to their homes and shut their doors, for they saw approaching processions of women in long mourning robes, their hair flowing and scattered with ashes, accompanied by flutes with sad and plaintive sounds; and they recollected that it was the first day of the feast of Adonis, when the women with tears and rent garments and scattered ashes weep and lament for their darling.

Julian esteemed himself fortunate to enter the city upon the day of this Pagan festival. Soon he met the lofty car upon which the gold and ivory statue of Adonis was laid upon a couch spread with the softest purple. The gardens of Adonis followed. These were symbolic of the influence of the sun upon vegetation in the most genial season of the year, and consisted of vases and baskets filled with earth and sown with wheat, fennel, lettuce, quick-growing seeds, which, by the effect of concentrated heat at the centre of the vases, sprouted, and became in a very short time of a vivid green, symbolizing by the fresh verdure, which faded no less rapidly, the powerful influence of the sun. Flowers of every hue were also borne in this procession, and "all pretty things *that fade*," to symbolize the gloom which follows, when Adonis or the sun withdraws to spend the winter months with Proserpine in the shades below.

Then followed, borne by young virgins just entering adolescence, golden baskets filled with cakes of fine wheat and honey, fashioned in every form of flowers, birds, butterflies, and creeping things. Verdant canopies were borne aloft by female slaves, where young nightingales flitted from bough to bough, and white doves, sacred to Aphrodite and Adonis, murmured in sweet tones their song of love.

The Christians in Antioch were placed in a most embarrassing position. They would fain have gone to meet Julian. They wished to express their appreciation of his noble qualities, as they would also have followed the precept of their Master, to render homage where homage was due. But how could they countenance by their presence in the street this Pagan abomination, this most corrupt of the heathen festivals, the Thammuz of the Old Testament, which the Syrian damsels went out to Lebanon to lament "all through a summer's day"? We have described only the graceful ceremonies of the first day of the festival. It went on increasing its excitements, till it ended in orgies too dreadful to mention. No wonder that Parthenia contrasted the chaste and beautiful ceremonies of the Christian Church with these debasing customs of Paganism.

Libanius had returned to his native city, and the Emperor upon this, his entrance, sought impatiently among the crowd, at every turn, the face of his friend. Julian had the rare good fortune for a Prince, to feel that he possessed a real friend. Forbidden as a youth to hear the lectures of Libanius, he had them stealthily copied for his use, and thus they were invested with the charm of stolen fruit; when he became a man, he sought the society of the philosopher, and lived with him upon the footing of a reciprocal and unostentatious friendship An adherent of the old religion, Libanius sympathized in all Julian's measures, and rejoiced to see the temples of the Pagan Gods opened, music and poetry again taking possession of the groves, and Apollo and the Muses restored to their ancient places.

Notwithstanding all this, Libanius went not out to meet the Emperor when he entered Antioch. The eye of Julian sought his friend in all the crowds, and at last perceived him afar off, making no effort to approach him.

"There is one," said the Emperor to the person nearest him, "who loves me as well as even my mother did, and yet he will accept nothing from me."

"Sire, an enemy would say, that, in refusing the gifts of his Prince, he would place himself upon the same level with him."

"No, he is not proud, neither is he attached to my fortune, but to my person."

"Fortunate man," said the other, "to possess the esteem as well as the favor of his Emperor; but believe me, Sire, his ambition towers too high! He would be paid for his disinterestedness by the favors he would exact from an equal."

"Let him; in all gifts of the mind, he is far above princes, and I find his heart of as pure gold as his intellect."

Many days passed, and Libanius did not approach the anterooms of the palace. When asked the reason, he said, that he had been the friend of the Prince in his adversity, and that he would never be the courtier of the Emperor.

Julian wrote him a note, treating with piquant raillery his desertion of his friend, and asking at what price he should purchase his society?

Libanius returned the tablet with an answer, in the same tone of delicate irony, but he went not to the palace.

"What!" said the Emperor, "does he expect me

to go to him, and upon my knees beg for the alms of his conversation?"

At length Libanius presented himself. Julian with embarrassed and sensitive friendship excused himself for the elevation which had been forced upon him, and pleaded with Libanius for perfect equality in private, when he was with his friend alone. He wished, he said, to have his own unworthiness corrected by a friend. The interview ended, the Emperor turned suddenly upon him, and asked him to share his solitary and frugal dinner.

"I never dine," said the stoic.

"Ah, well! let us sup together."

"Supper gives me the headache. Or at least I am too ill to-day," he said, observing Julian's mortification.

"At least come and see me often, I pray you; forget not our old and tried friendship."

Libanius answered gravely, "I will come, Sire, whenever you send for me. I cannot render myself importunate to the Emperor."

"So be it," said Julian, and he kept his word. At this price he enjoyed the conversation, the praises, and the reprimands of his friend. In all this Julian is more to be admired than Libanius. The latter, by refusing the favors of the Emperor, placed himself upon a level with his Prince, extremely flattering to a subject. He wished to be paid by exacting attentions for the disinterestedness of refusing favors. Julian wanted some one with whom he could enjoy the luxury of sincerity. Others were sycophants, and with all others he was an actor, at least since the death of Eusebia. With Libanius he wished to have no false relations: he was a *friend*, one of those rare beings of which only one or two are to be met with in a lifetime.

The Emperor had formed a most agreeable idea of the city of Antioch, of the genial influences of the climate, and the purity of the atmosphere. A large portion of the inhabitants were Christians, and this great people, though enervated by the seductive influences of the climate and passionately loving the theatre, were yet proud to bear the Christian name, which had its birth within its walls. Christians, and lovers of pleasure! Julian was as little consistent in an opposite direction. A Pagan, with manners of singular austerity, superstitious and philosophic, he could not fail to displease the Antiochians, both as a restorer of Paganism and as an enemy of pleasure. He tolerated no debauch, and lent himself to no spectacle except such as made part of the religious festivals. Antioch loved all pageantry, except such as related to the worship of the Gods. In one word, they had nothing in common except a spirit of caustic raillery, so that Julian was not long in discovering that he was despised.

At first, observing their predominant taste for amusement and pleasure, he persuaded himself that they had only a superficial attachment to Christianity, and that, by the preparation of fêtes and spectacles inseparable from the Pagan worship, he should draw them off to Paganism; and that he should gain their hearts by that affability which had succeeded in Gaul and elsewhere. He had not reflected sufficiently upon his own character, neither upon the genius of this capital of the East.

"They were first called Christians in Antioch." Since that day a large part of the world had been conquered by Christian constancy. The belief, if not the spirit, of Christianity had penetrated social manners and institutions. In Antioch the Church had enjoyed all the verdure of its spring. In its young and vigorous growth there was a magnificent efflorescence of virtues, of ideas, of intellectual riches. This happy season could not last. The flowers must pass and the leaves must fall, but the root became more firm, the trunk stronger, and harder to endure.

The Church, even in its third century, had developed with its growth all the elements of division.

In many of its bishops, intellectual power had taken the place of evangelical morality. Doctors in the school succeeded the martyrs in the prisons; the Pagans listened, astonished to hear the systems of their philosophers more clearly and eloquently explained by the Fathers of the Church than in their own schools. Together with the intellectual growth of the Church, divisions and heresies increased, and gave place to the greatest disorders. Heresies were to Christianity what systems of philosophy had been to Paganism, with this difference, — those systems were the truth of the Pagan religion, while the heresies were the errors of Christianity. Divided as the Church was into innumerable sects, like a river parted into a multitude of streams, each changed by the impure channel through which it has passed, yet it was continually purifying itself, from the infinite purity at the fountain of its waters.

Julian had studied all other religions. They contained in themselves the principle of dissolution. Christianity alone, from its Divine origin, possessed *life* in itself, and the power of purifying away its errors. But Julian did not recognize this truth. He admitted the virtues of the Christians, but he refused to recognize their source, and believed that, by stifling the various sects of Christians beneath the ancient worship, he should suppress them altogether. This was the error of one who saw but the exterior of things, the movement upon the surface, and did not perceive the essential idea reposing at the foundation.

Julian had not been able to recognize the signs through which this new epoch in the history of humanity was made known. In the words of another, "Every deep-moving truth sends before itself scattered messengers, who predict the new-coming event in the fortunes of humanity. Together with these messengers of the new, appear men in whom feeling and imagination overweigh clearness of thought, souls of more warmth than penetration, who compare with the perfected appearance of the old the unformed and incomplete aspect of the new; they turn from the prose which they see everywhere around them, to the rich forms of the ancient faith, and wish to bring them back for themselves and the world."

At the same time Julian was the child of the Christian era, and more indebted to, and more penetrated with, the principles to which he was opposed, than he knew, or would acknowledge; he held upon the old faith, as the child clings to the breast of its nurse after it has ceased to receive nourishment therefrom.

He then who had the sad distinction of being the

first to bear the name of "Apostate," he who turned his face to the past, and his back upon approaching ages, the grand *conservative* of the fourth century, was now to persecute and endeavor to destroy Christianity in the city where it received its name.

There can be no doubt of the religious sincerity of Julian. This sincerity of faith led him to fanaticism, and from fanaticism to persecution. When a person has committed a fault which is irreparable, pride makes him seek a shelter even in the fault itself. Not that Julian regarded his persecution of the Christians in the light of a fault, but he was too sagacious not to see, however much he might wrap himself in pride, that what he called the "Galilean superstition" was what its Founder had said, the grain of mustard-seed, the branches of whose vigorous growth already spread as a shelter to the nations.

The Christians were now the educated, the learned men; they occupied the chairs of eloquence and belles-lettres; they were everywhere the educators of youth. It was a refined and subtle cruelty in Julian to forbid them to teach the Greek and Latin authors; to make it criminal to call the ingenuous youth around the platform of their eloquence. By his edict, he robbed, ah! how many Christian families, of their daily bread, and he added a cutting sarcasm in the words of the edict: "Does not your Founder say, 'Let the little children come unto me?' Cease to explain the heathen writers, if you condemn their doctrines; or if you do explain them, approve what they say. If you believe that Homer and Hesiod are in error, go and explain Matthew and Luke to the children in the churches of the Galileans."

The most oppressive instrument of persecution was the law which obliged Christians to make full satisfaction for the heathen temples destroyed by their order. Too poor to make restitution, they suffered the most cruel wrongs from the Pagan magistrates in virtue of the Roman law, which delivered the *person* of the insolvent debtor into the power of the creditor. They were scourged and imprisoned, and on one occasion a Christian bishop was anointed with honey and suspended in a net between heaven and earth, exposed to the stings of insects and the burning rays of a Syrian sun.

CHAPTER XXV.

JULIAN AND THE CHRISTIANS.

JULIAN, with sincere but ostentatious devotion, went always to the earliest sacrifice. At the rising of the sun he immolated a victim to Apollo, his favorite Divinity. The sun was for Julian the Logos, the Son of the Father, the kindling WORD which gave life to the universe. His zeal led him to slay with his own hand the snow-white bullock, to kindle with his breath the fire upon the altars, to consult the entrails, to pour the incense, to scatter the perfumes, and himself collect the sacred ashes.

As the Emperor descended on foot from the grove where the early sacrifice had just been completed, he overtook two men, who from their dress he supposed to be Christians. The Christians indeed affected no singularity of dress; of these two, their robes were spotless and their heads bare, and the earnestness of their conversation showed that it was upon a subject of infinite importance to them. Julian could not repress a smile of derision. "These are the men," he said to the person nearest to him, "these are the meek and abject sectarians who expect to destroy our gorgeous and sublime worship of the Gods." Addressing himself to them, he asked, "What mischief are you Nazarenes plotting at this moment?"

"Your Majesty," answered one of them, "will always find us the most inoffensive of your subjects."

Julian was anxious to find some other fault than their religion, of which to accuse the Christians; he would have been glad if they had organized a rebellion; but their sins were those of omission.

"What, then, are all your secret meetings for, at the dead of night, if you are not forming a conspiracy against my government?"

"Sire, not so; each one of us is living in the midst of his family, surrounded by the ignorant whom we instruct, and by children; giving no offence to any."

"And is it true also," asked the Emperor, "that you resent no injuries?"

"Sire, loving our neighbor as ourselves, we do not strike those who strike us; we do not go to law with those who despoil us; if we receive a blow, we turn the other cheek; if they demand our cloak, we offer our tunic also."

"You are then a community of wolves and sheep, where every one would prefer to be the wolf."

"No, Sire, we live in loving communion; the children receive our most tender care; we honor aged persons. The poor, and we have many such, are supported. It is the command of our Master, that those who possess the goods of this world shall help those who do not."

"Thus you cherish a hive of lazy vagabonds."

"No, Sire, all must work according to their strength. And as we regard woman as completely the equal and the intelligent companion of man, she also takes her part in the cares and in the counsels of our community."

"You banish, as I hear, all the arts of seduction, and condemn amusements; going neither to the amphitheatre nor to the spectacles."

"Yes, Sire, we renounce your bloody amphitheatre, and endeavor to keep our youth from the spectacles which harden the heart and lead to every vice."

The Emperor was of the same opinion with regard to the spectacles and amusements of the city; he was silent, however, and one of the men ventured to ask him if the edict had really gone forth commanding the Christians to rebuild the heathen temples, and restore all confiscated property; adding, that it would reduce their community to beggary.

"Why not?" asked the Emperor, with a sneer. "Your admirable system enjoins you to renounce the goods of this world, that you may more easily arrive at the kingdom of heaven; we wish to facilitate your journey by easing you of the weight of earthly riches."

"Ah, Sire! how many of your best subjects will you reduce to abject poverty!"

"Well, is it not the vocation of a Christian to *suffer?* But learn from a heathen, that riches are not the greatest good. If I could render every individual of your sect richer than Midas, I should esteem myself no friend to him, unless I could reclaim him from his impious revolt against the immortal Gods."

The Christian made the sign of the cross, and said, "Sire! commanding, as you do, all the resources of the Empire, you can adapt your promises and rewards to every order of Christians; but we trust that your bribes will fall powerless before the constancy and faith of our brothers."

"See the gorgeous trappings of your bishops, and

how they contend for the richest seats, and for the material goods of the world. Then your Christian quarrels have convulsed every city and every village where they have entered; you Christians, as you call yourselves, are more cruel to each other than the wild beasts are to men."

"Ah, Sire, the heresies which have divided the Church are the grief of every Christian."

"The expenses of the bishops and their followers," said Julian, "as they travel at the public cost, from council to council, to decide upon articles of faith, and to reconcile the quarrels of the disciples of your crucified man, threaten to destroy the kingdom."

"Sire! every institution, divine or human, which would influence multitudes, must invest itself with outward splendor — "

"See your Paul of Antioch," interrupted Julian, "driving to the Basilica with his milk-white mules and golden harness. The jewels upon his sandals are worth a province. He, the follower of Him who had trod barefoot the stony paths of Judæa! See the perfumed handkerchiefs of the women waving him into the pulpit, and their delicate hands clapping and applauding his tumid sentences."

"Pardon me, Sire. Look again at the noble Basil, Bishop of Cesarea; his whole fortune is given to the poor, to the orphan, the blind. See his houses for the sick, the stranger, the destitute; they form a town of themselves!"

"Yes, they form a town and eat up the country. Then your eternal differences upon subjects so open to ridicule, that they furnish comedies to the theatres of our Pagans."

The Christians were silent, and, as Julian said no more, one of them ventured at length to say, "Ah, Sire, we are willing to be ridiculed, could we be spared those cruel exactions and fines which destroy our community."

"Consider them as a part of your coveted martyrdom," said Julian, and he laughed that scornful laugh which so distorted his features that even his friends found it hateful. "Your Galilean," said he, "came to bring a sword, and his followers should be glad to feel it."

CHAPTER XXVI.

DAPHNE.

At five miles from the city of Antioch was the garden of Daphne, one of the most enchanting places in the classic world. It was ennobled by fiction and poetry, for the change of Daphne into a laurel had been transported from the delicious valley of Tempe in Thessaly to the banks of the Orontes. An immense grove of cypresses and laurels was divided into luxurious paths, beneath whose shade the rays of the sun could scarcely penetrate. Delicious and abundant fountains gushed out, and scattered their liquid diamonds in showers. The limpid beauty of the sky, the perfume and enamel of flowers, associated with the fable of the ravished Daphne, united to make this one of the most seductive spots in all the Pagan worship.

Till the time of Gallus, the worshippers of Apollo resorted to this grove to imitate as much as to worship him. Here was a temple in honor of the

God celebrated in all the East for its magnificence. It was supported by marble columns of a rare beauty; gold and precious stones shone with profusion and good taste. In the midst, surrounded by the bending forms of Diana and the Muses, stood the statue of the God, formed of the purest marble, and so exquisitely finished that it was compared with the Jupiter of Phidias. The youthful God of light and music held his lyre in one hand, while from a cup of gold he seemed to pour out a libation to the Earth, as though he sought the venerable mother to restore the lost Daphne to his arms.

A thousand streams of the purest water rendered this enchanting paradise always verdant. Concealed harps produced mysterious melodies, and from every crushed plant arose aromatic odors. This peaceful retreat was consecrated to joy, to luxury, and love; but amid the corruptions of Paganism, purity found no place where Nature had been so liberal of her best gifts, and a man of grave and pure character would have blushed to be seen there.

It was the feast of Apollo, and Julian, eager to celebrate it in the most costly and magnificent manner, hastened to Daphne, dreaming on his way of the solemn pomp of his victims, adorned with garlands; of libations, of perfumes and incense, of choruses of beautiful children clad in white, whose souls should be as pure as their spotless robes. As he drew near, he was appalled at the silence and solitude of the grove. He entered the temple, and found there neither incense, nor offering, nor victim.

As Sovereign Pontiff, Julian demanded the offerings. A decrepit old priest approached with a lean goose in his hand.

"Shameful!" cried the Emperor, in violent anger; "is this all that so great a city offers to its tutelar Divinity, — a single gray goose, — and not even a costly bird, when each tribe should have brought an ox?" A keen sense of the irony of offering a goose to Apollo soon appeased his anger, as it found vent in sarcasm.

"No doubt," said Julian, "the cry of the goose will pass for the poet's song, and his hiss for the inspiration of Apollo. It will not be the last time, I fear, that the goose will represent the swan of Apollo."

"The oracle has been dumb," said the old priest, "since the noble Cæsar Gallus ordered the bones of the Galilean martyr to be interred under the altar of Apollo."

"The bones of Babylus?" cried Julian, stamping on the ground. "The court of Apollo may well be the purgatory of the Galilean bishop."

In the mean time the report had spread that the

Emperor had gone out to Daphne, to the temple of Apollo, and the crowd was soon augmented by senators and courtiers, mingling with the lowest of the people, who usually made up the cortege of Julian. He stood upon the steps of the altar.

"It is an intolerable scandal," he said, addressing the senators, "that you treat the Immortal Gods with such contempt. A city, with a territory so vast, and at a time when the Gods have dissipated the darkness of Atheism, allows the fête of the God of its fathers to pass without offering to him a single bird, when every tribe should have sacrificed an ox at least. But if the city is too poor for this, let them unite and offer a single bull. When you make a festival, or give a birthday feast, you spend your money with full hands. But here there is no sacrifice, no grateful offering in the name of the citizens, to its benefactor. You permit your wives to ruin you in favor of the vile Galileans. They love the impiety of these miserable wretches, whom they feed at your expense. You set your wives the example of despising the Gods, and dare to believe yourselves innocent. Who among you does not lavish vast sums upon his birthday or that of his wife, and here in your great sanctuary there is not a drop of oil for the lamp, not a grain of incense for the altar!"

The Emperor looked round and saw every countenance unmoved, every voice silent, and he felt in the bitterness of his heart how vast was the progress of Christianity in Antioch, and how indifferent even the Pagans were to their Gods.

When he paused, shouts arose of "Julian! Julian!"

"Silence!" he cried, with a voice of thunder. "Vile mortals that you are! You put *us* in the place of the Gods! You prostitute to *us* the incense which you steal from the altars! It is the cursed Galileans who have caused all this. But for them —"

"Ah! do not curse them," cried a voice. "Sire! Curse them not, they are the best of your subjects. Our own poor would perish in the streets, and upon the steps of our temples, if Christian women did not succor them; if young virgins among the Christians did not refresh their parched lips, and with pure gentle touch wipe the dews of death from their brows."

"Silence!" cried Julian, exasperated! "Are you *all* Galileans! Are you *all* infidels! Let the martyr's bones be scattered to the winds! Purify the temple from the defilement of a Galilean sepulchre! See that the flowers and the incense be again restored! I will myself take care that the altar of Apollo shall never again become the shrine of a lean goose."

The report spread through the city, with wonderful rapidity, that the Emperor had ordered the bones of the martyred Bishop to be disinterred and cast out from his sepulchre in Daphne. The Christians were moved to the very depths of their souls.

"The Emperor will pass this way," said Monica to the Christian women assembled in her house ; "let us show him that we are the friends of the martyr, and steadfast in the faith he so much hates."

Parthenia's Christian belief had opened a gulf between herself and Julian ; but tender and faithful memories of the past prevented her from wishing to wound or insult the religion which did indeed, from her present point of view, seem to her a wretched delusion. She was silent, therefore, when Monica proposed, that, as the Emperor passed in his return from Daphne, they should greet him with one of the psalms of the Christians.

Parthenia gave no assent, and, as she sat there silent in her unimpaired beauty, she was calm from the very depth and fulness of her emotions.

At length shouts were heard, and Julian drew near, with his usual cortege of the idle and the vagabond portion of a great and luxurious city.

To all those who had no homes, the Emperor's appearance in the streets was a signal to start and follow in the train of a prince, who loved popularity, and who was as liberal in his gifts as the sun in his noontide beams.

As Julian drew near the portico, Monica and the young women of the church who met at her house raised their shrill voices in the words of the ninety-sixth psalm: "For all the Gods of the nations are idols, but the Lord made the heavens." And also the words, "Let God arise, and let his enemies be scattered."

The attention of Julian was arrested, and as he looked up at the windows of the house, his swarthy cheek became crimson with anger. The excited crowd caught the words, "Let God arise, and let his enemies be scattered." The Pagan mob became furious; they cried out to stone the women, to throw them to the beasts, to bring fire and consume them and the house. Julian alone could restrain them from instantly executing their threats. With the aid of his officers he dispersed the excited mob, and then entered the house, with no attendant except the captain of his guards.

Monica had thrown off her veil, and stood there in the presence of the Emperor, her noble Roman brow pale, but with a majesty he had scarcely ever seen in woman. She saw herself joining the long procession of martyrs for the faith she gloried in avowing, and her heart leaped within her for joy at the prospect. Torture and the fagot were before her, but she gave fearlessly the order to the women to repeat the offensive words: "Let the enemies of the Lord be scattered."

Julian, pale with rage, ordered the captain of the guard to strike her on the mouth. The officer shrank back from the majestic countenance of the woman, and the Emperor became conscious that another was present. His eye caught the pale countenance of Parthenia, just as the crimson of shame was rushing over it at the order he had given. He also felt how unworthy of him it was, and in the presence of this noble Athenian, and, bowing to Monica, he turned towards *her*. "Beautiful Parthenia," he said, "what is this I see, and how are you here, in the midst of the enemies of Julian? Is it madness, or demoniac influence, that brings the priestess of Pallas, the noble Athenian virgin, the disciple of Plato, in contact with the ignorant and frantic Galileans?"

"Say not so, noble Prince," she cried, while a tide of joy rushed to her heart and glowed upon her cheek. "It is not madness, or if you call it so, it is more precious than all your wisdom, than all your philosophy."

Julian's astonishment for a moment kept him silent. Then, turning to her with grief in his voice, he said: "It is then true that the noble Parthenia has joined the enemies of Julian, the calumniators of her Gods!"

"No, Sire! Parthenia can never belong with the enemies of the Emperor."

"But can she have deserted her beloved Athens, those glorious Grecian skies, the blest temple of Pallas Athena?"

"Ah, Sire, it is a woman's destiny to follow those with whom chance or fortune connect her life. And I — ah, Sire! I bless the day, and the cause, which brought me to Antioch."

"Do not say, noble friend, that you have connected your fate with these enemies of the Empire, with these superstitious and abject Galileans."

"Sire, it is only since I have known them that I have begun to understand the meaning and the purpose of life. In the temple of the Goddess, when I went there to pray for light, all was dark in my soul, as in the books of our philosophy. But now, trusting in the love and wisdom of another, I have found serene and joyful hope."

"Who has Parthenia found so wise, so faithful, so exalted above herself, as to rely upon his wisdom and truth?"

"Ah! Prince, do you ask? Can you not divine that in him whom the Christians call their Christ I put all my trust?"

Julian's eyes flashed with anger. He must have surmised the change in the Athenian maiden; but this bold avowal from her lips excited his scorn. "The dead man!" he cried, "the son of the carpenter! the crucified malefactor!"

Parthenia turned her head aside, and while she made the sign of the cross, a tear started to her eye. A new and ardent convert, she felt her heart throb with pain and grief.

Julian was softened. He asked gently, "Does this new faith fill the aspirations of one who sat at the feet of Plato?"

"Sire, I have pure joy in believing in the Christ. But no woman can be happy while seeing her friends deprived of all resources, cut off from their honorable employments, and their children condemned to poverty."

"To suffer is their vocation, and poverty is their badge," said Julian, with a sneer; "but you must admit, fair Athenian, that I have not been, like some of my predecessors, a persecutor of the Christians."

"Scorn is a heavier burden than stripes, and contempt more bitter than imprisonment. The loss of honorable employment, and of the confidence of others, is an affliction to a refined nature more severe than death itself."

"Stay, fair Athenian! Will those who love the wisdom of Matthew the publican, and listen to the oracle of Peter the fisherman, will they condescend to interpret the divine Homer, or to gather the honey from the lips of Plato?"

"Sire, was not your own childhood fed with Grecian and heathen wisdom, distilled through Christian lips?"

"Yes, my mother was a Christian, and a lover of Homer; but this is far from the purpose. The Gods themselves command me to punish their enemies."

"Ah, Sire! you punish the best of your subjects. You compel those who are the bone and sinew of your Empire to abandon their homes, and their children are given up to poverty."

"I only facilitate their entrance into the kingdom of heaven, where they affirm that a rich man cannot enter."

"You take from us the merit of our good deeds, and will not even allow us the honor of martyrdom," said Parthenia.

"O Jupiter!" cried Julian, "how canst thou allow those Grecian lips to plead the cause of thy enemies?"

"The Emperor is justly incensed at the insult offered to him in this house; but is it not beneath the imperial Julian to punish a disrespect aimed at himself alone?"

Monica, who had scarcely restrained herself from speaking, now burst forth: "You will not listen! God has closed your eyes that you cannot see, and your heart that you cannot understand."

Julian turned somewhat fiercely to her. "Woman," he said, "you disobey your own teachers, who say that it is shame for a woman to speak, except to her own husband in the privacy of her own apartment; for that I honor the Christian teachers. It is the only word of wisdom which has fallen from their lips."

"Our religion alone," said Monica, undaunted by Julian's sneer, "has given woman her true position. With you Romans, and even with the refined Athenians, we were domestic slaves; — this was not enough degradation for us, and you have added Asiatic luxury to our effeminacy, to sink us still lower. Had not Christ, with tender and beautiful regard for woman, raised her to be the equal and the friend of man, how hopeless had been our condition!"

"Now, by the Immortal Gods!" Julian began. But what he would have called upon the Gods to sanction was here interrupted by the entrance of Olympia, followed by both her children, one holding by her robe, the other, who had failed to catch the robe, stumbling at every step — for he had just learned to walk — and recovering himself to keep up with the other. This last was a lovely infant, clothed only with a little low-necked shirt, one sleeve of which had fallen off, and the beautiful shoulder and breast were bare, presenting the perfect form of infant beauty.

Olympia threw herself at the feet of Julian. The bashful emotion flushed her fair cheek with crimson, and her beautiful arms, bare to the shoulder in her Greek dress, recalled those exquisite statues the Emperor so loved. "I am a Greek," she said, "a lover of the Gods of my country, and for the world I would not despise them, or join with others in disobeying the Emperor; but I know the Christians, I am filled with proofs of their goodness, their nobleness, their generosity. O Sire! do not take their bread from them! Do not deprive these children and others like them of their fathers! Do not imprison them! Ah, Sire, your servants are cruel! They torture and destroy your best subjects."

Julian was dazzled by this beautiful apparition. It has been often said that beauty could not move him. The excessive activity of his brain and its ever-busy schemes left his heart slumbering or insensible. Many women knelt to him, and he always granted their petitions; but beauty in so exquisite a form he had scarcely ever seen; he held out his arm and raised her.

"Who are you," he said, "and how is it that a Greek, and a lover of the Gods, is with those who hate both?"

At these questions the blood mounted and crimsoned the brow of Olympia, not because of the Emperor, but from the presence of Monica. Her eyes filled with tears; but turning to the youngest boy, she took him in her arms, and said, "I am the mother of these children, and I love these Christians more than my life —"

"Can so much loveliness ask anything of them or of the Emperor that cannot be granted?" said Julian.

"O Sire! restore them to their homes and their possessions. Grant them the same privileges that you do your other subjects."

"That they may turn them into curses against their Emperor? No, fairest Greek, to us the eloquence and the arts of Greece; to them let us leave their ignorance and their poverty."

"I cannot thus distinguish, Sire. Love is my religion. Where I give this, I would give all other things beside: a Grecian woman's heart is filled with her home only."

Monica now interposed: "Sire, it is the grief of our home, that this siren has so wound herself into the heart of my son as to make him forget his duty to me and to the Church."

"Is she not his wife, and is not that her place?"

"Yes! I am his wife before all the Gods, the Christian's God as well as the Gods of Olympus, and they would divide us from him; his children and his wife they would tear from him, and send him to a solitude in the desert, to a monkish and desolate life of fasting and mortification. And me, — ah, Sire! dividing us they would kill me! Without his love, away from him, I shall die!" And she drew her veil around her and burst into an agony of weeping.

"And these are your Christian hearts, and what you call your Christian duties, — to tear asunder the sweetest and most sacred of all ties, and sacrifice two lives to the Moloch of your ascetic and self-denying religion!" said the Emperor.

"Sire, our religion condemns the ties which unite, which connect together these two children; for such they are," said Monica.

"Ah, yes! your Christian superstition—for I will not call it a religion — demands your canting prayers, your whining beggars, your goods thrown to vagrants and impostors ; and then to drive to despair those who in obeying their hearts would create a paradise, where you would make a Tartarus ! "

Parthenia, who had remained silently attentive, merely placing her arm around Olympia, as she drew her children close to her knees, now said: "How happy would it be could they look upon her as one of those domestic Lares, or angels rather, who bring love and gladness to every family ! — for such she is."

Monica now came forward, cutting short Parthenia's remark, and, taking both the children in her strong arms, signed to Olympia to follow. The latter, whose temper seemed all submission, and whose face expressed a settled sadness, did not hesitate; she only pressed her lips upon the arm of Parthenia as she withdrew it, and followed the matron.

As soon as they were gone, the Emperor turned towards Parthenia, and his eye softened from its flashing and scornful brightness. "The pure vestal, the priestess of Athena, has not informed me why I find her so far from the temple of her love, and from the matchless sky of Athens," he said.

"A daughter must follow the fortunes of her

father; but, Sire, I never can regret that weariness of life and desire of change brought me to this Syrian city; for here I have found that pearl of infinite price, for which I would willingly exchange all else of life."

Julian's lip curled with a scarcely repressed sneer.

"Ah, my lord, I am a woman neither learned nor eloquent, but the few sublime ideas of the Christian faith, the grand but simple truths it teaches, cast all our Pagan Deities, with their low, sensual lives, into the shadow of death."

"Thus, like the bee of Hymettus, you have been able to extract some drops of honey from the bitterest herb that grows."

"And your own Gods are broken idols, yielding no support," said Parthenia.

Julian was silent, and a cloud gathered upon his brow.

Parthenia added: "Let me entreat the Emperor in behalf of these Christians who have so offended. Clemency is most noble in the powerful, and to pardon an insult is greater than to forgive an injury."

"Let them insult their prince! they offer a greater insult to the laws. Yet the Antiochians call me cruel. 'You oblige us,' they say, 'to obey the magistrates and the laws.' How cruel!"

"Sire!"

"Call me not Sire, nor Lord! I cannot endure these flattering titles."

"Those who applaud you in the temples of the Gods, and meet you in the theatre with shouts and noise, you may call flatterers; but not one who, pleading for those who have offended, cannot forget—"

"Let us at least forget these Galileans! They are not worthy of the eloquence of that Athenian tongue," interposed Julian.

"If the Emperor forgets them, will he not also forget their offence?" pleaded Parthenia.

"After all, they are less contemptible than those laughter-loving Antiochians, who take delight only in dancing-men, dancing-women, and dancing-boys, and despise the Emperor because he also does not dance!"

"A rational life, like yours, is in their eyes the worst of folly."

"I do not reproach the Antiochians for being in 'lying and in wanton dances skilled'; why should they reproach the rusticity of my manners?"

"The Antiochians have not time to look beneath the very outer surface. But let me offer the Emperor a precept from one of the books he despises too much to search for himself,—'Cast not thy pearls before swine.'"

Julian laughed. "Ah! I have been much my own enemy. I came to this free city uncombed and bearded. They took me for a morose old man, when, with the advantages of dress, I might have passed for a handsome youth."

Parthenia smiled.

"Ah, you doubt! They blame me also, because, like the changeful chameleon, I cannot be all things to all men. They think it strange that, in a city where there are as many dancers and more players than there are citizens, there should be any respect for sovereigns, or anything but insult for the laws. The very name of obedience, either to the Gods or the laws, only disgusts them."

Parthenia could only show her interest by silent attention.

"They cry, how cruel and unjust to require moderation in the rich, or to restrain the poor from slander. In truth, fair Parthenia, I reproach myself for being so stupid as not to perceive that, to please this city, I must revel the whole year. I would fain bring a little order into the city; but to deprive them of the power of saying and doing whatever they please, is an offence against liberty of the deepest dye. They allow their wives to be their own rulers, that they may be as licentious as possible; they lay no restraint upon their children, lest they also should be enslaved, and when they advance to maturity should respect their elders a little, and then by degrees should reverence their prince, and thus becoming temperate, just, and honest, should be corrupted and totally ruined."

Parthenia could only smile at the bitter irony of the Emperor.

"I hoped, fair Parthenia, that to rule with mildness and moderation would atone for my want of beauty. But since the length of my beard, my dislike to the theatres, my adherence to equity, my earnest endeavors to banish extortion, my remittance of a fifth of what they used to pay in taxes, has given such offence, I shall hasten to leave this fair city."

"You do not know, Sire, how many of your Christian subjects honor and reverence those very virtues of moderation and equity."

Julian seemed not to hear, but went on: "If I should attempt to alter my conduct, I should probably exemplify the old fable of the kite. The kite, it is said, had a voice like other birds; but being ambitious to neigh like a high-bred horse, and not being able to attain this accomplishment, she lost the other. I am afraid, in trying to be polite, I should cease to be rustic. For you perceive, fair Parthenia, I am on the verge of that age when, as the Teian poet says,

'Gray hairs will mingle with the black.'

Pardon me, fairest, for thus intruding my griefs upon you. They are caused by the ingratitude of those I have obliged, and are therefore the effect of my own folly. This will teach me to act with more discretion in the future."

The Emperor rose, and, abruptly bowing, left the apartment.

CHAPTER XXVII.

THE HOSPITAL FOR STRANGERS.

Anxious to imitate the beneficent institutions of the Christians, and oppose Christianity with arms borrowed from itself, the Emperor visited the houses of relief and hospitals founded by the Bishop and supported by Christian men and women, which, even in this luxurious Antioch, surpassed in number all the places of public amusement in the city.

In order to preserve a strict incognito, the Emperor dismissed his guards, and divested himself of every sign of royalty, and even of that offensive beard so abhorred by the Antiochians.

The hospital for strangers, to which he first directed his steps, was a city of itself, — a city of sorrow within a city of luxury and pleasure. Here found shelter that suffering humanity which had been cast out from the dwellings of the happy. Here angelic Pity opened her arms to succor the broken-hearted, collected from every part of the world. The sick, the lame, the blind, the wounded, the sore in body or in mind, found refuge, pity, and healing; or, if past cure, the kindly bosom of Mother Earth closed over their griefs, with prayer and benediction from angelic tongues. It was only necessary to pronounce the word *stranger*, and here they were at home.

The Emperor saw in the court the light carriage of Parthenia, with its beautiful Thessalian horses; for since she became a Christian she had given freedom to the Syrian slaves who formerly bore her litter.

Although, in order to preserve his incognito, the Emperor had divested himself of every sign of royalty, yet, after going through the male divisions of the hospital, he was obliged to show the imperial order to gain admittance to the female wards. As he entered one of the well-ventilated and beautifully clean apartments, where on low pallets lay the victims of their own vices, or of the irreparable guilt of others, he saw Christian women at every pillow, and among them he recognized the stately form of Monica and the pure spiritual brow of Parthenia.

As he approached, Parthenia knew the Emperor; but he placed his finger on his lips, and she understood that he wished to remain unrecognized. In her simple Greek tunic of white wool, she was kneeling beside a young girl who seemed scarcely past the age of childhood. The spotlessly fair skin, the heavenly azure of the half-opened eyes, and the pale golden tresses of hair which fell down upon her breast, showed that she was a child of the North, perhaps from that far-off island of Britain, from which, in an earlier period of Rome, those who came were called angels.

Parthenia was drying, by the tender touch of her soft hands, the dews of death from her brow, when the young girl opened her eyes as from slumber, and said in a tongue which Julian understood, for he had often heard it in his beloved Lutetia, "Are you my mother?—Ah, no! I only dreamed." This was said in a tone so wrung with sorrow, that tears started to the eyes of Parthenia.

"I dreamed that I was in my home, the cabin by the river, and that I gathered the cool oak-leaves for garlands, and that my mother held me, as the Roman soldier tore me from her arms. Ah, you are not my mother, but you are an angel come to tell me that the dear Lord will receive me, and that God will forgive me." She said this in a dialect unknown to Parthenia; but the intuition of her heart told her that this victim of the wrong of others needed only the assurance of pardon to close her eyes upon a world where she had been one of those little ones of whom Jesus said, "Woe unto those who offend them, for their angels do always behold the face of their Father in heaven."

Parthenia whispered in her ear words of comfort and of prayer. The young girl looked at her perplexed, with wistful expression; the beautiful Greek tongue of her comforter was wholly unintelligible. Julian's quick perceptions found the remedy. Kneeling by Parthenia, he translated her whispered prayer into the ear of the dying girl. As he rose, he looked for an instant at the beautiful Greek. "Ah!" he thought, "could those cool, soft hands be laid for one moment upon my throbbing brain, would they not check its schemes, — would they not press the brain itself, which too much thought expands, back into its quiet, peaceful channel, and leave me leisure for that cloistered life, which was my choice, before power and ambition laid their commands upon me?"

As he turned to go, he said: "Your port here is open to all who are wrecked of fortune; you harbor good and bad, whatever may be their crimes. Do you not offer a reward to the wicked?"

"Sire, it is sufficient that they are wretched. If we asked after their merits, I fear we should find few worthy."

"Ah, these are the fruits of our civilization. Look at our gorgeous and senseless lives, and then look here: one follows the other as the harvest follows the sower."

"Christianity is to bring a remedy for all these ills," said the Athenian; for thus enthusiastic souls believed in that early age of our religion, while *we* find the remedy as far off as ever. "Its bounty is like that of God," she continued. "It sheds its light and its dew upon all alike. Those who have lost all but life come here. We ask nothing, we refuse none."

"And thus you win all," said Julian, bitterly, as he left the hospital.

"Ah!" thought the Emperor, as he returned to his palace, "it is not their ostentatious simulation of humble virtues, and the absence of luxury and ornament in their dress, of which even some of their women are vain,—it is not these things that thin our ranks,—these are not our enemies! It is their hospitals, their tenderness to the poor, their humanity to strangers, their bounties poured out like water! Ah, they have learned the secret."

He was interrupted at the entrance of his palace by one of his priests, who came to tell him that Daphne was purified, the bones of the martyr scattered, and the worship in the temple restored to its original magnificence.

"All this is of no avail," said Julian, "while we leave these Galileans, these impious Galileans, to take care of our poor, to build hospitals for those who should not be strangers to us. We leave the poor and the stranger cast out into absolute want." And quoting his favorite Homer, he added,

> "By Jove, the stranger and the poor are sent,
> And what to these we give, to Jove is lent."

"Ah, Sire! he sends double, ah, treble, the number of rascals," said the priest.

"We style Jupiter the Hospitable, and we are ourselves more inhospitable than the Scythians. These houses for strangers, built by the impious, put us to shame." And the Emperor again repeated from his favorite Homer, "We lend to Jove what we give to strangers."

"Pardon me, your Highness, Jove's poor are not so numerous as Mercury's thieves."

"The Gods are called by us the 'household Gods,' and Jupiter is the 'domestic Deity,' but we treat our relations among the Gods worse even than strangers. But, leaving these, explain to your colleagues what they ought to be, in order to serve the Gods truly; for Jupiter is as much pleased with the pure thoughts of religious men, as he is with the purity of Olympus."

An incredulous smile just flitted across the face of the priest.

"It is an easy thing to abstain from shameful actions. Let them avoid all licentious jests and all immoral discourse."

"Ah, Sire, we must then stop their ears and clip their tongues."

"All studies are not proper for a priest. Let all those fictions which are composed in the form of love-tales be wholly abstained from, and serious studies pursued."

"You would not have us imitate your Majesty, and covet the reputation of universal erudition?"

"Bad thoughts as well as bad books should be avoided; for the guilt of the mind and that of the tongue are, in my opinion, of an equal dye," said Julian; "but the thoughts should in the first place be guarded."

Notwithstanding the reverence of the priest for the Emperor rather than for the priesthood, he stood uneasily under this homily.

"The hymns of the Gods should be learned," continued the Emperor. "They are many and beautiful, and should be sung in the temples."

"But, Sire, Apollo has not showered his gift of music upon all. The croaking of frogs would be less hideous than the voices of some of our priests."

"Let those who cannot sing address the Gods in prayer, three times a day, or at least at the dawn and in the evening."

"Sire, can we find a priest who, since the siege of Troy, has risen before the dawn?"

"Let them follow the example of the Emperor, who, before the dawn has flushed with crimson the loftiest of these hill-tops, has written countless despatches and sent his messages upon the wings of the wind."

"Who can ever hope to imitate the Emperor, even in those minor virtues of industry and punctuality?"

"Better imitate him in what the refined Antiochians call his savage rusticity. Because he does not send to summer climes for roses to adorn his winter palace, they call him a savage; and because he leads a life of rigid self-denial, they call him a brute."

"Hard indeed would it be to imitate the ascetic life of the Emperor. Even the Galileans indulge themselves with the solace of wife and children," said the priest.

A smile of contempt curled the Emperor's lip. "What business have priests with children? You should live in celibacy, like the anchorites and hermits. I tell you again, it is not sufficient for priests to be blameless. If you would stand against this blasphemous impiety, you must excel all others in piety and in good works. Are the Christians ever seen in the theatres, or drinking in taverns?"

"They do indeed preserve an outward ostentation of goodness; but in secret, Sire, if we listen to report, we know not the crimes they commit."

"No, we do not indeed," said the Emperor; "but the Gods of Olympus, or the Infernal Deities, will furnish some cause against them."

It was not many days before an opportunity was presented anew for punishing and persecuting the Christians.

CHAPTER XXVIII.

THE HERMITS.

A LOFTY chain of precipitous heights, crowned by perpetual verdure, except where broken by rocky precipices, down which poured mountain streams, rose on one side of the city of Antioch. These heights were adorned by a luxuriant vegetation of the vine, the fig, the myrtle, and the laurel, beside the loftier growth of the oak and the sycamore.

These solitary hills opened secluded retreats and quiet solitudes, where those hermits and anchorites who had fled from the violence and sin of the world passed their days in prayer, meditation, and fasting. These were the men who were afterwards formed into religious communities, and subjected to the strict rules of their order. But at this time these solitaries consisted principally of men of education and refinement, who, under mistaken ideas of the duties of Christianity, fled from the world, in order to live a peaceful and passionless life, ascetic indeed and stern, but often elevated and spiritual. There were also many gentle and devout spirits, who in times of so much violence could find no shelter so peaceful as these natural solitudes; so secluded and so beautiful, "that they were in danger," as said St. Basil, "of forgetting all duty and real self-sacrifice in the midst of a luxuriant nature, blossoming flowers, and singing birds."

The stars had not yet faded from the sky, but one by one, as they dropped beneath the sheltering hills of Antioch, they left upon them a deeper flush of the rising day. The solemn silence and solitude of the dawn were unbroken, but as objects became more distinct, a young man was seen issuing from one of those recesses in the hills that we have spoken of. He wore the usual dress of a hermit, a single garment or tunic, confined at the waist by a cord, sandals, and a wide-brimmed hat, as a shelter from sun and rain. This young man was slender and pale, as though inward passion or enthusiasm had consumed the outward bloom, and the pallor was made more striking by the short, silky beard, black as ink, which shaded his lip and cheek.

As the mists of the valley ascended, and were colored by the rising sun, he stood an instant looking at earth and sky, and then towards the city, whose silence was still unbroken by the toil and tumult of labor, or of pleasure. A moment seemed to have passed in silent prayer, when he started with hurried steps towards the great high-road which led to Antioch. This was the young Theodorus, whom we met in the temple of Pallas Athena in Athens. Could we have directed our vision to other points, we should have seen the Christian recluses everywhere issuing from their retreats, and hastening towards the city. They had been summoned by the Bishop to assemble as for some great event; and as one after another they emerged upon the great thoroughfare, that broad, paved, and shaded avenue leading to the city, they presented a dark body of enthusiasts, with bearded faces, pale and emaciated, where all the vitality seemed centred in dreamy or flashing eyes.

As the young Theodorus met a gray-bearded recluse, he asked, what was the object of this early summons from the Bishop.

"Where have you been dreaming," asked the other, "not to have learned that the bones of the martyr have been cast out by the impious, and collected by order of the Bishop for reinterment by the faithful?"

"Every new demonstration of the Christians will only rekindle the anger and the zeal of the Emperor."

"He cannot rekindle the cold ashes of a faith in which every spark is nearly extinct. He bears himself the whole weight of the heathen sacrifice."

"Yes, it is a fine spectacle to see the Emperor of the world split and lay the wood; with his own right hand slay the victim; then blow the fire with cheeks all distended in the presence of a few old women, who, if he did not reward them with an alms, would only laugh at him."

"And to see the little man at the fêtes of Venus, marching between two ranks of her votaries, trying by rising upon his toes with long strides to make himself a giant, his shoulders raised, his beard pointed outwards —"

"He who is himself so strictly chaste! Ah, how far will fanaticism carry a really wise prince!"

"He will soon pass from fanaticism to severer persecution," said the other; "but would to God that the Church could be roused from its lethargy by persecution!"

The recluses now arrived at the gate of the city. Passing through the streets, they found the houses occupied by Christians hung, from roof to pavement, with black drapery, and all appearance of life and festivity removed. The square, where stood the magnificent octagon church, although so early, was full of people, and they perceived that preparations were making for a great celebration, which, instead of the usual festivity, wore all the attributes of mourning. With this aspect of grief, the glorious Syrian sky which rested upon the hills around the city offered no sympathy. The vaulted cupola of the church was embraced by the blue vault above it, as though there could be only love and joy upon the whole earth.

Although hosannas and hymns were sung, no joy appeared in the countenances of those who formed the procession beneath. This was headed by a large silver cross, borne by three persons, and followed by the Bishop, and by the priests and deacons in mourning robes. Immediately after them came the lofty car upon which rested the bones of Babylus. This was followed by the Christians, matrons and virgins, in mourning robes, and veiled. Then came boys bearing incense, and the pupils of the Christian schools, all clad in spotless white. After these children, the fairest portion of the pageant, came the melancholy train, the banners of the martyrs, a countless multitude, bearing upon a black ground the names of those who had suffered, and the instruments of torture and of death through which these constant souls had opened to them the agonizing but glorious passage to the presence of their Master.

As this part of the procession came in sight, all the Christians among the immense throng fell upon their knees and uttered groans and cries. A spectator would have thought that the whole pleasure-loving city of Antioch had turned from amusement to follow the melancholy canonization of a martyred Christian.

As they entered the magnificent church, hung with pictures and blazing with precious stones, every voice joined in chanting the Psalms. "All the Gods of the nations are idols." "Say among the heathen, that the Lord reigneth." The organ was not yet introduced into churches, but this immense choir of human voices, taught as they were with infinite expense and pains to join harmoniously in singing praises to God, filled the immense building, and the echoes of ten thousand voices vibrated to the ears of the Emperor in his palace.

Darkness had descended ere the church was again empty, and the interment of the bones of Babylus the martyr in consecrated ground was performed by torch-light; the reflection of this multitude of torches enlightened half the autumn sky of Antioch.

The Emperor was in an upper room of his palace, occupied, as usual, through the night, with his secretaries. He was traversing with long strides the apartment, dictating with almost breathless rapidity to four or five reporters, in as many different languages, letters of business, or friendship; orations, learned dissertations, essays; sending directions and orders to the various officers of the government; hints to priests, physicians, musicians, philosophers; for there was no art or department of science into which Julian did not look. These rapid dictations were afterwards prepared by their respective secretaries for Julian's signature, and sent on by couriers to the remote ends of the Empire, almost with the rapidity of modern times.

It was past midnight, and the pressure of business seemed scarcely to lessen, when Libanius, with the privilege of friendship at that hour of the night, was announced by the waiting page.

"Do I intrude on confidential business?" he asked.

"With friends there are no secret hours," said Julian, embracing him.

Soon he drew the attention of the Emperor to the occurrences of the day and the significance of this demonstration of the Christians, which included such numbers that the whole city seemed to be Christian.

"Bah!" said Julian, "it is only the bent of this pleasure-loving city for excitement. If I were to order a procession of apes to-morrow, the whole city would turn out to see it."

Among the Emperor's secretaries there was more than one Christian, and he signed to his friend to follow him out upon the balcony. The exquisite Syrian night, with a cloudless moon, was only a paler day, — paler, more tender, more touching, more balmy sweet. The city was silent now, — the noise and tumult had sunk away to rest, — and the two friends stood silent also, looking at the stars, which the full moon had paled.

"Notwithstanding these cursed Galileans," said Julian, resuming the conversation, "my star is still in the ascendant."

"Pray your Majesty, which of these bright planets may I worship as your star?" asked his friend.

"Ah, you can scarcely perceive it in this pale, serene sky. But," and he started, "do you not see that bright and glorious star, moving so rapidly along?"

"By the Immortal Gods!" cried his friend, "that is no star, — no, not even a shooting meteor!"

"No, Jupiter forgive me!" cried the Emperor. "Ah, what demon has sent that ball of fire?"

As they both gazed in consternation, this seeming ball of fire descended directly upon the temple of Apollo in Daphne. Like many Grecian temples, it was open to the sky, and the meteor or ball of artificial fire smote the noble head of Apollo, the statue of gold and ivory supposed to be the work of Praxiteles, and melted the exquisite features to burning streams of metal. Instantly the temple caught fire, and the beautiful marble pillars placed there by Julian, the statues of the Muses, all fell to the ground, wrapped in one sheet of flame.

The Emperor, full of consternation, rushed to the temple; but soon he perceived that nothing could be saved. Precious stones, costly pictures, golden vessels, the Muses attending upon the God, all perished together. The laurels and palms surrounding the temple, shrivelled and blackened, stood stripped of their shining foliage, like mournful ghosts, weeping their former splendor.

Julian at length ordered all efforts to cease. He stood silent, with concentrated anger burning in his breast. On this occasion no philosophy came to his aid. His favorite temple, the oracle which had foretold his greatness, which had also promised him the ascending power of the ancient religion, had fallen powerless, as he persisted in believing, under the incendiarism of the detested Galileans. Julian, who believed in magic, and in Pagan miracles, scorned all Christian faith in supernatural events, and inwardly resolved to punish the Christians as the authors of the fire.

CHAPTER XXIX.

THE ANGER OF THE EMPEROR.

SALLUST, the Prefect of the city, had been late at night with the Emperor, but had left him before the burning of the temple. The stars were in the sky when a messenger came to summon the Prefect again to the presence of Julian.

"No," said the slave who was sweeping the outer court of the palace, "I will not venture to disturb the slumbers of his highness. It is not my office."

"Call those whose office it is," said the other; "they are numerous enough."

"And get a beating? No!"

"I will go myself," said the messenger. "The Emperor's anger rages. I do not fear the Prefect as I do him in his anger."

As his servants prepared his luxurious bath, the Prefect could but curse the hardy habits of the Emperor, who had only to dash into the Orontes, as the sea-breeze came sweeping up the valley of the watercourse, to restore all the waste of twenty-four hours of intense labor. The Prefect, on the contrary, resorted to all the luxurious appliances of an Eastern bath, and the innumerable arts invented by the effeminate Antiochians, to restore the vigor and the beauty of the wasted body.

The Emperor was walking his apartment with those hasty strides habitual to him when disturbed. His small stature and violent gestures, notwithstanding his noble head and flashing eyes, gave him the appearance of a dwarf simulating the prowess of a giant. Sallust was a Pagan of a mild disposition, who abhorred blood and all the sights and sounds of violence. As he entered, the Emperor paused in his rapid walk, and turned abruptly to the Prefect.

"Give orders," he said, "that every Galilean in this city be bound and imprisoned, till we can devise further measures."

"Sire," said Sallust, respectfully, "the prisons of your whole Empire, from Britain to the deserts of Arabia, would not suffice for the Christians of this city."

"Men, women, and children, every one of them shall be punished," continued the Emperor.

"Will you act over again the part of Herod?" asked the Prefect.

"Ah! that tender prince was too lenient. He

should have destroyed one more, the son of the carpenter, and the world would have had peace."

"Sire," asked Sallust, "are you convinced that the burning of the temple was effected by the Christians?"

"By their infernal conjurations, making it appear the work of accident, or of lightning."

"Believe me, Sire, you cannot grant the Christians a greater joy than that of gaining the honors of martyrdom."

"Every second man among them," said the Emperor, "shall enjoy that glory."

"Pardon me, Sire; will your own fame gain as much by this order, especially with posterity, when the cause is forgotten?"

"You see the fruit of my clemency! I do not punish opinions, but deeds like that of last night, burning and plundering the most precious temple of our worship. Jupiter and all the Gods depart from me, if I leave their enemies unpunished!"

Sallust was a mild Pagan, a hater of deeds of violence; he ventured to suggest to the Emperor, that to close the great church of Antioch, and condemn the eloquent preachers to silence, would be a severe punishment to the Christians.

"And to the whole city," said the Emperor, "who push to hear these eloquent declaimers!"

"The women, Sire, lead the fashion here. Even the young and beautiful, who have brought offerings to the altars of Diana and Venus in the morning, go thence to clap and applaud the Christian preachers!"

"Ah, yes! I hear that they kiss the hem of the robe, the hands, and even the lips, that they call golden, of their favorite Chrysostom."

"The Antiochian ladies claim the largest liberty, Sire; they seduce their children to the religion of the Galileans, by the promise and the charm of pleasure."

"In consequence, they renounce all subjection; first to the Gods, secondly to the laws, and lastly to us, the guardian of the laws."

"But, Sire, if the Gods connive at this licentious city, and take no vengeance on its enemies, should we be enraged against it?"

"You recall me to my duty," said Julian. "Because the Gods are forbearing, shall not I punish their enemies?"

"The Christians assert," said Sallust, "that the intercession of Babylus pointed the lightning against the doomed head of the God. A more probable solution of the fire, is, that the philosopher, Asclepiades, who had passed some hours in this palace with your Highness, on his return placed the small image of Juno, always, as you know, Sire, his companion, upon the steps of the altar, and, lighting his wax tapers, left them to the stray breezes of the night, and they, more devout than the philosopher, kindled — "

Julian looked keenly at the Prefect, and commanded silence by a gesture, which was obeyed. This was the probable solution of the fire; but it was the will of the Emperor to attach the guilt of the incendiarism to the Christians, to give him a pretence for more severe persecution.

He turned again to the Prefect: "Let instant preparation be made to arrest all those who assisted at that absurd procession of the bones of Babylus."

Sallust bowed.

"Let not those recluses from the mountains escape. Though secret and noiseless, their part has been most effective."

"Sire, we shall endeavor to obey you."

"Wring from them, if necessary, the confession of the fire, by the question."

"Believe me, Sire, torture will effect nothing in these heroic souls; they will rush to those iron embraces as to the arms of a mistress!"

"You remind me that there are certain women among their number more effective in *winning souls*, to use their own jargon, than all their bishops. Let them be scourged."

"Sire!"

"Every one of them!" The Emperor paused. "No, there is one, a Grecian muse in form; an angel, if we had angels, in the expression of her face. Her I would have exempted, — protected from all harm."

"The fair Parthenia? Sire, the daughter of—"

The Emperor placed his finger on his lip and bowed. The Prefect knew that the interview was ended.

As Sallust returned with his guards to his home, he passed the house of Monica, where a number of Christians were collected who had passed the night in prayer, and in strengthening and comforting the weak and timid among them.

Parthenia stood at the window of the balcony, still hung with black, that looked out upon the great square of the church. The faintest flush of breaking day began to gild the dome, when she was startled by a rush of people, with officers at their head, who pushed rapidly past the steps, and, tearing away the locks and bars of the doors, began their work of spoil within the church. The golden vessels and candlesticks, the pictures and ornaments of the altar, were borne forth, and last the statue of

Christ, which had held the holiest place above the altar, — all were given over to the heathen. There was no mob, no violence; all was done in order, under the direction of officers. This accomplished, the doors were barred, and the holy place, the sanctuary of the Christians, closed against its worshippers. Then they knew that it was the Emperor, and that his anger was deep, and his vengeance certain.

Parthenia was thinking of the time when Julian's influence was all-powerful upon her, and although a mysterious thread of destiny seemed to connect her in some degree with him, she believed that her faith in Christianity could not now be impaired by any influence which he had held over her mind in those happy days in Athens.

The tender memories of that time had paled her cheek, and an aged man who was addressing the company of Christians, attributing it to fear, looked at *her* as he said: "What have we to fear? Can it be death? But you know that Christ is our life, and in dying we shall live! Is it exile that you fear? The earth, in all its extent, is the Lord's, and you cannot go from his presence. Can it be the loss of riches? We brought nothing into this world, and we shall carry nothing out of it. All the evils of this world are contemptible in our eyes; we laugh at all fears, we shun no poverty, we wish for no riches, we do not tremble at death."

A new life was about to open for the Church in Antioch. It had for a long time remained in peace in this effeminate city, and had become lukewarm and luxurious, and had lost its original stern and heroic virtues; but there were many in this room at this very moment who rejoiced in the prospect of persecution, and were ready to meet martyrdom with joy. Monica was one of these, and she longed to exhort the others, and was ready herself to risk everything for the cause.

After singing a hymn together, during which tears streamed down many faces, and the women sobbed as they embraced their children, they agreed upon a secret sign by which they would know each other in their assumed disguises. After this a solemn covenant was taken, in which, calm, fervent, and even joyous, they devoted themselves body and soul, their strength, their estates, and their life, to Christ and to each other.

Parthenia felt an intense loneliness; she had no child, no sister there; her father was estranged from her new faith; and these late formed friendships with the disciples of her new religion had not yet knit together with her those sweet and intense relations which so often bound Christians to each other and to Christ. Her interview with Julian had stirred her soul to its utmost depths. Busy memory went back to Athens, to those serene, happy days when her own soul reflected the transparent sky of Greece, and Julian was the sun in whose light and warmth she lived. The memory of those golden hours, those moments marked by diamond sands, had driven away the present. The cruel question would not be unheard, "Had compensation for all she had lost come with her new faith?" She started and her knees trembled beneath her. "O God!" she sighed, "am I a traitor to both, — to the past and to the present? O Jesus, help me!" It was well that a new interest soon drew her from herself.

CHAPTER XXX.

THEODORUS.

THEODORUS, the recluse of the mountain, had followed Parthenia from Athens to Antioch, drawn by that irresistible attraction, carefully concealed within his own breast, to which he gave no name, which expressed itself only in silent and distant adoration. This sentiment of adoration, even for a human being, which the imagination exalts so infinitely above us, mingled with a devotion of soul which brings the object into a near relation to the heart, ennobles and purifies the youth who submits himself to its influence. Where there is such disparity as between Theodorus and the Athenian maiden, there can be no fruition of joy; but the sentiment itself sanctifies the heart it has entered, and it is ever regarded in future days as the period when life was the sweetest, the richest, the holiest, the most truly lived.

Theodorus was again ascending the mountain,

after that night of unparalleled excitement, with soul uplifted, so that he was only a few steps from heaven. He had wings at his heart, wings upon his feet. In the tumult of the night, in the mingling of the processions of the Christians, he had been often near enough to exchange a few words with Parthenia; he had touched her hand, he had warned her of a false step, he had turned aside and received himself a missile thrown very near her. She was aware of this last service, and smiled upon him, and the smile, like that of the sun in later ages, had caleotyped itself upon his heart, to wear out only when the heart itself dissolved. He was now returning to his hermitage, to prayer and fasting, and the ascetic life to which the enthusiasts of that age devoted themselves. Parthenia and himself had become converts from the service of Pallas Athena; they had been catechumens of the same class, and had been baptized nearly at the same time. How often had he watched that spiritual profile and those folded hands, as she knelt at the Christian altar, and, in the innocent purity of his young soul, his prayers had fallen, unconsciously, beneath the Supreme, and had rested upon her.

Theodorus was too much lost in sweet meditations to observe that he was followed, till the stroke of a sword was laid upon his shoulder. He turned and beheld the guard of the Prefect. They had chains which were fastened upon his wrists, and he was driven back to one of the prisons, already crowded with Christians. Julian's anger burnt fiercely. The prisons were crowded, and he, the philosophic and lenient prince, had given orders that confession of the incendiarism should be drawn forth by torture.

As Theodorus passed through the courts of the prison, his eye sought anxiously among the women, but he saw no form resembling hers. His heart beat more freely. The Athenian had then escaped, for she was too conspicuous to be forgotten. Night had again fallen upon the city, — a Syrian night, which is only a paler day; the stars were faint and veiled, and not a breath stirred the summits of the trees.

Parthenia had returned wearied to her couch, when her handmaid came weeping to tell her that Theodorus had been seized and hurried to prison. She rose instantly, and with prompt forethought assumed her dress of a Grecian priestess. As a Christian maiden she would have been seized and imprisoned. Then she scattered upon her beautiful hair the golden grasshoppers, to indicate that she was the daughter of Athens and entitled to the protection of Julian in the streets of Antioch.

Thus disguised, she reached the gate of the prison. There was nothing strange in this, for wherever there was suffering, there were the Christian women to soothe and alleviate.

As she reached the prison gate, she came suddenly upon the Jew, Cartophilus. He could scarcely speak from surprise. "Fair Athenian," at length he said, "I rejoice to see you thus, referring to her robe as priestess; but what can have brought your angelic presence into these abodes of guilt? At least accept such protection as a poor Jew can offer you."

"I incur no danger," she said. "Mercy is ever a passport to suffering."

The delicate Jew shuddered, for he began to perceive her errand.

It was a low and dark room devoted to the infamous purpose of torture, admitting light only through the roof, and at night by torches. The door turned upon rusty hinges, for Julian's short reign had been too humane to allow this prison to be used, and soon Parthenia stood like an angel of mercy among the dark, mysterious instruments.

Theodorus stood bound in the midst of the dark figures. "See," said the Jew, "that beautiful youth. He is like the young David or your own Apollo. Surely he is not a subject for the question. His frail and delicate limbs could bear no torture."

Parthenia became pale as ashes. She felt a deadly sickness, and came very near to swooning; but she rallied herself. "Can I not bear this," she said, "when to-morrow it may be my own fate?"

Theodorus's face wore an expression of joy, which changed to ecstasy when he saw Parthenia.

"I know these Christians," she said to the Jew; "they come to torture and to death, as others come to a bridal."

"Let me lead you hence," he said; "this is no place for woman, — no place for you!"

"Why, then, did I come here? Surely not to leave my friend in his agony?"

She stood at his side. The soft folds of her veil were laved in the cooling water, and she bound them gently on his brow. She raised her eyes and heart to heaven for strength, and then whispered in his ear, "O be strong, and God shall comfort thy heart!"

He smiled faintly. "Jesus is near me," he whispered; "his angels are about me!"

She bathed the bleeding lips. "Jesus is waiting to bless thee," she said; "God will give thee a crown of rejoicing, and a place at the right hand of the Father."

"Noble Athenian," said the Jew, "Theodorus is now beyond your care" (he had fainted); "come, let me conduct you hence."

Parthenia turned to the officer. "O, leave him in that blessed unconsciousness! I beseech you, wake him not again to pain and agony."

"Take care of yourself," said the brutal officer; "you have need, for Julian hates beautiful women. Besides, these Galileans feel no pain. These iron arms are to them like silken tresses, and these pincers give them the kisses of love. This boy will come from his downy couch, rejoicing like a bridegroom."

Parthenia shuddered, and the Jew again urged her departure.

At this moment, Theodorus revived, and turned his eyes towards her. "One of God's angels stood by me," he said. "Ah! she has not yet departed."

Parthenia gave cordials to his lips. "God is ever near you," she said; "you will wear the white robes of the martyr, and Jesus will bless you!"

"O," said he, "I am happy, too happy!" and again he swooned.

"It is too much!" said the Jew, and hastened from the prison.

"God has granted him an oblivion from pain," she said, turning to the officer. "O, I beseech you leave him in these cold, but pitying arms of death! Be merciful! He will never confess; you can wring nothing from him."

"No, by Jupiter," said the officer, "the spirit in this womanly boy is stronger than Hercules. It is thus with all these Galileans. In every prison in the Empire, there are men and women who will not open their lips till doomsday."

"The Emperor is merciful; he will thank you when his anger cools," urged Parthenia.

Her prayers were interrupted by the appearance of a detachment of the Emperor's guard, who entered without caution or ceremony. Two of them approached the Christian maiden, and respectfully signed her to follow them. Her friends among the crowd began to weep, but she was herself fearless, for she believed in the Emperor's friendship. The Jew had hastened from the prison to the palace, and in his interview with Julian had informed him of the scene he had just left; and the Emperor had given instant orders that Parthenia should be removed.

CHAPTER XXXI.

THE SUBTERRANEAN TEMPLE.

The night had become intensely dark, the torches being everywhere extinguished, and as Parthenia was hurried, between the two officers, through the street, she felt the night air blowing from the river. Presently, at the margin of the Orontes, a massive gate was opened, and as quickly closed behind her, as, accompanied by the two officers, she began to descend a path which led deep into the earth.

To the Athenian priestess all the mysteries of the heathen mythology were familiar, and she soon perceived that they were descending the secret path to the temple of Hecate. She knew, although she had never visited it, that in Antioch a temple, to which three hundred and sixty-five steps beneath the earth conducted, was consecrated to this dread Goddess, and that magical ceremonies were there resorted to, to frighten recent converts to the Christian religion, and induce them to renounce their new faith.

At length they reached the foot of the descent, and she was left alone. It seemed to be the object of whoever had led her there to weaken and terrify her mind, for she was left in profound darkness, and wholly unconscious of the nature of her prison. She extended her arms, touching every object, till she felt the cold marble of the altar, and traced above it the form of the dog-headed Goddess to whose worship it was consecrated. Then she felt secure. She knew that she was in the temple of a heathen Deity, and she offered a fervent prayer to the true God, the Universal Father, and to Christ, his Revealer to her heart. Then, wearied and exhausted, for she had not slept for two nights, she leaned upon the steps of the altar, and fell into deep slumber.

She had not reposed long when the sounds of sweet music mingled with her dreams. With difficulty she aroused herself from the heaviness of sleep to find the temple brilliantly illuminated, showing upon its walls incrustations of precious stones, and ivory, and gold, beside all the emblems of the triple Goddess of magic, and mistress of the lower world. Hecate was believed to wander by night along the dark places of the earth, seen only by dogs, whose baying announced her approach. She was worshipped as an averter of misfortune and a protector from the ills lurking in the darkness of night.

Behind the altar the Goddess stood in the form of a beautiful woman, the bust of polished marble of exquisite proportions, but surmounted by the head of a dog. This altar was covered with cates of various forms, and offerings partaking of the earth. In her years of darkness the Grecian maiden would have knelt and sought the protection of the Deity of the place, but now she knelt and blessed God that the darkness had passed away.

The music, which had approached and receded in exquisite strains, now ceased, and soon was heard the approach of footsteps, and the voices in various keys, both loud and low, of the dogs. A curtain in the remote part of the temple was lifted, and the priestess of Hecate appeared, followed by her canine attendants. Wrinkled and bent by the iron hand whose touch none can withstand, her head bound with the foliage of the oak, in which writhed living serpents, tamed by art, whose eyes glittered and whose tongues darted vivid flames, she scarcely deigned to notice Parthenia, but proceeded to prepare her altar and to make ready for her incantations and ceremonies.

Having finished her work of preparation, she came to the side of Parthenia, and whispered, "Have no fear! I know the secret wishes of your heart, and my art will soon reveal to you your future destiny, and that of the Empire also."

"I have no faith in your art," said Parthenia, coldly, "and I do not presume to connect my fate with that of the Empire."

"Are you wiser than those wise men who read the secrets of destiny in the stars?"

"Look at me! I wear the dress of the priestess, and I know all the sorceries of priests and the arts by which knavery imposes upon credulity."

"Yet there *is* an occult science that wrings from destiny the secrets of the future."

Saying this, she threw upon the altar a preparation of drugs which she had concealed in her robes, and the whole temple was instantly filled with a dense vapor, and from the altar rose spiral flames of vivid colors, while a sickening perfume, together with the vapor, weighed heavily upon the brain of Parthenia. She knew that this was produced by potent drugs, intended to dull the senses; she endeavored to free herself from the oppression, determining to keep all her powers of mind in clearness and activity.

"The bright star consecrated to Hecate, the dog-star, never lies," said the priestess, "and what has been revealed to the wise is, by our pictured art, revealed to the simple."

While she was speaking, the dense vapors gathered into a curtain on one side of the temple, and where the light diverged as in rays from a central sun, the curtain opened and a dim and distant landscape was revealed. By degrees the vapors cleared, and Parthenia saw more and more distinctly revealed a broad and splendid country, with vales and hills, bridges spanning a wide river, farms, villas, towns, and villages. In short, the whole Campagna of Rome, and the Imperial City itself, where the Grecian maiden had never been, but instantly knew as Rome in the distance. But the central object was a magnificent heathen temple, the area in front entirely filled by an immense procession, consisting of the crowded congregation of all nations. There were priests and priestesses of every Deity, in festive robes, with all the emblems of their worship, in all their highest prosperity.

She saw that the temple was dedicated to Minerva, the Goddess of Rome, and that the splendid festival which was taking place in the capital of the Empire was to indicate that the heathen worship was re-established in all its splendor, even there.

Her eyes by a strange fascination were riveted to the scene, and to the two figures ascending, at the head of the procession, the steps of the temple.

She saw that one was Julian in his robes as Sovereign Pontiff; but whose was the veiled female figure at his side? She looked again. The breeze had blown aside the veil, and she saw beneath, her own features wearing a joyous and excited expression.

A shade of scorn now mingled with her astonishment. Could the Emperor have ordered this strange phantasmagoria? and what could have been his object? Lost in conjecture, she turned from it and covered her face with her veil.

A few moments passed, and a vivid flash of light compelled her to look up. The Emperor himself stood near her. He was dressed with unusual care, in his gorgeous purple robes, and in other respects he was carefully adorned and perfumed. All historians unite in admitting the extreme beauty and majesty of Julian's head. His eyes, flashing like diamonds, had also a penetrating glance, and a soft and dreamy light, that made his fixed expression, when turned upon one, irresistible.

Parthenia in an instant rose to her feet. Was the Emperor also a part of the illusion, or was he really at her side? The color flashed crimson on her cheek and brow, and then she became deadly pale. It was partly fear that blanched her cheek, for though she had reason to believe in the friendship of Julian, she had not been deaf to the thousand stories she had heard, of the blood he had shed, and the sacrifice of life, both of young women and children, in his researches after the principle of life. Christians delighted to repeat stories of his cruelty, which could not fail to be recalled when she found herself alone with him in this underground temple, where no cry of hers could reach a human ear.

"Beautiful Greek," said the Emperor, "the Immortal Gods protect and bless you!"

"Pardon me, Sire, I believe but in one God, who alone possesses the power to bless or to injure."

"Do you not believe in the dread Goddess to whom this temple is consecrated,—she who has just now uplifted a corner of the dark curtain of the future?"

Parthenia looked steadily at the Emperor, and his eyes fell at the calm glance of her own. "It was beneath the character of a noble prince," she said, "to order so puerile a device to impose on the senses of a simple woman."

Julian believed in the power of the Infernal Deities, and in Hecate,—in divination and in auguries. How far he understood the deceptions of the priests is not known.

"She in whose temple we stand rules the destiny of mortals, as the unerring minister of Zeus, in whose hands are the issues of all things."

"You forget, Sire, that you are speaking to one who has been admitted to all the secrets of the heathen necromancy, and whose senses are not easily deceived."

"Thy faith in the Immortal Gods may have been for a moment shaken, but it can be as easily resumed as the Athenian virgin resumes the spotless robe of the priestess of Pallas. Is not Hecate the universal mother?"

"The earth is indeed our mother, and with an equal love she bestows her gifts upon all her children."

"Alas, fair Greek! have you lost that ancient and beautiful faith in the living spirits who breathe in all the elements, — the lovely beings who dwell in the caverns of the earth, who give beauty to the living groves, who breathe enchantment over falling waters and leaping streams, who whisper in the evening breeze, and with unseen hands lead on the star of love, who roam through the groves, and whose touch revives the flowers, as their breath renews their perfumes? Have you renounced this lovely faith in unseen beings?"

"Even then, Sire, I felt the emptiness and void of our religion. The beautiful forms of our worship — perfect, I acknowledge, in their outward grace — contain within but bitter ashes; the fervency and calm prayer of the Christians, the enthusiasm of their faith, are only less sublime than their daily actions."

"Can you, doubting our own beautiful myths, believe the vulgar and puerile fables of the Galileans?"

"Pardon me, Sire, I am an ignorant woman, and I cannot reason upon these transcendent subjects. I believe in one God only, who is a spirit everywhere present, and whose providence watches over the destiny of mortals."

"You believe also in that Jesus, the suborner of men, the companion of thieves and prostitutes, who was never heard of till within three hundred years, and who did nothing in his whole life but heal a few who were lame and sick? Compare him with Æsculapius, and he sinks into insignificance."

Parthenia became crimson; her voice trembled. "Can the Emperor," she said, "despising the incapacity of woman, condescend to instruct her, or to punish her errors?"

"Fair Greek, report has done me less than justice. Would you esteem me more if I had been subdued by every woman to whom Venus had lent her zone, or if I had trembled before the cruel eye of Constantia? Noble women I have ever honored. Was not Eusebia my friend, whom I reverenced in my heart's core, scarcely less than Basilina, my mother?"

"Ah! Basilina was a Christian, and her lips taught you the tender precepts of Jesus. Ah, Sire, why did you renounce them?"

"Had all Christians been like Basilina, perhaps — But alas! look back at first to the bloody tragedy in which all my family perished by Christian hands; then to the haughty and imbecile Christian eunuchs, who alone controlled the mind of Constantius and held my destiny in their wicked counsels; the Christian prelates steeped in hypocrisy and living in ostentatious luxury; the Christian Church usurping all honors, grasping at all emoluments, and shedding the blood of others with the ferocity of wild beasts; — how could I hesitate between a religion which produced such results, and the revival of our ancient venerable worship?"

"Sire, you forget the Jewish precept about pouring new wine into old bottles."

"There is another Jewish command, 'Thou shalt honor thy father and mother.' The *past* is our mother. The venerable old religion of long-past ages is our father and our mother, while this new Galilean superstition is scarcely three hundred years old."

"I cannot argue. I am a woman who can only

feel, and the new religion satisfies the longings of the heart. Jesus says, 'Come unto me and I will give you peace.' Pardon me, Sire, it is true; I have felt the peace which is promised to those who believe in him."

A crimson spot burned on either cheek of Julian. He began to feel the awkwardness of his position, arguing with a woman, almost with a young girl. But why had he sought this interview? Why had she been conveyed to this under-ground temple? There could be but one answer to the question. The Prince had ever retained a fond remembrance of Athens. He wept when he was compelled to leave it. Parthenia had seen him weep, and he had preserved enshrined in his heart the fair image of the Greek maiden as the only woman he could have loved, the only being who had begun to move his heart to love. The memory of love is dear to every man, even if it has been unfortunate or fruitless. Like the reflected sunlight upon the morning of life, it lingers with a sweeter beam than that of the gairish day. A man thinks better of himself for having loved, and Julian remembered his residence in Athens as the period when he had most truly lived. It had been wrested from him by the order to return to the court and to marry Helena,—Helena, who was now in her unhonored grave.

Julian's enemies say that he was never known to feel the softer passions, and that his ideas of love were taken from Ovid and Juvenal. He had never dreamed of anything sacred in woman. That Christian idea had but just begun to penetrate through the sensualism of Heathenism, and to form a halo around the early virgin martyrs, which culminated a few centuries afterwards in the supreme holiness and worship of the mother of Christ.

The beautiful Athenian was the only woman that he would raise to the throne, and that not altogether because he loved or esteemed her, but because she had been the priestess of Pallas Athena, and doubtless would aid him in giving brilliancy to the heathen worship, and would add all her own grace and beauty to the ceremonial of religion. He could not believe that her Christianity was more than a passing fancy, which would be erased and dissipated by the splendid prospect before her. Beside, there had been Christian Empresses; and could not she also renounce all but the most secret allegiance to her faith, and aid him in the outward show of another worship?

"Noble Greek," he began, — but as he looked at her, the proud eye of Julian sank beneath the celestial blue of hers, so calm, so pure, that he could read no worldly ambition there, no passion or weakness which encouraged him to go on. Still, he could not go back. "Noble Greek," he said again, "I will not plead for Julian, for the Emperor,—his happiness is of small account; but for our ancient worship, for our beautiful temples, for our gorgeous ceremonies, for our art and poetry. I would plead with Parthenia to unite her efforts with those of the Emperor, to bring them all back to their ancient lustre and to their place in the heart of the Empire. It needs but—"

Parthenia had turned deadly pale. "Sire, you forget that I am a Christian."

"Forget? No! but what is the superstition of a day, which had its birth among a few fishermen of that obscure Judæa, in comparison with our ancient religion, which was born before the constellations were named? Let the noble Parthenia be persuaded to assume again her office and her robes of priestess, and all that is impure or unholy shall be banished from our worship; the reign of beauty and of truth shall come again; the altars shall bear only faithful offerings; victory shall again crown the song of heroes; soul-filled games and dances shall again enliven the festivals. The groves shall echo with the joy of happy hearts, and Apollo shall linger to prolong every hour of light. To restore this reign of the Gods upon the earth, I would, like Latona's son, take myself the shepherd's staff, and go forth to tend the flocks of Admetus."

Parthenia remained silent, with her eyes cast down, and the Emperor continued: —

"Life has been to me but a solitary, unloved path; and now, when I stand on the summit, it is but an icy pinnacle; but as I look forward, with thee at my side, it is all an Elysian stream, peaceful with the shadows of wisdom, gay with the sunlit ripples of joy. Let us forget, fair Parthenia, all that has filled up the interval since the lovely sky of Athens bent over us in the garden of the Academy, before the iron hand of Nemesis tore me from thee."

"The hand of Nemesis still holds her iron sceptre," said Parthenia.

"Fairest," said Julian, with a smile that seemed to illumine the temple, "love shall draw out the thread upon which are strung the golden years, and the beauty of our lives shall lull the Parcæ to sleep."

He had opened a glimpse into the paradise which the Grecian and Christian maiden, in moments of joy, had alike dreamed of. Could she take the first enchanted step? Alas, no! The two-edged sword of conscience barred the entrance. She turned from it, — and a momentary, but almost insupportable, pang of grief shot through her heart.

"Not even Nemesis can turn back the hours that we let slip from us. Alas, Sire! thy hand had power even then to stay our destiny, when Parthenia knew no wish but thine."

"Ungrateful! to remind me of him who held his cruel foot even then upon my neck, and whose spies would have given neither you nor me a second day of love," said Julian, turning pale with anger.

"Ah, Julian! I cannot bear thy anger."

It was the first time she had ever called him Julian; he was instantly softened, and said, "Anger shall never come between thee and me! Say but one word,—the word that is now trembling upon thy lips,—because in thy heart thou canst not hate Julian." And he turned upon her those eyes whose softest expression was irresistible.

It was impossible for the Grecian maiden not to understand the meaning of the Emperor. She was a woman,—she loved Julian, and ambition was not dead in her breast. To be Empress was a dazzling elevation,—yes, there had been Christian Empresses,—why not another? A violent conflict was going on within her, which turned her cheek pale as ashes, and caused her to tremble in every fibre of her frame. She loved him, but it was a sin to love him; and after some moments of silence, a fervent prayer for help was answered in her soul. Tears trembled upon her eyelids; she raised the cross which hung upon her neck to her lips, and kissed it fervently.

Julian understood the sign. The cross had once power over him, but now a slight shade of contempt mingled with the deep feeling of disappointment. Still he saw the tears, which had swelled beyond her eyelids and stood in two large drops; they encouraged him to urge his suit. He knelt at her feet, yes, the proud Julian knelt. But Parthenia had now recovered from her embarrassment. She saw that the Emperor sought her more as an ornament for the pageantry of his worship, than for herself alone. Her heart beat calmly again.

"Rise, Sire," she said, "that position becomes neither you nor me." At the same time she rose herself, and retreated a few steps from him. "Sire," she said, "I am deeply grateful; there have been hours in life when it would have filled me with overflowing joy to yield to a wish of Julian's; but now all is changed within and around me. That he whom the Emperor despises, that Christ has lived and died, and that I have believed in him, is all the world to me. To know and believe this is life and joy! It is all the wisdom and all the happiness that I can now desire. That thou canst neither understand nor believe as I do, opens a gulf between thee and me wider than the Empire."

"Ah, Parthenia, I hoped we might unite for one great object, and by one harmonious effort set the whole Empire to divinest music!"

"Sire, the only real good is the life which Christ has given us; the only evil is separation from God."

"The time has been when the Athenian maiden would not have turned away from the pleading of an Emperor, when he held in his hand the gift of the Empire," he said.

Parthenia, who had remained pale as death, now became crimson. "Shall I gain the whole world and lose my own soul? What would you give in exchange for my soul? O Sire, would you rob me of peace here and of felicity hereafter?"

"What do we know of felicity hereafter? The present is all that we can grasp; alas! we let the past slip from us. Is not a life of ecstatic joy on earth worth all the uncertain chimerical hopes of the future?"

"Sire, I am a Christian! Even at this moment the Christian subjects of the Emperor are suffering torture and death. The voice of their woe cannot penetrate these vaults, but it pierces the ear of God. Shall I unite with their enemy?" She paused, for she saw Julian's eye flash with anger. She could have braved death with the other martyrs, under the excitement of numbers and the inspiration of enthusiasm; but alone, in the night, in this subterranean darkness, her woman's timidity returned. She became again white as death, and trembled in every limb. Not that she feared any personal violence; O no! she knew Julian better; but she feared that she might betray her faith, and yield too much to the intimidation of his presence and character.

He also began to feel the futility of his efforts and the absurdity of his position with regard to the Athenian maiden. He gave the sign, and the temple became instantly dark and filled with the perfumes intended to deaden or intoxicate the senses.

Parthenia knew their power, and strove successfully against them. At length they were dissipated, and the pure light of the lamps, rekindled as it were by magic, revealed only the priestess and herself as occupants of the temple.

CHAPTER XXXII.

THE JEW.

ALTHOUGH the information conveyed to Julian by Cartophilus had caused, as I have said, the removal of Parthenia from witnessing the agony of Theodorus, the Emperor had summoned the noble Jew to an interview for a very different purpose.

Before entering upon his expedition against Persia, Julian wished to put in train his great design of rebuilding the temple of Jerusalem. This enterprise regarded nothing less than the destruction, at the same time, of the Christian religion, and the discredit of the ancient Jewish prophecies respecting it. Could he succeed in rebuilding that temple, of which the prophecies had declared "that one stone upon another should not stand," he would also weaken the prophecies respecting the coming of Christ, and thus the edifice of Christianity, deprived of the foundation of Judaism, would crumble to the ground.

"Noble Cartophilus," said Julian, "I see that you retain your Jewish costume; why is your ancient worship neglected? I approve your Jewish rites."

"Surely the Emperor is not ignorant that only in our temple on Mount Zion are we permitted to sacrifice."

"Certainly, I should know; I have been studying your ancient books, and I have learnt that the time has come to summon the wanderers of your nation to return to their ancient temple upon Mount Zion."

The Jew looked keenly at the Emperor, but he only bowed in answer.

"Are you not ready to gather again to your ancient city your oppressed and scattered people?"

"Jehovah knows my heart," said the Jew; "but the Jewish people are everywhere dispersed, everywhere the objects of contempt and hatred. Years must pass—"

"Listen!" interrupted Julian; "I have found in the papers of my predecessor new designs for taxing your people. I have cast them into the fire, and I will now release them from the excessive tribute they pay into my treasury."

"Sire!"

"Hush! The condition is, that you obtain through your prayers that I return victorious from my Persian war. I will then rebuild the walls of Jerusalem; and the holy temple, after which your whole nation sighs, shall rise again in threefold beauty."

"And will your Majesty go with us there to worship the Great Jehovah in his holy temple?"

"I would willingly return thanks in your temple to the Great Being, whether he be called Jehovah or Jupiter; but I could never place Zion above Olympus."

"If you believe in one Great Being, the everlasting source of good, I see not how you can fail to worship our Jehovah."

"Yes, but I believe that the Great Being has formed other Deities, which fill up the great intermediate scale between him and us. Helios, the God of the sun, is the revealed emblem of the Supreme God, and the object of our devout worship."

"You forget our great command, 'Thou shalt have no other Gods before me.'"

"There are various living ideals in the various Gods, who make themselves known to us as beneficent beings."

"The Christians say that God is made known only through his Son."

"Yes, and deny the great Helios, the living, animated, spiritual, beneficent image of the Supreme Father."

"But let us put aside theology till I return victorious from Persia Now, noble Jew, my dearly loved Alypius and yourself are appointed to summon from every part of the Empire workmen to Jerusalem, and I will give you orders upon my treasurers for the funds to rebuild the temple in all its former magnificence and grandeur."

"Sire! these sums will be immense."

"Faint-hearted! Cannot the Empire in all its provinces furnish funds for one temple? Nemesis be propitious, and we shall succeed."

"Jehovah be on our side," said the Jew, "and we cannot fail!"

Cartophilus was too shrewd not to penetrate the thin disguise of the Emperor. It was no love for their nation, no wish to restore their temple, which prompted this benevolence. The present scattered condition of the Jews was a perpetual testimony to the truth of Christianity. Could the ancient prophecies be falsified, the whole would fall together.

CHAPTER XXXIII.

THE CHRISTIANS.

THE prisons of Antioch were crowded with Christians of every age. The Church had enjoyed a season of repose since the persecution under Diocletian, and although it had apparently become supine and luxurious, when the persecution came, it was aroused as with the voice of the trumpet, calling the sleeper to awake, the rich and luxurious to shake off their fetters of flowers, and the indolent to put on the armor of steel for the battle. It is true that many succumbed and yielded to the rewards which almost always followed an apostasy; but the infamy of such a course caused many to return.

A severe struggle took place in the breast of Phorion. He had never been a very zealous Christian. A dreamer, he lovèd the philosophy of Plato; and had Christ not lived, he would have been happy as a Platonist. He was one now, with the added faith that Christ had lived and died. Under the repeated prayers and entreaties of his mother, he examined the Christian Scriptures, and admired and loved their touching histories; but he denied that Christ had revealed any new truths. That he "brought life and immortality to light," he said, was only a reinforcing of what had been revealed in the Jewish Scriptures. He had formed for himself a faith, in which he combined with the Jehovah of the Hebrews, the united truth and beauty of Platonism, the self-denial and tenderness of Jesus.

But the time had come when he could no longer dwell in an idealized religion; when the stern question was asked, "Is Jesus or Apollo your God? If the latter, scatter this incense upon his altar, and offer the daily prayer to his statue as it stands in the glorious temple."

To declare himself a Christian would, he thought, separate him from Olympia: he was not prepared for her decisive act, to throw herself into the power of the Prefect, deny her country's Gods, and go with him to prison and to death! With such examples of faith and womanly tenderness as his mother and Olympia, could he hesitate? No, his luxurious abode, his beautiful collection of works of art, his Sybarite habits of ease and luxury, all were left, and he went to the squalid and crowded prison where his mother had already been conveyed.

Exhausted, but exultant, suffering, yet full of joy, Monica lay upon her bed of pain in the upper room of one of the prisons of Antioch. Every stroke of the scourge had drawn from her, with the blood that followed, almost a shout of joy that she had been found worthy to suffer for her Lord. And now, as she lay faint upon her couch, she saw, or fancied that she saw, the lovely faces of angels clustering around her, and that she heard the blessed words, "Well done, thou faithful servant! enter into the joy of thy Lord."

A sombre twilight was admitted through the high grated window of the prison. Some scattered rays fell upon the pallid face and compressed lips of her son, Phorion, who had, as I intimated above, obtained the favor of sharing the same prison with his mother.

"Are you easier now, dear mother?" he asked.

"I feel no pain, my son! This wooden couch is a downy bed, and balm has been poured upon the wounds of the scourge. O my son! we can only rejoice that we have been found worthy to suffer stripes and imprisonment for the cause of our Saviour. Think of what he suffered for us, and our pain should turn to a song of joy."

He could not rejoice with his mother, but reminded her that Olympia would soon be there. "My mother," he said, "receive her to your heart. How intense must have been that love for us which induced her not only to declare herself a Christian, —a Christian in loving acts she has always been,— but to throw herself into the power of the Prefect, that she might share and soften our captivity. Dear mother, your heart is not still shut against her?"

Monica was silent. Phorion received this silence as consent; he knelt by the side of the couch, and pressed upon her already stiffened fingers a grateful kiss for what he chose to accept as her consent to his marriage with Olympia, which she had constantly opposed upon the ground that Olympia was a Greek and a Pagan, and that her son's highest duty must be to the Church, to serve her as a monk, to sacrifice all family affections to the vows of celibacy.

Olympia had not been imprisoned with the others, because the officers of Julian, supposing her to belong to the old faith, had left her with her children. But she had sought the dwelling of the Prefect, and obtained leave to share, accompanied by her two infants, the prison where all was hidden that made life to her. Her baptism, which she urged as the seal of her faith, and the ceremony of her marriage, the seal upon her vows of love, were to take place at the same time, through the presence of an aged bishop, who was also a tenant of the same prison.

She entered, bringing, as such lovely natures are endowed with the power to do, a flood of mental sunshine into the dark and gloomy prison. She wore the blue robe and white veil, the usual dress of married women at their Christian baptism, which she would not afterwards exchange for a marriage robe. The only witnesses of this betrothal to Christian duty, and renewal of vows long since accepted and fulfilled, were the Christians in the prison. The aged bishop, whose benediction was all they needed, bore already deeply scarred upon his forehead the marks of a former persecution, and his bared temples were ready for the crown of martyrdom.

"Dearest," said Phorion, "do you know that, in placing your hand in mine with the marriage vow, you share my fortune of privation and saddest poverty. Go back, beloved, to your father in Corinth; these babes shall go with and cheer you."

She looked earnestly in his face; tears quivered on her eyelids. "Silence," she said; "am I here to desert you again? Did I only love you in joy and happiness? and am I not your wife for sorrow and distress? Shall I leave you now, when your anguish makes you need me most?"

"Olympia," he said, "look upon these children; they may soon beg their bread in the streets of Antioch, and my steps may lead us down the dark path of a cruel death!"

"If they beg, I will beg with them, and rejoice in having been the wife of Phorion. I am here because I am yours, and I will never leave you."

The water and the betrothal ring were also there, and Olympia was baptized into sorrow, and wedded to him whose steps perhaps would lead her to martyrdom. But whatever her fate, it could not be disjoined from her love. She was not made for heroic deeds, or for "palm and crown"; the passion of her nature was centred in wife and motherhood; "in that she must live, or have no life." Whatever heroic deed this passion prompted, it was easy for her to do. She was here because she would not be separated from Phorion. She was here because she was determined to save him. How, she could not tell; but save him she must, or die with him.

The order that the Emperor had given to the Prefect, to exempt the Athenian maiden from all share in the persecution, had been strictly observed; but the little party of her friends in the prison, being ignorant of this order, were full of anxiety and grief when she did not return from her agonized watch by the suffering Theodorus. How great was their joy then, when, after her release from the temple of Hecate, she discovered the prison of their detention, and entered just as the preparations were completed for the baptism of Olympia.

Monica, who had ceased to speak, and whose eyes were already darkened by the films of death, instantly knew her voice, and whispered the name she had taken at her baptism. "Mary," she said, "come here, that I may bless you before I die!"

Parthenia informed them of Julian's clemency towards her, but was silent respecting the subterranean temple, and her forced nocturnal visit, as well as her interview with him.

Night and quiet at length returned, and sleep that comes to the most wretched hushed the sounds of anguish in the prison; and now the three friends knelt around the white-haired man, while with trembling lips and unsteady fingers he poured upon the beautiful head of Olympia the baptismal drops, and afterwards placed again upon her finger the ring which had been that of betrothal, now converted to the holy rite of marriage.

Monica had watched with dying eyes, from her couch of pain, the whole touching ceremony. She felt at last, with humble resignation, that it was the will of the Highest that Phorion, instead of devoting himself to the Church as a priest or monk, should bend to the humbler duties of a Christian father, and that, if he could not wear the martyr's crown, he must bow beneath the Christian's cross. Beside, her moments were numbered. She was no longer young, and her woman's frame yielded beneath the strokes of a scourge which was held by no timid hand. As the night advanced and the shadows gathered in that prison chamber, they veiled the departing spirit, and when her children knelt around her they heard the last whispered word, thanking God for martyrdom.

Olympia had become a Christian, and though willing to suffer for those she loved, she had no ambition to become a martyr. All her efforts were now bent to save her loved ones from the loathsome suffering of a crowded prison. In this purpose Parthenia came to her aid.

The order which the Emperor had given to the officers of his guard to convey her to the underground temple of Hecate remained accidentally in her hand. Fortunately, from her long connection with the heathen ceremonies, the intricacies and secret avenues of their subterranean temples were perfectly known to her, as well as the passwords and cabalistic signs of their secret associations. It would not be impossible, therefore, to convey Phorion to the underground concealment of the temple, till Julian had departed upon his Persian expedition. Olympia was in no danger, as it was unknown outside the prison that she had embraced Christianity.

Phorion consented at length to assume the concealment of the robe of the Athenian priestess, while the maiden disguised her graceful form beneath the manly cloak.

The night was intensely dark, and although the streets of Antioch are said at this time to have been as light as day with numerous torches and lamps, the obscurity near the steps which led to the temple favored their concealment. They heard the rushing of the Orontes, and Parthenia trembled in every limb when she presented to the keeper of the gate leading to the underground temple the order of Julian. The well-known signature of the Emperor was easily recognized, and, as the gate closed behind them, Phorion could not avoid a shudder of apprehension that his eyes had taken leave for ever of the blessed light of heaven.

CHAPTER XXXIV.

JULIAN DEPARTS FOR PERSIA.

THE longer the Emperor dwelt in Antioch, the more he repented having chosen this city as the place of his residence. His manner of life—laborious, serious, divided between the civil and the military service and affairs of state, his hours of relaxation given to study, or to his friends—appeared like a censure of the public dissipation and of the idleness of the citizens. His decided aversion for all spectacles caused the public pleasures to languish. He had hardly shown himself at the circus, and then with an air of such discontent that he seemed to reproach those who attended there for this condescension to their tastes. He was, they said, a misanthrope, a savage, whom nothing could tame.

Libanius, who appreciated and admired the noble qualities of the Emperor, and, like a true friend, often blamed, was yet often obliged to defend him.

"See," said one of the citizens, "these preparations for war; is the young boaster sufficiently firm on the throne to undertake conquests? — as if he had not enough enemies at home, without seeking them in foreign lands."

"The army," said Libanius, "adore the Emperor; they would support him if he conquered the great globe itself."

"He has put one world in combustion," said the citizen, "persecuting the Christians, and he will expose himself to certain ruin by this imprudent and premature expedition."

"The Emperor trusts in his star and in the favor of Nemesis," said a citizen, with a sneer.

"Intoxicated with success and pride in what he calls 'the favor of the Gods,' he deserves a reverse," said another.

"Ah!" said Libanius, "those who tax him with imprudence would be the first to accuse him of weakness or indifference if he remained in repose. At least you must believe in his clemency, since you say these things to me, who may well not spare you at my next interview with the Emperor. Nothing will satisfy you; you blame equally what he does, and what he does not do; even the drought and the sterility of the season is the fault of the Emperor!"

"At least you must admit that famine has followed him from Constantinople to Antioch," said the other.

"Ah yes! the fountains are dry since he profaned them," continued a senator.

"You must admit," said Libanius, "that the means which the Emperor pursued to alleviate the distress was a mistake, from which he was the greatest sufferer."

He had, in fact, imported a great quantity of wheat, which he sold at a price much below its value, hoping thus to open the granaries of the rich merchants also, at a lower price. They, however, were not so disinterested as Julian; they bought up his own wheat at its low price, and sold it again to the poor, with their own, at a greatly augmented cost, and thus increased the distress of the poor.

Julian, justly incensed, ordered the whole senate to prison. Libanius, anxious for the true honor of the Emperor, hastened into his presence to plead against so arbitrary a proceeding.

The same citizen accosted him again. "Friend," said he, "methinks you are too near the river Orontes to plead so boldly with the Emperor."

"The Emperor is no tyrant," said Libanius, "and such surmises as that only dishonor him."

When he reached the palace, however, he found

the Emperor less lenient than usual. He urged that the whole senate merited his just indignation.

"True," said Libanius, "they merit the indignation of the Emperor, but the Emperor should show the world that he can discriminate between offences against himself and crimes against the state."

"Ah, my friend," said he, embracing him, "you are the true guardian of my honor." And he instantly gave the order to restore the senators to their homes.

Julian had before this time incurred the bitter hatred of the Antiochians, which he repaid by the most biting contempt. In a city where the arts of luxury and effeminacy were honored, the serious and manly virtues of the Emperor could be the subject of ridicule alone. Fashion was the only law, pleasure the only pursuit, and the effeminate Orientals could neither imitate nor admire the severe simplicity which Julian always maintained. During the Saturnalia the streets of the city resounded with indecent songs, in which they derided the laws, the religion, the personal conduct, and even the beard of the Emperor. A tyrant might have proscribed the lives and fortunes of the citizens of Antioch; a milder sentence might have deprived the capital of the East of its honors and its privileges; but Julian, endowed with quick sensibility, and possessed of absolute power, refused himself the gratification of revenge, and retaliated only by composing, under the title of the Misopogon, or "Enemy of the Beard," an ironical confession of his own faults, and a severe satire of the effeminacy and licentiousness of the Antiochians. This satire was publicly exposed on the gates of the palace, and Julian then prepared to leave Antioch for ever. But though he could laugh, he could not forgive, and he appointed them a governor worthy only of such subjects.

When it was urged that the governor he had appointed did not merit the office, "I know it well," said the Emperor, "but the Antiochians deserve to obey a tyrant."

The senate and the people followed the Emperor outside the gates, praying him to forgive the past and to return to them.

Julian, pointing to his friend Libanius, said: "I see that you rely upon this just man to restore you to my favor; you count upon sending him to me after every fault, to beg for your forgiveness and to reinstate you in my favor. But you do not deserve that I should leave him with you. Though I bid him adieu at present, I shall summon him to follow me." Then the Emperor and his friend embraced each other tenderly, and Libanius melted into tears.

The army of Julian had already filed towards the Euphrates. They dispersed themselves in different places, whence they could unite when the Emperor appeared.

On leaving Antioch he took the road to Litarbe, and arrived the next day at Berœa, that city commended in the Acts of the Apostles for the readiness with which they became Christian. The senate of this city were nearly all believers in Christianity, and the chief of this senate had just cast his son out of his house because the latter had embraced the religion of the Emperor.

Julian invited father and son to sup with him, and placing one on each side of himself upon the couch where they supped, "Ah," said he, addressing himself to the father, "it appears unjust to me to compel the conscience. I do not compel you to follow my religion, why should you compel your son to follow yours?"

"How, my lord! do you open your royal lips in favor of this villain, this enemy of the true God, who prefers a lie to the truth?"

"Softly, softly, my friend! let us put aside invectives." Then, turning to the boy, he said, "You see I can do nothing with your father; I must take his place, and be a father to you in his stead."

Sapor, against whom Julian's preparations were directed, was a prince of an insupportable arrogance and pride, which, however, he was able, with a sufficient motive, to subordinate to his interests. His craft equalled his pride. Notwithstanding his hatred against the Romans and the superiority he had maintained through the reign of Constantius, Sapor would have consented to make peace had he been left master of the conditions; but Julian, possessed by the thirst of conquest, had resolved to add to the number of princes he had conquered this "king of kings, placed among the stars and brother of the sun and the moon."

As the Emperor's finances were exhausted by his immense preparations, in order to support this war he established a tax upon all those who would not sacrifice to the Pagan Gods; he intended to employ the money of the Christians to conquer Persia, and the leisure which this conquest would procure him to destroy the Christians afterwards.

Two great roads conducted into Persia. One leading to and passing the Tigris, the other through Assyria, along the banks of the Euphrates. Julian had collected immense magazines upon both routes. Having decided to pass the Tigris himself, he left upon the banks of the Euphrates, to defend Mesopotamia, thirty thousand of the *élite* of the army, under the two bravest of his generals. This army was to join him before the walls of Ctesiphon, the capital of Persia.

After passing the river that divided the Persian Empire from the Roman territory, the Emperor ascended a height from which he looked down upon his immense army, sixty-five thousand strong, more numerous than any previous Emperor had ever led against his enemy. The broad basin of the Euphrates was covered by his fleet, which was to accompany this army to the heart of Assyria, stored with provisions, medicines, engines and machines, flat-bottomed boats to form bridges for crossing rivers, in short, everything which the wisdom or the humanity of Julian could suggest for the comfort of his army. Among the incredible quantity of provisions there was nothing for luxury or pleasure. He had embarked a very large supply of biscuit and vinegar, but a string of camels loaded with exquisite wines and luxuries he sent back, saying, "Take away these poisoned sources of luxury and debauch; a soldier should drink no wine that he has not taken from the enemy; and for myself, I shall live upon the food of the common soldier."

After the river was passed by the whole army, upon a bridge of boats, the Emperor ordered the bridge to be destroyed, thus leaving no resource behind him for the faithless or faint-hearted.

There were two classes of men attached to the army, who were a constant source of irritation to Julian, and with neither of which could he dispense. These were the soothsayers and the philosophers. The soothsayers everywhere found prognostics of misfortune; the philosophers, despising these, relied only upon physical science. The first alleged their books, and the rules of their art; the second dared not attack the rules, but disputed upon their application, and opposed to superstition the experience of wisdom. In the last extremity, Julian was found, notwithstanding his superstition, to rely upon the philosophers.

The army, animated by their own courage, and full of esteem for their commander, did not need an address; but Julian, upon passing the dividing river, ascended a mound of turf, and made an oration to the army, exciting them to the most heroic ardor, especially the legions who had accompanied the Emperor from Gaul, and who now surpassed all others in attachment to his person. The oration was closed by a donation of one hundred and thirty pieces of silver to each soldier, and at break of day the whole army advanced into the territory of the enemy.

It is by no means the object of this book to describe the conquests of Julian. An epic poem might be written upon the campaign in Persia, so full is it of spirited episodes and miracles of heroism. Julian was himself never absent from the post of danger, darting with the rapidity of lightning in every direction where aid was needed. At the centre, which he commanded in person; at the head, where was his standard; in the rear-guard, preventing all sedition; soothing by his caressing manners and air of kindness all disputes and differences, but assuming when necessary an authority which quelled at once all discontent. He saw everything with his own eyes, and trusted nothing to report. All ambuscades and snares of the enemy were investigated by himself, exposing continually his own person, but guarded and cherished by the soldiers, every one of whom would have sacrificed his life for his beloved general.

The sieges conducted by the Emperor were often distinguished for their humanity. But in one instance, after long-continued labor and extensive mining, the city of Maogamalcha was taken, where the victorious army like a torrent inundated the territory, and put every inhabitant to the sword. The taking of this city required miracles almost of daring and perseverance. Julian's vanity, which had till then been little gratified, was now excited. "At last," said he, "there is work for the sophists of Syria; this exploit is worthy to exercise the eloquence of Libanius."

He distributed crowns of laurel to those among his soldiers who had distinguished themselves, making their eulogy in the presence of the whole army. After having divided the booty among his soldiers, reserving for himself three pieces of gold which he cherished as souvenirs, they brought him a little fellow, both deaf and dumb, whose guardians had been killed, and who instantly attached himself to Julian with the tenacity which such unfortunate beings often display.

This little mute made himself understood by signs with the utmost facility and grace, and he soon won the favor and love of the Prince by the spirited and delicate meaning he continued to give to his mute and caressing signs.

The Prince was amusing himself with his little captive, when certain of his officers craved admittance. They wished to present to him female captives of rare beauty taken from among the princesses of Persia.

Julian declined accepting the gift.

"Admit them only to your presence, Sire," said one of the officers, "they will be proud of subduing the Emperor, and you will not allow such grace and beauty to be assigned to meaner hands."

"Why should I expose myself to an influence more dangerous than all the snares of the enemy?"

"Does the Emperor admit that he could become the captive of beauty?" asked the officer.

"Why not? The greatest conquerors have thus been conquered, and philosophers have submitted to wear the chains of beauty. No, I will not see them!"

Upon another occasion, after the capture of a very strong place, Julian mounted the tribunal to thank his army, promising a moderate donative of a hundred pieces of silver. He heard upon every side murmurs of discontent; the sum appeared too moderate. The Prince instantly assumed that majestic but indignant air which became him well, and continued his harangue thus: —

"There are the Persians! Behold the Persians in the midst of opulence and luxury! You have only to enrich yourselves! The Republic is ruined, since unworthy ministers have persuaded their princes to purchase from the Barbarians a shameless peace, that they may have liberty to return to their pleasures. Hope nothing from the country; the finances are in disorder; the provinces deserted; the cities exhausted. For myself, of all my ancestral estates, there remains to me but an intrepid soul. An Emperor who esteems virtue only need not blush to avow his poverty. It is great to resemble Fabricius, and look upon glory as the only treasure. Here are glory and riches presented to your acceptance, provided you confide in my care and in the leading of the Gods.

"But if you yield to the spirit of mutiny, and pretend to dictate to me, go and renew the infamy of your ancient seditions! For myself, I shall die, as I am, Emperor! but full of contempt for this perishable life, which a fever may cut off in a day. Or at least, should I live, I shall leave *you!* We have here, and I have the honor to say it, many generals of singular merit; profound in every circumstance of war; capable of commanding, and of making themselves obeyed!"

This discourse, in which there prevailed a noble indifference mingled with modesty and pride, changed their murmurs into protestations of obedience, and with one voice raised even to the skies the authority of Julian, and the nobleness of his sentiments.

At length the patience and valor of Julian had triumphed over all obstacles that opposed his march to the gates of Ctesiphon, the capital of Persia. The city had the reputation of being impregnable, and Julian felt himself too feeble to attempt anything till the arrival of the thirty thousand troops which he had left in Mesopotamia. He defied the enemy to hazard a battle before the walls of Ctesiphon, but they answered from the shelter of these walls, that, if he wished to fight, he must come and seek the great king in his citadel.

The monarch had no wish to measure himself with Julian, but would gladly yield one part of his kingdom to save the other. He summoned Hermisdas, his brother, and entreated him to serve as mediator with the Emperor, and negotiate, at whatever expense, a treaty of peace; but Julian, desirous to play to the end the part of Alexander, refused to listen to any proposition.

The Emperor at length determined to re-ascend the Tigris, and seek the troops which he had been so long expecting; for without this addition to his army he could do nothing. The current was very rapid, and their progress extremely slow; and after some forced marches, the army not arriving, Julian admitted that to reach the frontier upon this route, without having acquired an inch of territory, would be too mortifying to the ambition of a youthful hero like himself. He returned, therefore, before the walls of Ctesiphon. He must rely on himself alone; but determine upon — what?

Julian remained in this painful uncertainty. The augurs gave no favorable answers; the stars were unpropitious. His midnight studies were continued long after the philosophers, wearied out, had retired to their own tents. He was alone; the sentinel only stood at the door of the tent, when a venerable Persian, whose beard, white as snow, descended on his breast, craved admission to the Emperor. High birth was stamped upon his noble brow, and his whole person bore the impression of refined culture and unequivocal nobleness.

Julian rose in surprise, and advanced to meet his visitor.

The other fell at his feet, and embraced his knees. "Behold," said he, "the servant of Sapor, the king of kings, who has fallen into disgrace with his master, and fearing destruction from all the avenues of life, the air, the food, the water, being poisoned to him, has fled, royal Julian, to you, and, hating his former lord, is ready to lay down his life to serve the enemies of Sapor."

"What would you ask of me?" said Julian, more and more surprised.

"Only to serve you, and thus to prove my hatred of the tyrant."

"Can you ask me to trust a traitor?" said Julian.

"Sire, the proof of my truth is, that I will render you in five days the master of Persia. Follow my counsel, and the king of kings will be at your footstool, and your army shall revel in Ctesiphon."

"And how? Your walls are impregnable, and half my army, my best troops, far off in Mesopotamia. Think you, that, if I could have stormed yonder walls, I should have sat idly here?"

"Listen! you have placed the kingdom of Sapor within two fingers of destruction. The fame of your exploits, the exploits of the invincible hero, has spread through all lands, and the hearts of my countrymen are faint with affright. They feel that entire prostration of all energy which presages the fall of an empire. The monarch also is all consternation."

"But what does all this avail me," said Julian, "unless by force or fraud I can enter those adamantine walls?"

"Sapor has indeed nothing to fear, while, a slave to your fleet, you merely coast these rivers. He can avoid a battle with ships or boats."

"What then would you have me do?" asked Julian.

"A conqueror such as the invincible Julian will know how to throw off such shackles. What prevents you from attacking Sapor in his citadel?"

"Ah, what indeed but an army!" said Julian, with a sigh.

"A true soldier should expect nothing except from himself and his sword. His right arm should gain all his honors."

Julian was silent, waiting for what would come next.

"Of what avail," continued the other, "are all these ships and magazines? Mere snares for cowardice. At the sight of these refuges, the sailors grow pale and indifferent. Had you not employed your army to contend against the waves of the Tigris, you would have conquered the enemy; Sapor would have been dethroned, and your army rich with the treasures of Ctesiphon."

Julian fixed his stern regard upon the Persian; his eyes alternately flashed with hope, or were veiled with doubt.

"I know every secret way to the city," continued the old man, "and subterranean paths leading to the heart of the palace. I will be your guide. You will need provisions for four days, because we must pass a desert. Hasten, my lord! victory is certain, it is infallible! My head, this white head of an aged man, shall answer for the truth of my words. I pledge my life, my liberty; keep me prisoner till I shall have proved my truth. Till then I expect no recompense for my zeal."

"It is your zeal which makes me doubt."

"Ah, I love a young hero, like yourself," said the Persian; "beside, that effete and stupid old man has turned my blood to hatred. But hasten, my lord! set fire to your fleet, lest it fall into the hands of the enemy."

Julian was dazzled by this daring plan. It was brilliant, bold, and singular, and, beside, his embarrassment was so great that he easily fell into the snare. By burning the fleet he should gain twenty thousand soldiers for his army, who had been hitherto employed in the service of the vessels.

The imagination of the young disciple of Plato was intoxicated with visions of glory. He should run through Persia as a conqueror, and perhaps penetrate as far as India. In vain his experienced generals reminded him of the deceit practised upon Zopyrus, and of the deserters who made Crassus perish. In vain Hermisdas entreated him not to place confidence in his countryman, and warned him that a Persian was capable of every deceit. He would not listen; but ordered his army to take food sufficient for twenty days, instead of four, and commanded them to set fire to the fleet.

The army were thrown into the utmost consternation. "Are we betrayed to the enemy?" they asked. "Has the Emperor secret intelligence with Sapor?"

The Persian could nowhere be found.

Julian began to suspect that he had been betrayed, and ordered the fire extinguished. The deserters who had accompanied the spy were put to the question, and answered, that a plot had been formed for the destruction of the Romans.

They saved but a dozen of their smallest barks, which were transported upon wheels to serve them at need.

But how did Julian support this misfortune, so overwhelming for his army, so humiliating to his pride, his self-esteem ?

He endeavored to enliven, to cheer his soldiers. As they had taken provisions for twenty days, he did not despair of meeting Sapor, and winning the battle, or by forced marches to reach a fertile and rich country, where the harvests were already ripe.

But the enemy had been before them, and set fire to the forage and burnt the fruits. The army were arrested by the fire, and knew not what path to take. It was difficult to advance, dangerous to recede, impossible to find food. That which they had taken with them was rapidly consuming. Julian concealed a deadly anxiety under an air of security, but he could not reassure his army against the horror of famine.

In defect of human prudence they consulted the Gods; but the Gods, after many sacrifices of oxen, which they could ill spare, seemed to condemn everything proposed. At length all suffrages were united in the project to endeavor to gain a small province in Armenia, which was dependent upon the Romans.

No sooner had they begun their march, than the troops of Sapor began to appear. The appearance of the enemy always animated the Roman soldiers, and they gained easy victories over these detached portions of the army of Sapor. Indeed, it was easy to conquer a large army commanded by the two sons of Sapor. But, unhappily, Julian had in his camp an enemy more formidable than the Persians, more deadly than all their arms, — Famine!

CHAPTER XXXV.

"THE GALILEAN HAS CONQUERED."

Julian had dismissed his generals and his counsellors; his friends lingered, but at length all, even Libanius, had left him to the solitude of his tent.

The soldier who prepared his food, for he had never indulged himself with a cook, brought him a little soup; he had tasted nothing through the day. It was black and uninviting. Julian put it away. "Carry it," he said, "to the tent of him," naming the soldier, "who is suffering from debility more than his general."

"Sire," said the soldier, "the food that was intended for your own table has all been distributed, as you ordered, to the soldiers who suffered: you allow me to provide only the most common for yourself, and do you also reject this, when famine is telling its sad tale upon your emaciated form?"

"Ah," said Julian, "the tale will soon be ended." He dismissed the soldier, and threw himself upon his couch for a few moments' sleep. The mute, who never left him, was sleeping at the foot of the skin which formed the bed of the Emperor.

Julian slept that uneasy sleep which refreshes neither mind nor body. He heard, as he fancied, soft music in his tent. Half awake, he opened his eyes, and saw, faint and dim, a veiled figure gliding before him. He was instantly wholly awake, and with breathless attention fixed upon the vision.

The Genius of the Empire stood before him, such as he had seen in Paris before the crown was forced upon him; not festive and radiant as he then appeared, but pale, drooping, his eyes heavy with tears, and the brilliancy of the royal diadem which he wore upon his head soiled and dimmed, the jewels scattered, while he bore an inverted and empty cornucopia on his arm. Julian extended his arms towards him. The Genius looked upon him with mournful eyes; then veiled his head, and slowly, with averted, tearful gaze, quitted the tent.

Julian arose from his couch, and went out into the night air. The intense darkness gave place to the softer shades which precede the dawn; faint blushes began to kindle along the eastern sky, but the great planets Mars and Jupiter were not yet dimmed.

The fires upon the altars were again kindled, and the Emperor, with almost a regretful pang, sacrificed his last beautiful white heifers. Alas! all those for which the soldiers were hungering were slain upon the altars of the Gods, to implore their sorely needed aid, or to avert their anger!

Returning to his tent, the Prince observed upon the verge of the horizon apparently a ball of fire, swelling and inflaming to a fiery red. His agitated spirits made him alive to superstitious fears.

"What portentous and threatening omen is it?" he asked. "The planet Mars, does he wear that angry and fearful aspect? or is it my own brilliant star thus fallen and about to set for ever? Or can it be," he continued, "only an exhalation from the damp air of the night, which a breath will dispel?" While he gazed, it sank heavy and dark beneath the horizon. Whatever it might be, Julian trembled!

He called his servants, and bade them summon the augurs. They assured him that it portended only misfortune, and ordered that the army should remain in camp, and spend the day in sacrifices and prayers.

Necessity and famine were stronger than superstition. Immediately the trumpets sounded, and the order to march was given.

Julian, who led the van with all the skill of a consummate general, was perpetually called back, to repel the Persian army which hung upon their rear. He charged with fury, beat them back, and again galloped to head his troops.

The intense heat of the weather had compelled the Prince to throw off all but the lightest armor, and also to lay aside his cuirass. On the second day, while he led the van, he was alarmed by the intelligence that the rear-guard was suddenly overpowered. He snatched a shield from an attendant, and hastened to its relief. He was instantly recalled to the defence of the front; and as he galloped forward, the centre of the left was assailed by a furious charge of elephants and cavalry.

By his well-timed evolution of the light infantry, the barbarians fled; and the Emperor, standing in his stirrups, without his helmet, his hair streaming on the wind, animated the pursuit with voice and gesture. His trembling guards reminded him that he was without helmet or armor, and conjured him to abandon the pursuit. As they still exclaimed and entreated, a cloud of darts and arrows were discharged behind by the flying enemy. A javelin, taking an unerring aim, after grazing the skin of the arm, pierced the ribs and buried itself in the Emperor's side.

"Ah, I am hurt!" he cried, "and seized the dart to draw it out. The sharp edges cut his fingers to the bone, and Julian fell fainting from his horse.

The guards flew to raise the Emperor from the ground, and placing him upon a buckler, he was borne to his tent.

The faithful physician, Oribasius, the friend of his youth, one of those to whom Basilina had committed her infant son, was instantly at his side; Libanius heard the appalling news, and rushed to aid his friend; Sallust was leading on the enraged soldiers to avenge their Emperor. As soon as the wound was bandaged, Julian rose from the ground, crying out, "A horse and my shield!" and he would have rushed again to the battle. The effort was too great, and he fell fainting again into the arms of his friends.

Oribasius examined the wound anew; tears, in spite of his efforts to repress them, streamed down his cheeks as he turned to the friends collected in the tent. Then they knew that the wound was mortal.

Julian, extended upon a lion's skin, his usual couch, retained a cheerful and even joyous expression, while a mournful silence prevailed throughout the tent, tears filling the eyes of all who approached him, and even the philosophers, unused to weeping, were oppressed with grief.

An oracle had formerly predicted to Julian that he should finish his days in Phrygia. Superstitious to the last, he said to those weeping around him: "Be not dismayed, my friends. Julian is not yet conquered. Nemesis is baffled! I trust the oracle which told me that I should die in Asia Minor, in a Phrygian city."

"Alas!" said one of those standing near, "this very spot is called Phrygia."

A cloud darkened the face of Julian; he threw his arms aloft and cried, "GALILEAN! THOU HAST CONQUERED!" A deep silence prevailed in the tent. After a few moments, he resumed all his cheerfulness. "Dear companions, friends," he said, "why do you weep? Nature only demands of me that which she has lent me for thirty years, and I discharge the debt with ready cheerfulness."

Libanius, entirely prostrated by grief, could scarcely endure the smile which quivered upon the pallid lips of his friend; he sat by his side, with face averted.

"My friend," said Julian, "how often have we talked of this hour! How often have we learnt from philosophy that the soul is more excellent than the body! And should we not rejoice, rather than grieve, when the noble part is disengaged from that which drags it down to earth?"

"Ah!" said Libanius, "could we but accompany thee! But fear not, my friend; my soul will overtake thine in the Islands of the Blessed!"

Julian did not detect his meaning, and continued: "An early death is often the reward which the Gods vouchsafe to piety. How grateful am I to the Eternal Being, who has not suffered me to perish by the secret dagger of conspiracy, or by the slow tortures of disease."

"Or by the cruelty of a tyrant," said Libanius.

Julian pressed his friend's hand. "I knew that I was destined to fall by the sword. I have not withheld myself from danger. The Eternal Being has granted me a glorious departure from this world. I thank Him most devoutly! Ah, my weeping friends, I would say more to comfort you; but I feel the breath, I hear the fanning of 'the wing of the Genius of death.'"

His friends pressed round, urging him to name a successor.

"Nay, my friends, my choice might be imprudent, and, if not ratified by the army, fatal to him whom I should choose. The little which remains for me to dispose of, the remnant of my private property, I would and do divide among these friends. But where is another who loves me,—where is Anatolius?"

"Ah, Sire," said Sallust, "Anatolius is happy!"

Julian, who until then had not shed a tear, now turned aside his head and wept.

This excited the grief of his friends anew, and the tent was filled with wailing and violent weeping.

Julian roused a little. "Ah, why will ye break my heart with your grief, and why disgrace with these unmanly tears the fate of one who in a few moments will be united with the stars!"

Instantly the friends were dumb; a deep and respectful silence was only broken by the piteous wailing of the little mute, Julian's petted favorite, who had been lying prostrate at the head of the couch, and whose presence had been unobserved. All the avenues of the tent were crowded by the eager faces of veterans, down whose shaggy beards flowed the anxious tears. They pressed upon each other to catch one glance of him more beloved than any Emperor of Rome had ever been.

"O my honest braves!" he cried, "would that the Immortal Gods had granted me the power to make you all rich and happy! But, alas! Julian is poorer than the poorest of you all. His only riches is the possession of his immortal soul!"

The midsummer night advanced with slow and

humid steps. The southern constellations looked down upon the tent, and the sweet influences of the Pleiades were not stayed by the departing soul of him who had always believed himself peculiarly connected with the stars. Silently the moments dropped like pearls from his thread of life, which the angels gathered into the treasury of eternity. Soon the great mystery would be solved for him, and he would learn whether unseen angels or the messengers of the Gods would conduct his soul into the presence of that Divine Creator and Soul of the universe, in whom he had always devoutly believed.

Midnight had struck with that deadly echo which toned itself upon every heart. The Emperor asked faintly for water. He drank, — a dying smile lingered upon his lips, but his soul had departed.

CHAPTER XXXVI.

THE CONVENT.

Monasteries for both sexes had arisen throughout Christendom. It was the influence of the spirit of the age, which compelled multitudes to flee from the world to ascetic and solitary seclusion. The mother and sisters of St. Basil, the contemporary of Julian, had founded a convent for women in the vicinity of Antioch, where the sisters and the daughters of senators and nobles hastened to bury beneath its sombre roof their beauty and their still fresh and blooming youth.

A short time after the events described in the last chapter, at the close of a day in autumn, a litter, borne on the shoulders of men, slowly ascended these heights beyond the city. It was followed by servants, and a little apart from the others rode a horseman whom we have seen before, whose Grecian features, harmonized by the influences of

Christianity, were still more softened by recent sorrow. As the cortege ascended the last height, and passed through an opening in the hills, they looked down upon an area of gently sloping fields, surrounded on three sides by hills, the fourth bounded by a rapid and sparkling river. This rounded valley was fenced by lofty trees of every variety, enclosing and shutting it in, like a solitary island of verdure. Fertilized by mountain streams, it yielded to the lightest culture every variety of plant and flower.

This company were met, as they paused upon the height, by refreshing breezes from the river, by the delicious fragrance of many flowers, and the singing of innumerable birds, which the unbroken silence of this retreat had allured as to a secure asylum.

"Here," thought Phorion, who had drawn near the litter, "might be found the sweetest fruit of solitude and repose."

"Here," said Olympia, "one might forget the world, and with one loved being enjoy an Elysium of peace," — and she pressed her lips upon the hand which rested upon the side of the litter.

In the centre of this lovely valley was the convent already mentioned, founded by thoughtful piety for recluses of both sexes; for St. Basil had himself established a convent for men, near that founded by his mother for the other sex.

At this period Christianity seemed to have failed of its divine mission to reform society, and within its circle there was no refuge for the gentle, the innocent, and devout spirit; no peace, no security, no home, but the cloister. "There was an almost universal feeling of the pressure and the burden of sorrow; an awakening of the conscience to wrong, a blind, anxious groping for the right, a feeling that what had hitherto sufficed to humanity would suffice no longer." But religious fear took the place of religious hope, and those assailed by the vision of seductive pleasures which they had not strength to avoid, or wrung with repentance for sins already committed, fled to the convent, there to atone by ascetic privations, by the maceration of the limbs and the scourging of the body, to Him who looketh upon the heart.

But all came not for self-immolation; the most numerous class, especially of women, came to bury for ever in the sombre shades of the cloister hearts broken by disappointment and made desolate by the inconstancy and the perfidy of others, — gentle and crushed spirits, for whom there was no future, except in the cloister. Here they met, from places far apart, from lands divided by seas and by mountains; faces of every degree and shade of beauty, forms bending under unuttered sorrows, yet all concealing the same wound at heart, for which the world contained neither balm nor simple, neither poppy nor mandragora. Each believed her own wound concealed from every other, but all knew that the voices, variously attuned in hymns, in chants, and in prayer, had all the same key-note of disappointed hope, of broken vows and love betrayed. All were like shattered vases, breathing in every fragment the perfume that once filled them with the fragrance of love.

Our party descended the winding path which led to this singular valley, just as the first rays of the rising sun seemed to throw a transparent veil woven of golden vapor upon the summits of the motionless trees. They approached the centre, the chapel of the cloister common to both sexes. In this early age of the Church, men and women could pray together without apprehension of evil. It was the matin hour, and the recluses, arranged on either side of the altar, each in his or her white robe, were kneeling immovable, with head bent forward in the attitude of profoundest meditation. Their exterior presented that deep peace of souls disabused of the delusions of the world, and already admitted to that eternal repose, that beatitude promised to the pure of heart.

As the recluses rose, Parthenia met the friends who had come to seek her. They did not immediately recognize her in the cloud of white-robed companions, who seemed like doves to flutter before them. She knew them instantly, and came forward to greet them with cordial welcome. Her dress was little altered from that she wore as priestess of Pallas,—the white robe of softest wool, but without the purple border; and instead of the golden grasshoppers or the wreath of silver laurel-leaves, she wore a veil of the same material, concealing her beautiful hair. She was pale, and much changed since we first saw her in Athens. They perceived that she had not yet attained that perfect abnegation of self which should belong to the life of the cloister. She had not yet "forgot herself to stone." She must wear her crown of thorns still longer, before she could win the crown and palm of the martyr.

A vivid blush of pleasure convinced Parthenia's friends that, as yet, she was no Stoic. She led the way to her cell, a small apartment of ten feet square, bare and empty, except for the narrow plank which formed her couch, and a deal shelf, upon which lay a beautiful copy of the Gospels, transcribed by herself. There was, also, shining like a star in the cell, a small statue of the Saviour, of carved ivory. Upon his head was the crown of thorns, and the expression was that of a divine compassion, an immeasurable pity.

Phorion and Olympia looked at each other. They were contrasting the bare, the uninhabitable aspect of this low cell with the lofty, luxurious home of the recluse in Athens. And she to whom beauty had been a religion and luxury, a necessity, stood there bare of all except her beautiful self, and the image of Him whom she had left all to follow.

Phorion and Olympia encircled her in their arms, and burst into tears.

She drew herself quietly from them. "Why do you weep," she said, "and break my heart?"

"How, dearest Parthenia, can you, who have so loved God's beautiful gifts, thus strip yourself of all?"

"Here are no flowers, no perfume, no ornament, no luxury," said Olympia. "Do you not give back upon the altar what God has scattered so profusely?"

"All are his," said Parthenia. "He asks only the *heart*, which it is so *hard* to give."

"Expiation, atonement," said Phorion, "are the cry of the Church, and the spirit of the age; but you, fair Parthenia, are free from sins, you have no burdened conscience to expiate."

"O come away with us," cried Olympia. "Return to Antioch. There is no longer any persecution of the Galileans. Jovian is the Christians' Emperor."

"It is not too late," said Phorion. "Beloved Parthenia, you have not yet taken the *vow* which will separate you from all you have loved."

"Return!" continued Olympia; "Julian, the impious, the persecutor of the Christians, is no more. The Gods he so honored have taken him to themselves."

"Fair Parthenia," Phorion continued, "are you sure that this life of seclusion and ascetic privation is that to which your youth and your cultured tastes will reconcile you? The death of Julian has left the Church triumphant. Christianity has obtained an easy victory. Life may now be serious and secure, with the Christian faith openly professed."

At the mention of Julian, Parthenia's cheek became more pale. His failure and his death had revealed to her the strength of the tie which drew her, and the riches of the soul which made that attraction so strong. But she did not go to the cloister to cherish a passion under the delusion of preserving a memory. "Pardon me," she said, "your words are kind, but they do not penetrate beyond the portal of the ear. The dreams which filled my life with illusions are past; my father is estranged from me; my fortune, in a time of famine, I turned into bread for the poor; this asylum presents to me all that I long for and need, — tranquillity, forgetfulness."

Phorion was in earnest. "I cannot accept your reasons," he began.

"Ah! but if here alone I can live for God, and for Him to whom I would give my heart," and she glanced towards the statue of Christ.

"It is not a change of place which will draw us near to God," said Phorion. "Wherever we are, God will come to us, if our heart is an asylum worthy to receive him."

She looked at Phorion with the smile of former days. "In leaving the dry husks of logic for the sweet wine of the Gospels, and Plato for Christ, I fain would meet with Phorion's sympathy."

"It is not that you have exchanged Philosophy for Christianity that I would draw you from the life of the cloister, but that you are a woman in the sweet prime of youth, and you should find your strength in your weakness, and give yourself to another."

Parthenia colored, first in anger; the flush faded, and a tear was on her eyelid.

"Fair Parthenia, shall your youth have no flower,

your summer no fruit? Listen to me! Love is the gift God has left the world, to keep it from despair. The heaped-up treasures of the world are not worthy to purchase an instant of its joy. Queens cannot exact it, but it blesses the humblest lot."

"Phorion, forbear!"

"I would that I could paint for thee the joys of wedded love; that daily fresh miracle where two souls become one."

Parthenia trembled, she merely said again, "Forbear!"

"The self-immolating aspect of this convent chills me like a sunless day of winter. Parthenia, return with us." He had taken her hand, and drew her to the door of the cell.

"No, Phorion! my youth is over. Love, the short joy of my youth, can never be rekindled. My choice is fixed, my resolution immovable. This is my home!" Turning to Olympia, she took her hand tenderly in hers. "Let us not waste these precious moments in unavailing regrets! Tell me of those I have left in the world, — Theodorus?"

"Theodorus is scarcely of the world. He has gone to add one more to the army of the monks of the Thebaid. He still declares to priest and bishop, that an angel in white raiment stood by him in his torture, sustained him when fainting, and presented cordials to his lips. He felt no pain: the perfume from the angel's wings gave him life and strength."

Parthenia smiled. "This perhaps will procure him in later days canonization among the martyrs," — a prophecy which the records of the Church have confirmed.

"Cartophilus? Have you no record of the noble Jew?"

"Report has surely reached you of the disastrous issue of the expedition led by Cartophilus, and by the order of Julian, to rebuild the temple on Mount Zion. The miracles they report have divided the believing, and converted the unbelieving. They record that rocks were rent and caverns opened; that the first spade thrust into the sacred spot was followed by streams of liquid fire; that invisible agents with their heavy blows struck back the frightened workmen; that balls of lurid fire and flashes of intense brightness blinded the architects who would survey the ground; that an earthquake shook the remnant of the old wall, and opened the earth to swallow up those who ventured near. Affrighted and appalled, believing in the Jehovah of the Hebrews, the workmen fled, and brought the report to Antioch and to Rome."

"And the noble Jew, Cartophilus, does he yet retain his scepticism, after all these miracles?"

"Cartophilus has ever been *almost* a Christian. By the aid of Moses, Plato, and Christ, he has thought out for himself a religion which enjoins the utmost purity of conscience. His life is pure: his immense wealth is devoted to noble purposes. The wonderful experiences of his career involve his early history in mystery, with hints of appalling incidents; his strange youthful enterprises, united with marks of extreme age, the immense and various information he has made his own, the beauty of his countenance, give him almost irresistible influence over men, and women also."

"How often," said Parthenia, "does he hint of events and incidents that he has witnessed, which would make him greatly older than his apparent age!"

"I have heard also of a strangely beautiful, but at her death very aged person, to whom he was betrothed in youth, who had kept her faith, and remained constant to him after very painful events which separated them for ever. This history of his early love belongs to the legend which makes him the contemporary of Jesus. He is said to be the unhappy Jew who, when Christ was bearing his cross painfully up the steep path of Calvary, cried out to him, in jeering tones, 'Go faster, Jesus. Why dost thou linger? Go faster!' Jesus turned to him without anger, and said, 'I indeed am going, but thou — thou shalt tarry till I come.'

"It is said also," continued Phorion, "that he has gone through several transformations; that at the close of every century the material part suffers a change, either by fire, water, or petrifaction, and that the immortal soul enters a new and youthful body, retaining all its faculties, its memory, and its accumulated knowledge."

"O misery to be cursed with such a life!" said Parthenia.

In conversation and in retrospection the day wore on, and after many hours, as the friends looked towards the west, they saw that the sun was declining; the clouds, purple and gold, were gathering around to form his setting canopy. With sorrow they felt that they must part. Once more they took each a hand of the beautiful woman, and again earnestly entreated her to follow them to Antioch, and to bless their own home by her presence.

Reluctantly, painfully, she drew her hands from them, and, glancing at the image of Christ, said, "Cease, my friends, cease to break — do not try to divide — my heart. Let the offering be pure and whole, and of every faculty of my being, to Him of whom I have learnt the worthlessness of this life in comparison with the life of the future!"

Are not both lives of nearly equal value, and were not those mistaken who sought in retreats of ascetic solitude, of unloving isolation, the only preparation for the life of love and joy in the future? Yet these retreats had their source in the deep heart of humanity; in the need the repentant soul felt for self-abnegation and self-sacrifice. Later in the history of the Church, women whom love or sorrow had driven like the wounded doe from their fellows, instead of seeking a cloistered solitude, bound themselves by religious obligation to a life of celibacy indeed, but to active self-devotion to the service of others. Have we improved upon either system? Are woman's noblest instincts and holiest affections better trained in the pursuit of the material interests of life, or even in the ardent, but narrow, love of the circle bounded by home and children?

But it was time to part with Parthenia at the gate of her convent. Silently they wrung the hands held out to them. Then, with that radiant smile sometimes seen upon the face of the dying, she pointed to the glowing west. "I KNOW," she said, "that we shall meet each other again in those mansions Christ has prepared for all those who believe in him!"

THE END.

www.ingramcontent.com/pod-product-compliance
Lightning Source LLC
LaVergne TN
LVHW021148110826
845150LV00005B/1161

* 9 7 8 1 4 2 5 5 4 7 5 4 7 *